Critical Issues in Criminal Justice

Critical Issues in Criminal Justice

Edited by

DONALD O. SCHULTZ, B.S., M.P.A.

*Police Science Instructor
Broward Community College
Fort Lauderdale, Florida
Formerly
Orange (California) Police Department*

HV
8138
.S34

CHARLES C THOMAS • PUBLISHER
Springfield • Illinois • U.S.A.

Published and Distributed Throughout the World by
CHARLES C THOMAS • PUBLISHER
301-327 East Lawrence Avenue, Springfield, Illinois, U.S.A.

This book is protected by copyright. No part of it
may be reproduced in any manner without written
permission from the publisher.

© *1975, by* CHARLES C THOMAS • PUBLISHER
ISBN 0-398-03331-5
Library of Congress Catalog Card Number: 74-18073

With THOMAS BOOKS *careful attention is given to all details of manufacturing and design. It is the Publisher's desire to present books that are satisfactory as to their physical qualities and artistic possibilities and appropriate for their particular use.* THOMAS BOOKS *will be true to those laws of quality that assure a good name and good will.*

Printed in the United States of America
R-1

Library of Congress Cataloging in Publication Data
Schultz, Donald O., 1939-
   Critical issues in criminal justice.

  Bibliography: p.
   1. Police — United States — Addresses, essays, lectures. 2. Police administration — United States — Addresses, essays, lectures. 3. Criminal justice, Administration of — United States — Addresses, essays, lectures. I. Title.
HV8138.S34   364   74-18073
ISBN 0-398-03331-5

DEDICATED TO MY SON

DONNIE

PREFACE

THE effects of our changing times have naturally had an impact on our criminal justice system. Corrections, the courts, probation and parole, the prosecutor's office, and, of course, federal, state, county and local law enforcement agencies have had new problems added to their historical dilemmas. In order to survive, the criminal justice system must change and continuously look for better methods of operation. Although all areas in the criminal justice system are important, the major emphases of this text is to explore new and recurring issues confronting the police service.

Some of the important issues explored in *Critical Issues in Criminal Justice* are: the police and politics; police and minority groups; the role of courts in a statewide criminal justice information system; team policing; lateral entry; police review boards; the police and their problems; the use of force; job performance evaluation; organized crime; police ethics; the traditional police organization; and police planning.

The text is written in a practical manner, blending theory with everyday police knowledge. The problems covered should not only be of vital importance to police administrators, but to all personnel sworn to uphold the law.

ACKNOWLEDGMENTS

The author wishes to thank Payne Thomas, publisher and personal friend, for his assistance. Also a debt is owed to the following authors for their contributions:

Lee P. Brown
George T. Felkenes
Robert R. J. Gallati
William H. Hewitt
Dr. John P. Kenney
Jack L. Kuykendall
Robert D. Pursley
David D. Robinson
Marvin E. Wolfgang

D.O.S.

CONTENTS

	Page
Preface	vii
Acknowledgments	ix

Chapter

1. POLICE ETHICS 3
2. THE POLICE AND POLITICS 14
3. THE USE OF FORCE 36
4. ORGANIZED CRIME 51
5. TEAM POLICING ORGANIZATION: A THEORETICAL MODEL ... 80
6. POLICE PERSONNEL ADMINISTRATION: LATERAL ENTRY 95
7. ISSUES IN JOB PERFORMANCE EVALUATION 159
8. POLICE REVIEW BOARDS: AN HISTORICAL AND
    CRITICAL ANALYSIS 172
9. POLICE AND MINORITY GROUPS: TOWARD A THEORY OF
    NEGATIVE CONTACTS 200
10. THE ROLE OF THE COURTS IN A STATE-WIDE CRIMINAL
    JUSTICE INFORMATION SYSTEM 221
11. THE POLICE AND THEIR PROBLEMS 236
12. TRADITIONAL POLICE ORGANIZATION: A PORTENT
    OF FAILURE 252
13. POLICE PLANNING: A STIMULUS FOR NEEDED
    ORGANIZATIONAL CHANGE 256
14. POLICE UNIONISM: IMPROVING POLICE AGENCY AND
    EMPLOYEE PERFORMANCE THROUGH
    COLLECTIVE BARGAINING 264

Bibliography 285

**Critical Issues in
Criminal Justice**

CHAPTER 1

POLICE ETHICS

Donald O. Schultz

ETHICAL practices are of major concern in the field of law enforcement. The police service is more closely scrutinized and open to more derogatory comments than any other occupational group. There are never any shades of gray concerning a police officer's or a police administrator's ethical practices. Either a police officer or administrator is honest or he is not.

It has been an unfortunate fact that the majority of police officers who are forced to leave law enforcement can trace their difficulties back to credit, liquor, or women. Credit is an easy commodity for police personnel because of the security of their position. Needless to say, a careful eye must be kept on the purchasing power of a usually only adequate salary. Any occupation which involves a great deal of mental strain easily leads to alcohol as an escape mechanism. For an occasional release it may be an acceptable means of therapy; however, dependence on alcohol is not only medically harmful, but occupationally fatal. Women are probably one of law enforcement's biggest problems. Many authors point out the fact that police officers are involved in divorces more than any other occupational group. The basic implications are that policemen just like to "play around." When all the factors regarding the amount of opportunity for extramarital relationships are weighed, the law enforcement community can be proud of the fact that only a small minority of its members have difficulty in maintaining restraint.

Some questionable practices have been used in the police service from time to time. The great majority of the police agencies today conduct themselves in a manner which makes them a credit to law enforcement. The balance of this chapter deals with ethical areas which have given some police personnel, police administrators, and police agencies problems not only in the past, but in some cases, remain present-day situations.

THE STREET POLICEMAN

Man's struggle to maintain a society of law and order is not without many conflicts, both moral and legal. The seed of liberty is guarded daily by members of the thin blue line. One of the purposes of this chapter is to explore the ethical nature of policemen and their differences of opinions, particularly the attitudes of those dedicated professional soldiers of law enforcement known as "street policemen," or "street cops." Few people are really aware of this basic separation within the ranks of the police service. Many carry the badge and wear the uniform, but only the dedicated are street policemen.

Moral and ethical standards vary greatly from one police agency to another. Many factors influence this, as well as the formal and informal organizational structure or hierarchy. The most important of all factors bearing a predominant role in any organization are the attitudes and moral convictions of the chief administrator. Even with this in mind, it must be remembered that he alone does not totally set the ethical climate.

Men who face tremendous danger almost daily are bonded together in a fraternity that can only be designated by the term "street policemen." Not all police officers know and feel what this term embodies. This chapter is then written to assist in advancing the rules, attitudes, and ethics which exist within this brotherhood. Many are called policemen; only the best are street policemen. Their loyalties are to principles, not men; their dialogue is different; they accept only the proven into their ranks, and they are fiercely patriotic Americans. They have always been and always will be the strongest link in law enforcement.

TICKET FIXING

The practice of "fixing" traffic citations by police officials is an old and illegal procedure. It is usually found in communities which still have the remnants of the spoils system in their political structure. In most cases it is a symptom of a far greater underlying problem.

Some may wonder just what constitutes "fixing" a traffic citation. In substance it is any act or failure to act which permits a traffic offender to circumvent established and lawful methods of adjudication. It can take many forms, but it always involves collusion on the part of at least one branch of law enforcement.

Because some sort of forms control must be exercised, most jurisdictions have serial numbers on their citation blanks. In most cases, the records system at the court level prevents a law agency or police personnel to fail to send the original "court copy" to the courts for legal processing. If, however, the county officials are corrupt, the court records and the court officers cannot be trusted any further than the law enforcement administrators who tolerate political intervention into the process of equal justice.

The majority of individuals whose citations fail to be prosecuted seem to represent the higher social element level of the community, i.e. a sister of a councilman, a bank president, or any relative or close friend of anyone with political connections within the community. The moral crime is obvious. Law enforcement officers are sworn to uphold equal justice as a duty and not just as an ideal. No less an authority than a retired police inspector, educator, and author, Paul Weston relates that ticket fixing is not only illegal but seriously affects the morale of the police personnel. When any segment of society can violate a traffic law or any other law without fear of fine or imprisonment, the foundations of our republic are weakened.

There have been cases both past and recent to demonstrate that when discovered, the community at large will not tolerate illegal "fixing" procedures. One of the more recent experiences to demonstrate this was the mass exodus of police officials from the Orange Police Department, Orange, California, after ticket fixing was discovered in that agency. It is then the duty of the police officers and the police administrators to see that their agency does not tarnish the image of law enforcement. Those who violate this obligation often explain their positions by exclaiming that the "fix" was an extension of an "interest of justice" as they diverted the citations from the bar of justice because *they felt* that the citations were not valid. In essence, they are criminally guilty of various state and governmental codes. They are also morally guilty within the standards of the accepted law enforcement code of ethics and have performed a disservice to the honest police officers who wrote the traffic citations in good faith.

In the end, the police officer or administrator who allows this illegal and immoral practice to continue with his knowledge has also then given his consent even if he is never involved as a participating agent. In our effort for effective law enforcement there cannot be any Nuremberg excuse. Failure to act to stop a "fix" is a personal responsibility, and this obligation cannot be transferred. When ticket-fixing practices occur in a police agency, the logical person who will expose and cleanse the department will be a dedicated street police officer. This has been the case in the past; it was the case in the Orange police scandal, and it is logical to conclude that the future will also be protected by the dedicated men who cannot be bought, threatened, and thus not swayed from a duty towards principles of law and to men who have justified graft.

There can be two effective means of eradicating this throwback of justice. The first is through the vigilance of the new breed who will not allow the past to haunt our future. The second is the possibility of a state central control of citations for all the agencies within its jurisdiction. A central control of all citations would not only prevent local politicians from interfering with the processes of law, but would also be helpful in future statistics and traffic studies on the state, county, and local levels.

OPEN ACCOUNTS

An open account in law enforcement has many definitions and connotations. Particular reference is made to the officer who receives merchandise from a marginal establishment and upon receipt of the merchandise informs the owner or clerk to "put it on my account." This transaction is many times done with the full understanding that the merchandise is payment for some past or future extrajudicial favor that has been or will be rendered to the owner of the business.

In other words, it is simply a payoff. The term open account means just what it states — the account remains open and *unpaid*. These petty bribes can range from a package of cigarettes to a bottle of liquor. Sometimes the account is even good towards the purchase of a new car.

From a police administrative standpoint, considerable difficulty arises in the detection and prevention of such problems. There is rarely a complaining party, and less often a victim, and more remotely a sustaining witness. When it is finally discovered, it has usually grown to a proportion that a discreet discharge of the police officer or police administrator is impossible. In one way this is good, as the bribing of a police officer is a criminal matter and should be treated as such.

As a rotten apple spoils, in time, most of the basket will, and so will a police officer who is on the take. In time, others who are also morally weak will follow suit under the guidance of the initial officer who has convinced them that double standards exist even in police work. The proverb, "God helps those who help themselves," has no place in law enforcement. The best advice which can be given to the embryo police officer is that "There is no such thing as a free lunch for a policeman."

Some examples of open accounts follow: A detective commander going into a local liquor store on his way home at night and picking up a bottle of whiskey on his account. The liquor store is owned directly or indirectly by a syndicate family. At the end of the month the account is balanced as no vice arrests have been made in the syndicate's establishments. An officer or patrol administrator obtains free tires, batteries, and other parts and services from a local gas station. For his open account at the service station the owner receives a continuous patrol check at his business during the night and early morning hours. This situation creates unbalanced police protection to the detriment of other businesses in the community who do not carry open accounts for law enforcement personnel.

BUSINESS CARDS

A business card in private industry is a necessity. It identifies the bearer as a representative of a firm and is a convenient system for recontact at a later date by the customer or client.

Professionals also know the importance of having their business cards with them at all times. In recent years the business card has evolved into many forms, sizes, and shapes in the interest of competition and artful eye appeal.

Law enforcement as a public business is one of the largest and most demanding. It is important in criminal investigations that victims and witnesses have a ready referral card at their disposal to recontact the investigating officer should they recall something that they failed to report when the initial contact was made.

A police business card should be printed in a conservative format, usually in block or Roman type. It should include the name, address, and phone number of the police agency, and the investigating officer's name and extension number. The case number block or space should also be included. "For business purposes only" or some other indication that the business card is not to be used for any other reason than for a reference for a specific case must be clearly inscribed on the face of the card.

Because of the nature of law enforcement, there have been some instances of misuses of the police business card. There have been cases where business cards have been changed into courtesy cards by individuals whose interests were not in tune with effective law enforcement. There have been some cases where police personnel have violated public trust by writing notes on the back of their business cards and then giving them to individuals who automatically had or thought that they had some immunity from arrest or traffic citations. In effect, the inscriptions on the back of courtesy cards usually state something along the lines of "This is to introduce _____, please extend any courtesies to him that you can." The courtesies expected are evident to any police officer who has the card handed to him in lieu of a driver's license.

Probably the majority of the courtesy cards have been altered by the persons who have received the card as a business card from police personnel. Because of this factor the police business card should have a design or blacked out reverse side to prevent alterations by either police personnel or by the citizen.

The most effective means of preventing any misuses of the police business card is through the line police officer. Under no circumstances should an officer ever honor a courtesy card. Effective law enforcement prohibits special favors for citizens claiming to be a "friend" or relative of a fellow police officer.

THE PURSUIT OF CRIMINALS

The pursuit of criminals and their apprehension are basic functions of law enforcement. The protection of the lives and property of the public is also not only a basic function but a sworn duty. Situations will arise from time to time where these two fundamental obligations may conflict with each other. When a conflicting situation does present itself, a decision must be made by the police officer involved to determine which duty is in the best interest of the public.

An example demonstrating an area of conflicting obligations might be the evolution of a simple vehicle pursuit into a high-speed chase. An arbitrary speed or set of specific guidelines cannot be justifiably established by police administrators as to when an officer should or should not terminate a high-speed chase. This can only be determined by the individual officer involved in the situation. Only he knows the basic ingredients required to formulate a correct decision. Only he knows the exact traffic and roadway conditions, and *his ability at that time* to effectively control his police unit and apprehend the violator. It must be the individual officer, not an administrator, who should weigh the balance between the danger of the citizens on the roadway and the danger to his own safety versus the psychological danger of reoccurrences should the violator escape because the police officer failed to continue pursuit.

The offender has an advantage over law enforcement personnel, as he has no responsibility to other users of the roadway except what he should morally do as a good citizen. If his freedom is paramount to him, he can set his own rules or stakes of the pursuit according to the risk he is willing to take to escape the penalty of the law. The police officer does not have this advantage. Even if he is willing to risk his life to apprehend the violator, his actions will be judged at a later date should an innocent citizen become maimed or killed as a direct result of the pursuit.

In decisions of this nature, the law enforcement officer must decide in favor of the value of the citizen's life if it is apparent that such a danger exists. Within all reason, he must, however, apprehend the violator as arbitrary "shut downs" in vehicle pursuits will result in more chases in the future by those willing to "test" the police officer of police policies.

COMPROMISING WITH CRIMINALS

Allowing petty criminals to escape the penalty of the law for information which will lead to the arrest of a major offender has always been an ethical consideration for law enforcement officers.

By the strict interpretation of the written law any violator apprehended is expected to be brought before a court of law and be judged by either a magistrate or a jury of his peers. To allow any person to escape the legal procedure appears to be a violation of the accepted code of ethics of law enforcement, which in part states, ". . . with no compromise for crime and with relentless prosecution of criminals." Therefore, any violation of this premise would be a moral violation against the written law by which police officers are expected to live.

Unfortunately, everything is not as clear-cut or precise as many of our rules may indicate. There is also the theory of the difference between the written letter of a law and the spirit by which it should be enforced. The often-referred-to compromising with informants on minor charges must be viewed in this respect if we are to become effective in enforcing the laws of major concern to society. Surely a drug addict who is willing to disclose his source of narcotics is of less concern to the community than the apprehension and prosecution of the narcotics pusher who is responsible for the human suffering of literally hundreds of addicts.

It must be remembered that these immunities to informants are not done in the spirit of allowing someone to escape through the bars of justice, but to apprehend a greater criminal who might not have otherwise been detected. The basic question then becomes, "Do the means justify the ends?" In the interest of the protection of our communities at large, the answer appears to be obvious.

REPORTING A FELLOW OFFICER

Through the centuries, in every walk of life, men who have informed on their peers have been held in contempt and distrust. This contempt does not limit itself to informants in criminal matters alone. How many times have we noted that the individual who informs the "boss" relative to all activities and errors of his fellow workers is soon found to be completely friendless at work. This reaction by the group is probably normal and reasonable.

In law enforcement, too, there are some police officers who spend a great deal of time and effort searching for the shortcomings of fellow officers. When this data is compiled, it is then brought to the attention of a supervisor for two purposes: The first is that the supervisor will think less of the patrolman who committed the errors. The second is that the supervisor may consider the informing patrolman rather clever, as he detected these errors and surely would not make similar mistakes. These informing police officers not only ruin their reputations but sow the seeds of distrust in the whole department. The field of law enforcement requires the closest ties between officers and distrust among brother officers can reap a fatal result.

In view of the above, it appears that the following would be a better procedure. An error committed by a patrolman should be discussed with the fellow officer who discovers the error. This discussion should be a free exchange of ideas, permitting both parties an opportunity to learn from the error. This is probably the best solution for harmony and a better quality of work performance.

For a more serious violation or error a different approach must be taken, depending, of course, on the circumstances and magnitude of the violation or error. A situation we might explore is that of a driver under the minor influence of alcohol who turns out to be an off-duty fellow officer within your department. The first offense might be handled by informal methods. Should the situation reoccur, a field supervisor should be informed concerning the condition of the officer. Ordinary citizens who violate the safety of the roadway by driving while intoxicated are removed from the roadway. This is done for their safety as well as for the safety of the general public. The above statement does not indicate that an arrest of a fellow officer who drives while he is under the influence of alcohol is mandatory; however, disciplinary action must be taken by the supervisor if possible. If an officer completely closes his eyes to this situation and at a later date the other officer seriously injures himself or someone else as the result of driving under the influence, the fault will be shared responsibility.

In summation, the reporting of a fellow officer's petty errors to influence a supervisor is wrong and injures the reputation of both the officer who commits the error and the officer who reports it. In the end, the department also suffers because of lack of trust between its members. For a serious violation, such as driving under the influence, burglary, theft, graft, etc., the well-being of the department must be the prime consideration. Personal feelings or obedience to the outdated unwritten law that a fellow officer can do no wrong must not take precedence.

THE TAKING OF A HUMAN LIFE

One of the most difficult decisions a police officer can face is if and when he should take a human life. For the hardcore members of pacifist religions, the answer is simple. No human life should ever be taken under any circumstances. A police officer who subscribes to this belief should immediately seek another occupation, as his decision may well effect the life of another officer or law-abiding citizen. In essence he should be able to justify the difference between *thou shalt not murder* and the accepted translated Bible version of *thou shalt not kill*. Surely, even the Bible demonstrates time after time the justification of taking a human life under prescribed situations. Legally an officer can usually defend taking the life of an escaping felon, a suspect committing a felony, a subject about to take the life of another citizen, or attempting to kill or maim another officer or himself. Within these classifications, however, each set of circumstances should govern the actions taken.

If a felon suspect is escaping from the scene of a crime, the officer should quickly evaluate; 1) the extent of the felony, i.e. is he a burglar or a murderer? 2) whether the suspect be apprehended *safely* without having to shoot him; 3) if there is *any* possibility of an innocent bystander getting shot; 4) if the suspect is a dangerous criminal, will his escape endanger the lives of fellow officers and innocent citizens?

Many pages could be written on this subject; however, the major concern rests in two areas, *the quick and the dead.* There is danger in both extremes.

The quick represents the officer who fails to evaluate a situation correctly and wrongly kills or maims in haste. His rash action will usually bring criticism against the police service, his agency, and criminal complaints against himself.

The dead are those who either failed to evaluate a situation correctly within a safe period of time, or for some reason could not bring themselves to take a human life. Among the numbers of these dead are also those good officers who depended on a fellow officer who could not face the responsibility to judge on the street level in sufficient time.

CHAPTER 2

THE POLICE AND POLITICS

Donald O. Schultz

ANY discussion or critical evaluation of the policeman's role in politics would be totally invalid and incomplete if it were not viewed from a historical perspective. Gerald O. Williams, author of the article "Political Police" in the March 1969 issue of *Police Magazine* states:

> Police from the earliest periods of history and organized government have existed as special bodies of officers, either civil or military, which have operated to detect and suppress political opposition to the government in power. Variously referred to a "Secret Police" and "Political Police" their objective has always been the same.

Political police have existed since the ancient Zoroastrian and Assyrian civilizations. According to Williams, the most complete information we have today deals with the political police system as it existed in ancient Rome. Organized normally as a military addition, Tiberius Ceasar's political police intelligence arrangement had a widespread organization of agents engaged in the surveillance and supression of political and religious factors adverse to the Roman government.

The word "police" itself, which like "politics" is derived from the Greek noun *polis* or city-state, gives us our first connotation of the involvement that political police might have played in the role of city-state governments throughout the Middle Ages and Renaissance, although during these times it seems as though they were in many cases nothing more than assassins.

Governments of the eighteenth and nineteenth centuries also utilized political police to counter the assaults of counter-revolutions and revolts which were against the best interests of the established government. Williams continues in his article and says, "Political Police organizations can thus be shown to be much older in their origin than are the organizations for the enforcement of the criminal law with which we are so familiar today."

Political police, which were developed during the French and German empires of the eighteenth and nineteenth centuries were subsequent developments of assassins and criminals being utilized for removal of political opposition. These organizations have become very important and omnipotent today in countries like Russia and China and virtually have a stranglehold on the lives of their citizens. Quoting from Williams' article we find that:

> When the political police of the Austro-Hungarian Empire, which served as a model for the security police systems of the 19th century Prussia and Germany, was being organized by Emperor Joseph II in the 1780's, the first formal dichotomy of function as between the political and criminal police was established. At this time, the regular law enforcement organizations of Europe were being established, and a delineation of function between them and the older political police was called for.

In a memorandum on the establishment of the Austrian Higher State Police, this division was announced by Joseph II. A public police was to provide the protection which the subjects were due for their persons and property. On the other hand a secret or higher state police should protect the prince and his government from all dangers from subjects as well as from foreigners.

Modern-day Russian secret police and World War II German gestapo units were subsequent developments of Joseph II's political police system.

AMERICAN HISTORY

According to a staff report to the President's Commission by James S. Campbell:

> Police participation in the political process in America has traditionally been limited and local. Limited to securing favorable legislation as to pension, working conditions and pay rates with occasional lobbying for or against proposals to

abolish the death penalty, legalize gambling, or raise the age of juvenile court jurisdiction, and in the local sense, that it invariably involved approaches by the locally organized police to municipal authorities or at most to the state legislators representing the district.

Many times charges would be made that the police were politically active in local campaigns, but generally the public has felt that the police should abstain from direct participation in politics. Early in the history of the United States, police were used against demonstrations, protests, strikes, and mobs, an example being the 1919 race riots. Many of these conflicts involved honest but misled groups of citizens. Many times instead of taking a neutral position in trying to restore domestic tranquility during these primarily political clashes, the police have tended to become active participants on the side of management or on the side of the conservative elements against the dissident elements. Historically, the dissident elements have quickly recognized police siding with whom they consider the enemy, and consequently they have directed their assaults and abuse against the police. The cycle obviously becomes vicious with the police on the short end. This has been shown by the results of confrontation between management and labor disputes in the thirties and between California landowners and migrant farm workers in the early forties, as well as various other conflicts.

Colonial Development

Political influence and law enforcement have seemed to be closely associated in the United States. During the early colonial period the sheriffs had a tremendous amount of political influence and frequently used their powers for political as well as personal gain. With the growth of the early towns the pronounced effect of their influences also grew. In those early days in America the sheriff, township constable, or village marshal, who were subject to popular election, were required to be engaged in politics.

Development of the Sheriff in America

In America the office of sheriff, a political office, has only lived because it has been a rich prize for the political system that controlled it. Raymond Moley states in his book *Politics and Criminal Prosecution:* "Ample political figures have found the office to their liking, including President Cleveland, who held the office of Sheriff of Erie County in (Buffalo)."

Largely because of the profits inherent in the fee system of compensating county officers, the functions of process server and jailer have replaced that of a peace officer and his value as a peace officer has become negligible, according to Moley. A field survey, *Police and the Community,* done by the University of California at Berkeley states:

> The Sheriff is the chief law enforcement officer of the county and as such has technically concurrent jurisdiction with city police in incorporated areas. He is also responsible for taking and caring for prisoners in the county jail.

Volume II of this report states:

> In Philadelphia the sheriff is elected for a four-year term and primarily is the execution arm of Philadelphia's courts. He serves court orders, warrants, writs and subpoenaes. He seizes real and personal property and sells it to obtain satisfaction on judgments, defaulted mortages or unpaid taxes.

Constables are also elected and they serve as executive officers of the Magistrates Court. By common law, constables in many cities still have power of peace officers. According to Roger Lane in his book *Policing the City;* "In practice, during the early 19th century, the appointment of Sheriff was for life."

Early American Police Politicalization

As related in a staff report to the President's Commission on Crime, *The Politics of Protest:*

> Political involvement of the police is not per se a new phenomenon in the United States. Indeed, it is well known that in the days of the big city political machines Police were in politics in a small way. They often owed their jobs to local alderman and were expected to cooperate with political ward bosses.

Yet there was traditionally another way — as an active arm of the status quo.

One of the early records of police actively involved in politics, states Lane, was in the 1850's in Boston, when the local marshal and his men decided to "dabble in politics" by having his men vote a certain way in a popular election. This action was subsequently frowned upon by the mayor, and he fired the whole night force in retaliation. In the 1860's a theory was expressed that "the relation of the Chief of Police to the Mayor, by its very nature required the most implicit confidence, should not be disturbed by any doubt of his friendliness of feeling." Here we see some of the first philosophical ideas about the separation of police from the influence of politics. Lane continues: "In 1863 the majority of the people in Boston felt that criminals held the political balance and the police were used for political purposes."

In 1878 a police commission was established to facilitate reforms in the police department. Some of the improvements were getting new facilities, provision of firearms and the adoption of new promotion policies void of any political influence. The lessons learned in Boston were lessons already learned by other cities, and that lesson according to Lane was that "political change at the top was not enough to solve Police problems."

Charles Reith states in his book *The Blind Eye of History:*

> Metropolitan police forces, most of which developed during the late 1800's when government corruption was most prevalent, have often been deeply involved in political corruption, this corruption being manifested in Police political appointments given as a reward for political favors.

Patronage appointments seemed to lower the quality of personnel and tended to entice participation of police officers with politicians although this is still an accepted practice today in many small cities.

Many of the problems which troubled our first organized metropolitan police forces according to a Task Force Report, *The Police,* presented to the Crime Commission, can be traced to a single root — "political control." As Bruce Smith in his book, *Police Systems in the United States,* related:

Rotation in office enjoyed so much popular favor that police posts of both high and low degree were constantly changing hands, with political fixers determining the price and conditions of exchange. The whole police question became identified with the corruption and degradation of the city politics and local governments of that period.

City leaders attempting to alleviate these problems sought to create police administrative boards to replace control exercised over police affairs by mayors or city councils. The President's Commission on Law Enforcement and Administration of Justice states that "this attempt to cure political meddling was unsuccessful because the people who comprised the boards were inexpert in dealing with the board problems."

Turn of the Century

On every side, the American administrative powers, at the turn of the nineteenth century was marked by lack of organization, decentralized responsibility, and an inherent attitude on the part of the public officials to cooperate. Roscoe Pound relates in his book, *Criminal Justice:* "Policemen as a rule changed as often as did the bosses of political power." Policemen who tried to fight the political system in this era, were in many cases transferred to punishment beats or other nondesirable positions.

According to Fred E. Haynes in his book, *Criminology,* police commissioners in New York up into the 1930's had an average term in office of about one year and seven months as compared to the police commissioner in London with an average of fifteen years on the same job.

RECENT EVENTS

In the early fifties a theory was expressed by Adlai E. Stevenson, a noted liberal politician, in his article "The Menace of Organized Crime" that "Crime and politics must be divorced. Police forces on what ever level of government must be severed from partisan control." For example, prior to 1952 no major policy decision or personnel promotion was made in the police department of Philadelphia without the approval of the mayor and the political cronies out in the city's wards. This included promotion and assignment to district police captains. Volume II of the California field survey further states that the police department was politically dominated and controlled in the sixty-seven years prior to 1952.

In response to this onslaught against police politicalization many police organizations incorporated into existing regulations strict rules prohibiting political activity except voting. In the last decade, mostly as a result of efforts to raise police pay scales to an even level with skilled workmen, more militant police associations, according to Paul Chevigny, became "trade union affiliated," others in loose state and national affiliations escalated their pressure tactics so that job action "blue flu" (police call in sick in total) and even threatened police strikes became common place in police municipality salary disputes.

The major attempts for police politicalization, however, was without doubt the cause of civilian review boards. As stated by the *Washington Post:* "The proposals for civilian review boards were fought against in the legislature, courts and news media." Some proponents of the civilian review boards felt that a politicalized police force united, well financed and closely related to conservative social and political forces in the community, posed a problem for those interested in preserving democracy.

A new role was starting to be perceived by the "Thin Blue Line" into the fifties and sixties. That role was one of a minority group, and their feeling was constantly being reinforced by an apathetic, unaware, unconcerned public who were unaware of police problems. Police began to become reinforced into a defensive group with cohesive solidarity.

THE POLICEMEN'S NEW ROLE

In a staff report, *Rights in Concord,* a response to the counter-inaugural protest, the policeman's new role in dealing with a mass of demonstrators for example, is basically that of an umpire. Since the umpire must be the instant decision-maker who stands in the eye of a potential storm, the policeman's job is an incredibly difficult one. To perform his task properly, a policeman should not become involved in the issues.

The conduct of government officials other than the police can make the policeman's job possible or impossible. Public officials can set the stage and lay down the rules for a demonstration in such a way that violent clashes between police and demonstrators are virtually certain to occur. Or public officials can condition responses of police and demonstrators in the direction of mutual toleration.

PRESENT INVOLVEMENT

Having covered the historical role that police have played in the world of politics from the era of kings and emperors to recent times, it is only fitting that we now view the present-day policeman and the role he has or continues to play in politics. As a general statement or rule, the power of the politician over police in the country as a whole has greatly diminished. It was only during the 1940's that this reform in most major cities won the police their independence from the old-line political machines and bosses. However, as is often the case, there are exceptions to this rule.

As a starting point of present-day police involvement in politics it is felt worthwhile to quote James Q. Wilson, a Harvard political scientist, whose recently published book, *Varieties of Police Behavior,* preceptively analyzes the police attitude. In it he detects a very definable "police attitude." He states "that the policeman develops from their work environment, whatever moral or emotional responses they may have brought to the job." The fact is that policemen in every city work within a social system which has already largely been defined by custom and practice before he entered it. This "police attitude" while informal in nature disposes the policeman toward rugged individualism, moral absolutism, and political conservatism. The conservatism is abstract and attached to distant ideals of honor and courage that rise above the reality of a society he feels is composed of uncooperative witnesses, of curious news media and reporters, and lastly of scheming politicians.

We could categorize the police in politics into two subheadings — *direct* and *indirect*. In distinguishing between the two we considered the following under *direct:*

1. Elected by citizens to a law enforcement position, for example the sheriff of a county.

2. Appointed to position in law enforcement by elected public official, for example the commissioner, public safety director, or chief of police appointed by the mayor, or in the case of some cities a city manager or commission.

3. Those elected to other public office having previously served as a law enforcement officer in some capacity, for example the former mayor of Minneapolis, Minnesota, the Honorable Charles S. Stenvig.

Within the *indirect* role of police in politics were considered actions taken by individuals or groups of police to openly support a political candidate or party and in some cases even joining various types of organizations (social and fraternal), unions, or other organizations such as the John Birch Society and the Minutemen.

Direct Involvement

1. Returning to the first heading under the direct involvement where we have a policeman *elected to a law enforcement position,* let us look briefly at the job cited — that of county sheriff. While he is an elected public official, he often is lacking in actual law enforcement experience or refuses to update himself in current aspects of it. He may often let the ideal of being reelected become paramount to his performance of duty as a police officer. This is not to say that elections corrupt a police officer who is an elected official but it does at least have a substantial influence on his life and job performance. Some county sheriffs have also given a "black eye" to law enforcement by their unscrupulous methods of retaining power and making financial gains to their individual benefit.

2. In the second subdivision we find those *appointed to positions in law enforcement by an elected public official* such as a mayor, city manager, or board of commissions. When this

happens, it goes without saying that being political appointees they owe their allegiance and loyalty to the man or men who appointed them. This may at times have an adverse effect on their performance of duty, though by the same token it may place them in an effective position to apply political influence gained largely on their record in the position.

In this context we will look at several large cities in the United States and see how the police and politics are entwined and the impact each has on the other. The cities discussed will be New York, Los Angeles, Chicago, and San Francisco.

The police may be called to protect the right to strike and picket in labor-management disputes. They may be confronted with the "marchers," sit-ins, and on election day it is they who add confidence and assure the peaceable use of the vote. However, as times have changed, the police have begun to take stands on more general social questions, sometimes in the political arena itself as we shall see in the discussion of the various cities.

Los Angeles: The party machines have never been a powerful force, but the police along with other groups of city employees have formed voter blocs that have often been important in the determining of the outcome of local elections. By and far however, they have concentrated on gaining higher wages and other material benefits in return for this support. As governmental employees they, as all other police in major cities, have usually tried to stay on the right side of city hall. Perhaps an example of involvement by a personage no less than the late police chief William Parker would be in order. He participated actively in the Christian Anti-Communist Crusade in 1960 and encouraged his police officers to attend their schools at special reduced police "fees." He, like many other noted police authorities and concerned Americans, considered the American Civil Liberties Union as a Communist front organization and was in favor of maintaining the "status quo" in regards to the ethnic groups.

New York: There are those who feel that even the most professional police department cannot be trusted to perform in the public interest if elected officials do not have a firm control of law enforcement policy. The police, like the military, should not be permitted to determine their own policies in a democratic society. Unfortunately, this control of police by elected officials is confused in the minds of many policemen and many ordinary citizens because of the kind of political domination of police departments reminiscent of the early 1930's. For such a case in point we look at the city of New York.

Leftist activist Mayor John Lindsay sought to assert his authority over his police department when in 1966 he installed his own police commissioner and made other changes in the department.

His results had been spotty at best against organized police opposition. The Patrolman's Benevolent Association did exert enough pressure however, to have the civilian board he established to review a complaint against the police abolished by a voter referendum.

San Francisco: The police had been controlled previous to 1956 by a three-man commission appointed by the mayor. Usually it consisted of one member who was above reproach and two political appointees by the mayor. Thus it can be readily observed that the mayor controlled the police and used them for his own ends. However, in 1956, a new reform mayor appointed three impeccable citizens to fill the commission slots. They in turn appointed a reform chief of police, Ahern, who kept the post until his death in 1958 when Thomas Cahill was appointed to replace him.

Police influence has been profound in many areas though it was usually in an indirect method scheme of things. In conjunction with these closer community efforts they formed special squads to work the minority groups as well as convicts just released from prison. They provided understanding of each others problems and helped to rehabilitate the ex-con with job opportunities he might not otherwise have received.

Various of the reform measures sought by the police have received only lukewarm reception by Chief Cahill and the community relations squads were returned to the control of the district captains under conserted pressures by them.

In showing their independence the police displayed Ronald Reagan for Governor stickers on the police vehicles in the 1966 election and ceased only reluctantly when Cahill issued a department directive forbidding it.

Chicago: Prior to 1960 the Chicago police were the epitome of police corruption and were generally held in contempt by the community. Traditional alliances between the police and politicians made the chief little more than a figurehead. Officers who had political influence knew they had little to worry about as long as their political counterpart remained in power. However, the downfall and reform of the police department happened in late 1959 when a number of policemen were found to be members of a large burglary operation.

Reforms followed, based on a commission set up by Mayor Daley. He appointed Orlando Wilson as chief of police who in turn started setting about making reforms despite opposition of the Patrolman's Benevolent Association.

Some reforms took place, it is true, but there are those who have expressed the belief that the mayor calls the shots right over the chief's head. This may have caused Chief Wilson to resign in 1967, and the feeling presented can be borne out by the handling of the demonstrations at the 1968 Democratic convention.

The influence of the mayor and other elected public officials varies, but the important thing is that today it's seemingly aboveboard, whereas in the past it tended to be of personal nature and was secretive as a rule. The objection of political control and domination of the police does not include, however, that the police function can or should be entirely divorced from the political process.

3. We shall now look at the last section of *direct* involvement — those *elected to other public office after having previously served in a law enforcement position.* For this we will look at the city of Minneapolis, Minnesota.

Mayor Charles S. Stenvig was a forty-one-year-old former burglary detective who ran on a third party reform platform with a campaign based on the "law and order" issue and backed by an army of volunteers on the street. He received 62 percent of the vote in the election. This is based on a full-scale revision of police procedure and support the police are getting from the mayor and other department higher-ups.

This tends to show in one case that the policeman from the office can be successful in the public elected office of mayor.

Indirect Involvement

Let us now look at the *indirect* methods of police involvement in the politics of our society. While it is true that a minority of policemen are actual members of organizations such as the John Birch Society, some discussion is felt in order. The John Birch Society hold ideals for the policemen by virtue of its sympathetic propaganda. One such publication of the Society decreed in California in 1965 that "demands for police review boards, false allegations of police brutality, rash Supreme Court decisions, demand for recall of police administrators and numerous other acts of harassment have made the police officer's job tremendously more difficult in these times of lawlessness in the streets." It is this type of literature which has great appeal for the hard-pressed policeman of our society. The same is true of the various other law and order oriented organizations.

The various fraternal organizations have also given the policeman a voice in the field of politics; as an example the case mentioned concerning the New York PBA which received enough popular support to defeat the review board in a voters referendum. The Fraternal Order of Police is doing likewise in the city of Philadelphia.

Procedures

The question facing the police officer is not one of whether or not to become involved in politics, but rather whether to be actively involved or passively involved. Police officers who chose to become actively involved include a mayor of Detroit, a mayor of Minneapolis, and a city councilman in Los Angeles, among others. The choice for them was not only one of active versus passive political involvement, however, for active partisan political activity is prohibited by regulation or policy in almost every major police department. Their choice caused them to leave law enforcement to enter the political arena. Let us assume that a police officer does desire to engage in political activity and does not wish to leave his profession. Can he do it? The answer is yes. There are restrictions and pitfalls, but the police officer can make his voice heard and his opinion felt without coming into open conflict with the municipality or state that employs him. The police officer can act as an individual or as a group member. He can participate in nonpartisan political activity, or in partisan political activity. The avenues to political activity are many and varied.

The first step to consider is the right to vote. The vote of the individual is sometimes downgraded or ignored as a vital item in the political picture. The importance of the vote of the individual, however, cannot be downgraded or ignored. It is vital!

From elections which decide the presidency of the United States to elections which determine the next city councilman, the vote of only a comparative few can be decisive. In the winner-take-all concept of our system of electing presidents by electoral vote, the popular plurality which sways the electoral vote is particularly interesting. During the 1968 elections, the pivotal state of Illinois threw its 26 votes to Nixon. The results could have been reversed, however, by only a change of one vote in each precinct. The 1948 upset of Thomas E. Dewey by Harry Truman was a close one also. Dewey lost Ohio by 7,107 votes and California by 17,865 votes, a margin of approximately one vote per precinct. The individual vote is even more important in the election of legislators. Those gentlemen, who have an even more direct effect of the legislation of concern to policemen, are often elected by an even closer margin. In 1956, Representative Hale of Maine was reelected by 29 votes; Congressman Sieminski of New Jersey won by 57 votes; and Representative Doliver of Iowa lost by 198 votes.

A selective effort to get out the vote can be very effective. During the 1968 presidential elections only 61 percent of the electorate voted. During the off-year of 1966 only 46 percent of eligible voters voted. The vote in state primaries seldom runs more than 30 percent, and is often lower in local elections. It is obvious that selective voter registration drives and pressure to get out the voters of each party can be the most rewarding effort.

A personal communication to the elected legislator can be

instrumental in the passage or failure of proposed legislation. Recently, in the state of Nebraska, a group of less than 100 citizens was successful in forcing reconsideration of a bill that had already been voted down in the state legislature. Fewer than 100 letters and telegrams caused a bill to be passed that will influence one and one-half million Nebraskans! A letter or telegram from even one voter can be influential. To help insure that it gets the attention that it warrants, there are several dos and don'ts which should be heeded. A legislator will normally place more weight on correspondence bearing upon pending legislation than upon general topics. Pending legislation should be identified by either its popular name or its number. If the bill is not properly identified, there is a possibility that a representative will not be able to identify it either. Comments should be concise and logical. A personal letter or telegram should be just that — personal. Form letters and coupons from papers and magazines, urging a particular view, are handy for head counts, but do not carry the same weight a personal communication does. Lastly, a communication should not be abusive.

Petitions and referendums offer a comparatively speedy way of forcing action on a subject when it has wide public support. The circulation of petitions by police officers would, in most instances, be prohibited or discouraged. A police officer's signature and support as a private citizen does help, however. Recently, in New York City, the mayor installed a police review board which was heavily weighted with anti-police and minority members. In the face of heavy opposition the mayor stated that his action was not subject to review by the voters. Subsequent legal action, a petition, and a referendum vote proved him wrong. Voters of both major political parties, the Conservative Party, and the John Birch Society rallied behind the Police Benevolent Association and threw out the civilian review board by a vote of better than two to one.

Individual, nonpartisan political activity can be effective. The same amount of effort exerted in concert with others, however, can be even more effective. Normally, joining with others in combined political activity will involve political party affiliation. Selection of a political party involves several considerations. Most important among these considerations is the compatability of the party philosophy with your own and the effectiveness of the party in promoting its program.

Historically, our country has always had two major parties, and occasionally, a third minor party which represents a radical or reactionary element which cannot be readily accomodated by one of the major parties. Senator Hugh D. Scott, the present Senate Minority Leader and a renowned political writer, has stated: "Independent movements usually fail through lack of continuity, grass-roots organization, and political know-how." The Socialist Party, the Dixiecrats of 1948, and Henry Wallace's Progressive Party of 1948 are cases in point. The two major parties have a great absorbant capacity. A persistent third party will find that, over a period of time, it has lost its platform. The planks have been incorporated in the platform of the major parties. Norman Thomas, the once perennial presidential candidate of the Socialist Party, stated shortly before his death that he did not feel it was necessary for him to run in the election, for one or both of the major parties had adopted his entire earlier platform.

On the state and local level, third party membership may be more successful. Even here, however, they are seldom able to muster a majority and are most effective in instances where they are able to force one of the major parties to bend to their position. This is normally done by being able to present a bloc of voters to one side or the other, rather than through fear that their candidate will win.

Normally, the next step after joining a political party would be to participate in supporting party activities, probably at the precinct level. It is at this point, however, that we run head-on into the general ban on active, partisan political activity by police officers. It is necessary then to consider another form of political activity that does not expose the police officer to charges of active, partisan political activity, but at the same time is the most practical and effective form of political pressure, namely participation in a pressure group that maintains an active lobby.

Lobbies in American Government and Politics

When divisions within a society become so conscious of their desires that they perfect a definite organization, draw up a platform of objectives and actively seek to bring about the realization of their aspirations by influencing elected and appointed officials, they have attained the status of a pressure group.

Stated above is one definition of what a pressure group is. Generally a pressure group is conceived of as a specific group of persons who feel their particular concern about public policy is the best. This group then goes about attempting by various methods to attain their goal. This organization may be well-organized or loosely organized. The group may represent a large economic concern or be practically penniless. Regardless of these factors it must merely be a group of interested persons who share basic attitudes and convictions on a common topic. Generally the pressure group is short-lived and rather temporary. This is caused mainly by the fact that the group is made up of persons who have become aroused over a single issue. When that issue is resolved, they disseminate until such time as they may organize again, with other individuals, to promote a different issue. Other pressure groups are more lasting such as the American Medical Association. This group has a large, well-organized following, adequate financial support, and prestige. Groups such as this do not tend to break up, but remain consolidated and pursue new issues when other issues are disposed of.

Law enforcement in general might be called a pressure group. The members of law enforcement organizations tend to have the same feelings about a number of issues. However, they also, to date, fall under the heading of the type of pressure group which is not well-organized. From time to time an issue arises which solidifies persons involved in law enforcement, but on the whole, there is not a strong enough national organization. This may be remedied with the advent of a national police organization. Members of the rank and file in law enforcement need this type of organization to look after their interests before state and national legislatures. A well-organized group would also help in the establishment of better public opinion in favor of law enforcement.

Related to pressure groups are lobbies. Lobbies are similar to pressure groups in that they attempt to sway public opinion and influence public policy. However, the comparison stops there. Where the pressure group is generally short-lived, the lobby tends to be sustaining. Where the pressure group generally is limited to one topic, the lobby is interested in the many facets of an issue. As an example, a pressure group of aroused citizens may attempt to influence a legislature to lower the speed limit near a playground, when this is accomplished they disband. But a lobby of the American Medical Association might attempt to influence a legislature for stricter drug control, and at the same time be interested in and lobbying for five or six other bills before the legislature. One should remember that "not all pressure groups are lobbies, but all lobbies are pressure groups."

Pressure groups form a lobby in Washington or state legislatures and are represented generally by lawyers, who prefer to call themselves legislative counsel rather than lobbyist. This is caused mainly by the fact that at one time, and with many people today, lobbyists had a bad reputation. People tend to think of lobbyists as unscrupulous and exerting undue influence of legislators. They believe that the purpose of a lobby is to bribe and force a legislator by any means to adopt the policy of the lobby. This has been true in the past and occasionally may be true today, but for the most part, this means of lobbying has been replaced with more acceptable means.

For the lobbyists' own good most of the state legislatures and the national congress have passed laws which regulate lobbying. This is accomplished through legislation which forces the individual lobbyist to register and keep on file a record of expenditures which are connected to his lobbying. Penalty for omitting to register or file financial reports has been made a criminal offense in some states, and is punishable, generally by up to one year imprisonment and/or a fine.

National police organizations should concentrate on the national congress and administration. However, local police pressure groups, such as local department associations (PBA's and benovolent leagues) could pressure and lobby in their own states and communities. This should be done, because the local departments know best where to and how to apply pressure in their own geographic area.

The pressure group and lobbyist can be an asset to the legislature and legislator. He generally has a wealth of information on the issue which he is representing. He has much more insight into the problems of the group he is representing and is better able to get the group's point across than is the group itself.

The police and law enforcement officials and the society as a whole would benefit from a law enforcement lobby in Washington. This lobby would have to be a full-time job and suited to the purpose of arguing for and pleading the cause of law enforcement. This lobby could have the effect of influencing and obtaining legislation which would be favorable to law enforcement, rather than some of the anti-police legislation which has been coming forth. This lobby could also appear before the courts as a friend of the court and explain the police position.

With the strength of the National Police Officers Association and other professional police organizations a strong lobby and more effective pressure group will probably come forth. As a law enforcement lobby, the lobby will probably be scrutinized more closely than the average lobby for unsavory practices and corruption.

Lobbying is very much like a public relations and advertising job. The techniques used by public relations men, advertisers, and lobbyists are very similar. All are aimed at winning favorable public opinion. All attempt to become and should be very adept at becoming, experts in the art of influence. A successful lobbyist knows how to write up a favorable bill and to whom to take it to get it started on its way to becoming law. The lobbyist must know from whom to seek help on different facets of legislation concerning law enforcement.

The lobbyists must also learn how to institute effectively the various techniques of influence. A few of these techniques are listed below with some brief explanations:

1. Attempting to influence individual legislators.
2. Testifying before committees.
3. Public advertising — television, radio, movies, pamphlets, articles, news.

4. Pressuring of constituents:
   a. Rifle — letters from chosen influential constituents to the legislator.
   b. Shotgun — appeal to all constituents to write to their congressman in an attempt to overwhelm the legislators.
5. Attempting to influence individual administrators.
6. Using courts to test constitutionality of a law.

These are but a few of the methods which might be implemented.

ADVANTAGES OF POLITICAL INVOLVEMENT

No longer can police take a defensive stand on every issue thrown at them. The time for debating on whether police should be outspoken or not is past history. Any group which has made strides in advancement has done so in an outright effort.

Unfortunately the word "politics" puts fear into the average lawman's heart and thoughts of graft into the citizen's mind. In its simplest definition politics means conducting the business of a government. Certainly the business of that government has to be enforced. Logically then, police are already involved in the mainstream of politics. The question then changes from how should we get into politics to how do we get involved?

There is only one path to follow. That is to come out in the open and stand up for those issues which are of police concern. Many candidates ran in the fall of 1969 on law and order tickets. A few policemen resigned their positions and were elected to office. Police are going to become more and more involved in this area. The people obviously are prepared to accept active involvement on the part of police in politics.

Certainly partisan politics will have to be eliminated, except in that police will be partisan for police concerns. No double standard can exist in the criminal justice system. Many people will undoubtedly be shocked at vocal involvement. These will be the anti-police minority though, and not the great silent majority.

One benefit of hearing a policeman speak out on issues is enlightenment. Manypeople in the "silent majority" are really ignorant of the many facets making up police work. They have never been confronted with law enforcement directly and simply have not had to think about it. These people have all heard the worn-out statements about how underpaid and worthy our police are, but it was normally only small talk and went in one ear and out the other.

During the last decade it has become fashionable to voice grievances in a boisterous way. The larger the group and the more aggressive their demands the greater their benefits seem to be. Police should not use coercion to achieve goals. But a few hints done in a well thought out manner can not help but assist police goals. This is the "now generation" for everyone else, so why not policemen? There is some truth in the old cliche "the squeaky wheel gets the grease."

A hard decision to make of course is where do we draw a line between what is political activity and what is dereliction of the sworn police duty. This line will probably not be clear until such time as the court system has decided them. During the meantime ground rules will need to be formulated for activation. We will take a logical approach to separation. Any activity which would be unquestionably detrimental to public safety must be ruled out. At the other extreme, activities which have little or no effect on public safety should be utilized. A good example of this might be to refuse a motorcycle escort for a dignitary who is a known anti-police supporter. This would drive across the point to him and his supporters that police have ways of communicating their feelings also.

A cohesive organization can muster support in numerous ways. They can send lobbyists to sway legislation. They have centrally directed goals and usually a solvent treasury to finance their means.

Many people who are afraid of police having any political power are hurting themselves. Suppose that a city has a high crime rate and very few policemen. The police they do have are local men hired at minimum wages. Consequently, they do as little enforcement work as necessary and it is of poor quality. It seems logical that the low wages have a direct bearing on the number and type of personnel employed by this city. Now, lobbyists push for a state standard and a bill authorizing an equal number of police per population. The city has to take a little tax bite, but now they hire outstanding applicants at a decent wage and get some qualified personnel. The crime rate is reduced, the city gets its money back in the long run, and the citizens are safer.

The police are much larger in numbers than many groups, but they are not united in a concentrated effort. At present there is no well-recognized national spokesman for police, but he or they will emerge as police become actively involved in seeking their goals.

The catalysts for police to stand up and be counted is everywhere. In addition to recent court decisions the anti-police elements have made police realize that they are no longer able to sit back and just bear the brunt of a changing society. Quite possibly the recent Supreme Court decisions are a blessing in disguise. The new breed of police are being trained to deal in a technical society where any breach of due process can free a criminal. Also this new breed is demanding compensation for its preparation efforts. Police salaries are being raised everywhere.

With an ever-expanding population our crime problem is multiplying. Even though the quality of police is improving the fact remains that crime does pay. It is estimated that a good organization can apprehend and bring prosecution in less than one third of all felony cases. This concern for growing crime has made law enforcement a bigger concern for the citizen.

Unless police choose to become actively involved in our increasingly complex society and its changing attitudes, they may receive less sympathy and understanding than they did in the past. Police have got to share their knowledge and experience with legislatures and courts. The police community is not a group apart from society; it is part of it. The time to act is now.

CHAPTER 3

THE USE OF FORCE

Donald O. Schultz

HISTORICAL ASPECTS

THE over-use of force, or perhaps force to any degree, so commonly referred to by today's public as "police brutality," is not relatively new to the American scene. Policing bodies have been plagued throughout history by critics as to their methods of quelling disturbances and the apprehension of criminals, whether it be by group or individual force.

One of the earliest examples of force was in 1786 during Shay's Rebellion. The state militia was called to quell rebel farmers who had gathered in front of the courthouse at Springfield, Massachusetts. A mob of about 600 persons, composed of small property owners and farmers revolting against their creditors and against high taxes collected in Massachusetts, had threatened the Supreme Court and prevented the court from allowing the foreclosure of farms and the imprisonment of debtors. A mob of this size was of course too large to be handled by a constable with a handful of men. The state militia, under the command of Major General Benjamin Lincoln, was able to subdue the rebels by the use of group tactics. Lincoln's men, armed with rifles and fixed bayonets, formed a wedge-type riot formation to move the rebels away from the courthouse. Although for the most part the wedge-type formation worked successfully to move the farmers from the courthouse, a few were shot and beaten by the militia because of the strong resistance encountered.

During the 1800's most of the law enforcement duties in the majority of the United States were handled by local sheriffs. Force to these men was usually either at a minimum or maximum. The sheriff or his deputy would ask an unwanted man to leave town. If he did, the only force used would be verbal. If he did not, he would either be put in jail or shot.

In 1835, a group known as the Texas Rangers was organized. These men were the first form of state police. Dealing with cattle rustlers, outlaws, Indians, and marauding Mexicans from across the border, the use of force by these men was handled quite similarly to that of the local sheriffs. The Texas Rangers have always been a well-organized as well as a very respected group.

The year of the great railroad strikes was 1877. Never before in America had labor disputes been so widespread, so damaging to commerce, or so marked by violence. Between the onset of the strikes of 1877 and the close of the Chicago railway in 1894, railroad strikes, boycotts, and strike threats became common. The federal government at this time was constantly trying to suppress these strikes. The strikes often got out of hand before the government was called in. The usual goal of intervention was to halt the strikes and to restore law, order, and regular railway service as quickly as possible. Usually the government agents could stop the strikes with a minimal degree of force. Many times however, railroad workers had to be taken into custody for interfering with the government.

In 1905 there were more strikes. These, however, were statewide coal strikes. It was during this time the Pennsylvania State Police came into being. Armed with clubs, hand guns, and rifles, the police stopped many of the coal miners from destroying community property. The Pennsylvania State Police were accused of strike-breaking by the public, but force was at a minimum, and the miners went back to work.

A historical example of an excessive amount of group force can be depicted by the Bonus Expeditionary Force of May, June, and July of 1932. The Bonus Law of 1924 had given every veteran a certificate payable in 1945. The veterans, hungry, homeless and out of work because of the depression, wanted the bonus paid immediately. Coming from all areas of the United States, some 10,000 Bonus Marchers went to Washington, D. C. to bring pressure on the Senate to pass the bill. Crowds of veterans stood on the Capitol steps, marched around the building and visited senators. For eight weeks the Bonus Marchers patiently and painfully camped in the open extemporaneous shelters to wait for the outcome of their demands. These destitute ex-servicemen petitioned their government for food and care, as well as the Bonus in a time of distress only to find that a federal policy of no-aid had been invoked against them.

No-federal-aid-for-the-poor — this was the verdict of the government. "Aid to anyone at this time is virtually not a financially sound idea," was the statement of President Herbert Hoover. The Bonus Marcher's hope for aid had been rejected and now their future seemed doomed.

Up until this time, the local police agency had kept the Bonus Marchers in line, but now since the bill had been rejected, Secretary of War Huntly, on a perfunctory command from President Herbert Hoover, the Commander-in-Chief, called out a contingent of the United States Army under the command of General MacArthur to disperse the marchers.

This swift movement of the marchers from Washington by police, cavalry, infantry and armor, proved very disheartening to the majority of the public. During the evacuation two unarmed veterans, William J. Hushka and Eric Carlson, were shot to death. A nine-month-old baby died from gas when a passing soldier threw a gas grenade into a house — this to the public was an excessive use of force by the government.

Although law and order cannot be maintained without some loss of individual freedom, the methods imposed on citizens during the late twenties and early thirties were really harsh.

Policemen, in their eagerness to detect crime and to apprehend and bring criminals to justice, sometimes overlooked the importance of the government function as a safeguard of personal liberty.

DEADLY FORCE

Deadly force is that force likely to cause serious physical injury or death. The firing of a weapon, except on the range during practice, should always be considered a deadly force even though the intent of the officer was merely to frighten or to sound an alarm. Once the weapon has been fired, the officer has used potentially deadly force. This would normally include the use of the baton or nightstick, chemical mace, and most "come along" or submission devices. However, these can very easily be utilized in such a manner as to also constitute deadly force.

Without exception, the cardinal rule emphasized by all of the law enforcement agencies is that *an officer may use only that amount of force, either deadly or nondeadly, which is reasonably necessary for the accomplishment of his mission.* Any unnecessary use of force, or unreasonable harrassment, places the officer outside the protection of the law and subjects him to either disciplinary action by his department or liability through the court system.

Every now and then a police officer is critized in the press for excessive use of force or discharging of his firearm. He is usually charged with poor judgment or with exceeding his authority. At the same time, his chief is often criticized for not having properly trained the man in his responsibilities. It is charged that the department does not have an adequate statement of policy as a guide to the officers in these important matters. Actually, most departments do have a statement of policy covering the discharge of firearms by officers. Also, as for training, almost without exception, a training course in which the practical work is always accompanied by a discussion of the circumstances under which force and weapons should and should not be used. Still, we frequently see articles, similar to the example cited earlier, charging officers with indiscriminate shooting and describing them as being "trigger-happy." Everyone will agree that the decision to shoot someone is the most momentous decision a police officer can make. Once the trigger is pulled, the action is irreversible; the decision, irrevocable. So, it is of paramount importance to have a clear-cut statement of policy to guide the men in making such decisions.

RESPONSIBILITIES

One of the primary responsibilities which the chief of any law enforcement agency owes not only to those officers under his jurisdiction, but to those people to whom he is responsible for safety and protection, is the formulation and promulgation of clear and concise policies concerning the expected actions of those officers in his department. One of the most vital areas of policy necessity is that of the use of force in the performance of assigned duties. The chief executive must establish these policies, of course, with the concurrence and approval of the government which he represents, to insure backing in their implementation and enforcement. These policies must be in such detail as to furnish adequate guidance to those expected to comply with their provisions but not so minute, or filled with trifles, as to stifle *any* initiative or freedom of action by the officer. Also, these policies must be constantly updated as decisions of the courts and trends in law enforcement change. Although there are few universally accepted guidelines which law enforcement agencies follow in formulating policies covering situations where particular types and degrees of force are called for and authorized, several areas have been found to be fairly similar.

FIREARMS

By far the biggest area of controversy, as far as the use of force is concerned, is in the area of firearms utilization. Most police departments have general orders or departmental directives furnishing fairly specific guidelines for the use of a weapon at a fleeing person guilty of a misdemeanor. A Baltimore Police Department directive comments on this thusly, "Under no circumstances shall a member of the department shoot at a person who is running away to avoid arrest on a misdemeanor charge, as the law recognizes that it is better to allow a misdemeanant to escape than to take his life. Members must always bear in mind, 'When in doubt, Don't Fire,' (Cardinal Rule)."

The General Order issued by the Chief of Police of Kansas City concerning the discharge of firearms is fairly representative of most other departments and is quoted as follows:

A. An officer may discharge his firearms for any of the following purposes;
    1. To defend himself from death or serious injury.
    2. To defend another person unlawfully attacked from death or serious injury.

3. To perfect the arrest or prevent the escape, after notice, when all other means fail, of a person whom the officer has reasonable grounds to believe has committed a felony.
   4. To prevent a felony involving force, surprise or violence.
   5. To kill a dangerous animal, or to kill an animal so badly injured that humanity requires that it be destroyed to prevent further suffering.
   6. When an attempt is made to rescue by violence a prisoner who is in lawful custody of an officer.
B. Nothing in this order shall restrict the discharge of firearms on a firearms range or while participating in an authorized training mission.

The Baltimore Police Department adds one additional purpose as follows: "to give alarm or to call assistance when *no* other means can be used."

Another requirement laid down in the majority of directives is the submission, in writing, of a report whenever a firearm is discharged by a member of the department in line of duty, giving full particulars, except when it is used on the range or while participating in an authorized training mission.

One situation, although not specifically mentioned in available departmental directives, which must be considered by an officer before he fires his weapon is that of the possibility of injury or death to innocent persons not only from direct fire but from ricocheting and "returning to earth" type bullets. Several of the departments indicate that their guidance to officers is that if an innocent person may be hurt, withhold firing except in the actual protection of *life*.

Moving Vehicles

Another area of constant problem to law enforcement agencies is in that of firing at a moving vehicle or when the officer is in a moving vehicle. Again, although not specifically mentioned in directives, most police departments generally agree that it is best to attempt to apprehend the individual through the use of police communications media and cooperative police work, if possible. The danger to innocent persons from unexpended or ricocheting bullets or out of control vehicles usually far outweighs any justifications for high speed chases and exchange of gunfire. However, a car should not become a sanctuary for a criminal at whom an officer is otherwise justified in firing if the officer is close enough to fire accurately, if the shot will likely be effective in stopping the car and/or suspect and most important of all, if the danger to innocent persons can be basically eliminated.

It is felt that, almost without exception all departments stress and insist on compliance with the rule — "When in doubt, don't shoot."

THE BATON

The baton or nightstick is an effective weapon for the police officer skilled in its proper use. The police officer who knows how to use his baton with propriety performs his duties with an extra measure of confidence and with the advantage of effective counterattack over the aggressive lawbreaker. The regulation baton has durability and is designed to meet all the requirements for police service *without* weighting or leading.

A sharp blow to the collar muscles, shoulders, or biceps is very effective. A well-aimed blow to the kneecap, shin bone, or upper leg can end a fight quickly by paralyzing nerves without causing permanent injury to the adversary.

Blows to the body with the baton are designed primarily to paralyze a muscle or nerve center. Jabs to the stomach are intended to take the suspect's breath away. Mild state of shock usually results to the victim in either jabs or blows.

When used correctly, the baton is an effective weapon against punches, kicks, bottles, or other similar attacks or weapons. It is useful in the application of "come alongs" and may be employed in many crowd control situations.

MACE

Mace, which has almost universally replaced tear gas, especially in the larger cities, is designed to enable officers to perform their duties in a more efficient and humane manner when dealing with persons who intend to do bodily harm to themselves, other persons, or to the police officer. If used properly, the chemical Mace will reduce the risk of injury to the officer or other persons.

Mace may be used in any situation where it becomes necessary for an officer to subdue or bring under physical restraint any person while the officer is performing his official duties, regardless of whether or not the officer is making an arrest. However, once a violent person has been subdued and brought under control, there is no further justification to use the chemical Mace against the person.

The Charlotte Police Department directive very accurately covers its use and reads, in part, as follows:

> The Chemical Mace may be used in situations where physical resistance is encountered when making an arrest; where physical combat is imminent or to stop physical combat; when subdueing violently insane persons or in any situation as a self-defense weapon. The use of the Chemical Mace protects the attacker, as well as the officer, against injury. Good judgment should prevail in its use as in the use of any other device. Do not overuse it. Do not use it where lesser means will accomplish the objective.
>
> The most effective use of the Mace is a well-aimed, one-second burst. A one-second burst will attain a range of approximately (15) feet, the maximum range of the Chemical Mace. The Chemical Mace projects a shotgun patter of heavy droplets of a specially prepared liquid base solution and a highly refined form of CN, strongly irritating to eyes, nose, and skin.
>
> Aim at the face of the attacker, the eyes being the "bull's eye." Upon facial contact the droplets release vapors of CN irritant which cause profuse tearing. At the same time the droplets wet, spread, and cling to the skin causing a burning sensation and a sense of apathy occurs in the recipient. He will be incapacitated for an average of fifteen to twenty minutes.

Some definitely prohibited utilizations of chemical Mace include:

1. use as a threat to make a person comply with an officer's verbal order, when no physical violence is imminent;

2. use against any person in retaliation for their verbal abuse of an officer;

3. use, either actually or as a threat, to elicit information from any person.

THE NUTCRACKER

Law enforcement agencies have for years attempted to develop an inexpensive, yet effective and relatively noninjurious device for use in restraining apprehendees. A variety of expensive hardware has been tested but the nightstick and handcuffs remained the basic tools of restraint. Now, police in Detroit think that they have the answer. They have developed a new ten dollar weapon known as the "nutcracker," which consists of two foot-long plastic sticks joined at one end by four short nylon cords.

Pointed at the suspect like a dowser's divining rod, the weapon works on two simple principles — speed and pressure. Before the offender can escape, or if he resists arrest, the sticks are clamped around his arm, wrist, or hand. The cords act as a hinge. If he resists, the arresting officer merely squeezes the sticks, inducing severe, immobilizing pain. Either way no permanent injury is usually inflicted because the pain will usually subdue the offender before any physical damage occurs.

The nutcracker is equally effective in mob control and dispersal. Holding onto only one stick, the patrolman swings the other like a flail. Any attempt to grab the swirling stick may result in a broken or badly bruised limb. A blow on the head can fracture a skull. Says a Detroit police official: "With six men carrying the sticks we can penetrate fifty men and bust up their formation and come back out."

On the strength of Detroit's success with the instrument, Michigan state police and forty-five other municipal and county police organizations are now testing the nutcracker.

POLICE DOGS

A K-9 squad is used at times for the following:
1. preventive patrol, both motorized and on foot;
2. tracking and building search (This includes calls such as holdups, car and foot chases, purse snatches, etc.);
3. to protect police officers and other persons from injury or

death;

4. to effect the arrest or prevent the escape of a convicted felon or of a person who the police officer has reasonable grounds to believe has committed a felony;

5. at the scene of riots, imminent riots, or other unruly crowd situations upon approval of the Chief of Police, Patrol Division Commander, Commander of the Special Operations Division, or the on-duty Watch Commander;

6. for special assignments when authorized by the Commander of the Special Operations Division.

Needless to say the utilization of dogs in situations indicated in subparagraph 5 above is usually used as a last resort. Various antipolice organizations have been able to convince many that police dog techniques are vicious, and some departments have given up their K-9 corps under public pressure. The psychological effect of even the presence of specially trained dogs in the area of mass disorder or riot conditions far outweighs the adverse public opinion generated.

AUTHORITY FOR USE OF FORCE

The authority and responsibility for the use of force to restore order lies first with local government. Many cities have the attitude that restoring order is solely a police function. That cannot be and is not so! While it is true that the police play the major role, all of the city's resources must be applied. City plans for civil disorder, such as *Procedural Instruction 68-2, Control of Civil Disorder, Kansas City, Missouri,* dated June 16, 1969, are detailed in their efforts to tie all resources into an effective force under the control of the police department. Officials from many cities, states, and the federal government have received instruction in city planning for civil disturbances at the Civil Disturbance Operations Course (SEADOC) taught by the United States Army Military Police School at Fort Gordon, Georgia. All attendees received a typed city plan which emphasizes a coordinated city effort.

All too often a city will not have sufficient resources to meet its needs in the application of force to restore order. When this is so, horizontal or inter-local arrangements can be made to a degree depending on the legal requirements of the city and state. Some of the arrangements which can be made are for additional police, assistance in fire fighting, use of hospitals, use of airports, and use of sanitation facilities. California has established a master law enforcement mutual aid plan. Under this plan, law enforcement officers may be transferred from outside the local area to aid in restoring order. The transferred officer is paid by his own city. State law gives him legal standing in the area to which he is transferred. Application for such assistance is made first to the county sheriff and then to regional authorities who can get help from any part of the state. Should a city be unable or unwilling to restore order, the state has the authority and responsibility to do so.

The first force applied by the state is the use of the state police. Normally, however, the state police are committed before the situation gets out of hand and as a means of increasing the numbers of the local police. The most potent force of state authority in the application of force is the National Guard. The trend today is toward earlier commitment of these state military forces. This may be explained by the greater violence and duration of modern disturbances and the requirement for the police to maintain normal law and order functions. Some feel that the early and repeated use of military force is a mistake, as the use of such force results in greater demoralizing effect and reduction of the shock value of that force. Whatever the local feelings are, plans to call and use the National Guard must be included in the overall city plan. An aspect here is the legal standing of the guard member in relation to the police, the citizen and the courts.

The final and least called upon force is that of the federal military to include the Federalized National Guard. The authority and responsibility of the federal government depends on the requirement of necessity. More specifically, when state authorities are unable or unwilling to maintain law and order, the use of active Army or Federalized National Guard forces in civil disturbances is based upon both federal statutes and the U.S. Constitution's provision that the President is Commander-in-

Chief of the Armed Forces and charged with faithful execution of the laws. The Constitution also guarantees each state a representative government and protection against invasion and domestic violence. Further, the Fourteenth Amendment guarantees to every citizen certain constitutional privileges and immunities and equal protection of the laws.

THE APPLICATION OF FORCE

We can now turn to aspects of the actual application of force. "The guiding principle for the application of force at any time should be minimum force, consistent with mission accomplishment." Because of today's mass media and of training in the subject, we have seen that the careful use of police force can prevent violence.

When it has been decided to apply a degree of force, the force commander must be guided by the fact that the suppression of violence, without undue force, is a basic policy. Commanders will have the problem of the soldier or police officer who internalizes the abuse heaped on him and strikes back. The individual must be made to understand that the reckless or malicious use of force may subject him to civil or criminal liability or both and that the greatest assets a control force has is its discipline, unity of purpose, and immediate response to leadership. The internalized application of force at MIT (5:30 PM newscast, November 5, 1969), which showed several police officers breaking from the organized police formation and charging the students, was a breakdown of purpose and control. It appeared that way on TV and that is the way it was reported. *Newsweek* also pointed out that the police unit as a whole displayed a great deal of restraint and purpose. While police officers may have a strong desire to strike out at those who vilify them, violence is not the answer. Punishment is not the job of the police officer.

Research has proven that most police departments use degrees of force adapted from the United States Army and contained inDepartment of the Army Field Manual, 19-15, dated March, 1968. These degrees of force are designed to accomplish the mission of restoring order with the minimum use of force. There can be no hard and fast rules concerning the application of force as situations will vary. Degrees of force enumerated in any set of regulations can be only guidelines.

The first step is to conduct a show of force. This may vary from a police squad armed with batons to a sizeable military force with bayonets and automatic weapons. It is to be noted that the goal of many rioters today is to effect a physical contact with the police; thus the show of force may not be as effective as it once was, since this is what is wanted, a force to fight with.

The next stop is the employment of riot control formations. Again, the force will vary from police with batons to troops with bayonets. Demonstrators know that if they fight, the police officers will use their batons, but that the federal troops will not usually use their bayonets. We often find that the demonstrators will sit or lie in front of the police. An arrest unit should then be employed to arrest the demonstrators nearest the police line.

The Use of Water

Another degree of force is the use of water. Water is most effective on cold days and on a narrow front. It is more effective if a dye is placed in the water to aid in later identification. This will help to break up a mob as the dye will cause the individual to lose the protection that the mob gives for his actions. It should be kept in mind that water, under high pressure, can do a great deal of damage to the human body and to property.

Selected Firing

More recent disturbances have passed from the use of a show of force to fire by selected marksman. These specially trained men must be available in the area of the disturbance to reduce indiscriminate firing. Also, a specially selected and trained marksman, armed with proper weapon, will be able to silence sniper fire more quickly, thus allowing the area to be cleared with the least amount of harm to either side.

Full Fire Power

Finally, we must consider the most severe measure of force, full firepower. This is and must be a last resort. Every other technique must have failed. The aspects of this degree of force is all too apparent.

Again, it is to be noted that it may not be possible to employ degrees of force. Situations may develop in our republic which will require as a first step, the full firepower of the control force.

LEGAL RESPONSIBILITIES

We turn our attention now to the aspect faced by the individual police officer and soldier, his legal responsibilities for his action in the effort to restore order.

Each state will have different laws affecting state and city forces. In some, the National Guard will have the power of arrest and in others he will not. While some states will declare a person guiltless if a rioter is killed while being arrested, it does not mean that if the killing was an unnecessary or malicious act, that the doer is in fact guiltless. A police officer or National Guardsman may be tried in a criminal court or a civil court for his actions. If a member of the control force internalizes and loses control of his actions, he may well suffer at a later time.

The legal standing of federal personnel is better defined than that of state military forces. First, the federal force member is responsible only to his military superiors. In no case will he take orders from the state forces. The National Guard may control active Army forces after the National Guard has been federalized. As with state forces, the member of the federal force may be held responsible for his actions in civil and criminal courts. However, the federal force member will be tried in a federal district court, which would eliminate the emotions that might be present in a state court.

The individual who is a member of a control force must direct all his efforts to the mission at hand. He must not attempt to punish and must remember that he is responsible for his actions, even when under orders. He must have patience, must be calm, must be fair, and must be firm. He must be prepared to make the mob respond and must not bluff. The officer or soldier must not take sides and must stand his ground as part of the team.

SUMMARY

No one, for one minute, would doubt or question the ready existence of adequate means of bringing to bear on almost any situation sufficient raw power, be it by an individual patrolman with his sidearm, baton, Mace, or some other impressive device or technique, or by a riot control element with its tear gas, dogs, or water as crowd-breaking procedures. The foremost consideration must be the legal and moral aspects of the utilization of these items of equipment or methods of mission accomplishment. The use of these, even in the slightest degree beyond what is absolutely necessary in the accomplishment of their responsibilities, is inexcusable and worthy of the public's attention, criticism, and possible censure.

CHAPTER 4

ORGANIZED CRIME

Donald O. Schultz

AMERICA has given birth and refuge to many different groups, cults, beliefs, and organizations in the two hundred years of its existence. None of these has presented such a threat to our way of life as the development of an organization which, since it was first recognized in 1890, has become bigger, richer, and more sinister until today it is so powerful that it touches almost everyone and affects the whole of American life. Many Americans still find it difficult to believe that their nation harbors an evil entity capable of stealing billions while destroying the honor of public officials, the honesty of businessmen, and sometimes the lives of ordinary citizens. Yet the evidence has become all too credible. (1)

It exists for the sole purpose of robbing the American citizen of everything he holds and if needed, of even his life. It recognizes none of the moral or ethical codes of any society other than its own; practically every type of business and industry in the United States is currently being exploited or penetrated by an awesome, powerful, and no-holds-barred competitor — a conglomerate of crime. This criminal conglomerate employs thousands, nets billions annually, operates nationally and internationally, possesses an efficient and disciplined organizational structure, wields a depressingly effective lobbying apparatus, insulates itself against legal action, destroys billion-dollar corporations and cripples smaller companies and, according to many, rates as the most serious long-term danger to the security and principles of this nation. (2)

The vast majority of the American people would say that we are now living in a period encompassed by acts of violence and civil

---

1. "Cosa Nostra — The Poison in KUR Society," *Reader's Digest* (December, 1969), p. 119.
2. *Deskbook on Organized Crime* (Washington, D. C., Chamber of Commerce of the United States, 1969), p. 3.

disorders. Our present total disregard for law and order was surpassed only during the era of prohibition when this society was plagued with such notorious gangsters as Al Capone, John Dillinger, "Maw" Barker, and hoodlum gangs which spread terror and lawlessness throughout this nation. But it was during this era that the real and most dangerous threat to every community within the United States was born. It is difficult to believe that the imperfections of our social institutions and of our government have provided the basis for the origin and development of an organization which has become known as the "second government." (3) Its management has been the least understood and revgnized of any malady within our society. Echoed warnings by many authorities investigating this criminal threat have been made public, but to no avail. A former chairman of the highly respected and effective New York State Commission of Investigation issued this sobering statement: "With the exception of the war in Vietnam, crime in the streets and organized crime are probably the most serious problems which confront the country today . . . in the long run, organized crime is probably the most serious, and unquestionably one of the most dangerous." (4)

What is organized crime? How did it develop? Why has it become so capable of such moral and economic destruction that it demands total submission to its desires and controls? This chapter intends to illustrate the areas covered by the above questions and to show how this group has obtained its stranglehold on America, its origin, its present location, its legitimate and illegitimate businesses, the way it daily affects the lives of every American, what can be done to overcome this organization, and a recommended course of action that must be taken if this society is to survive as a free and democratic form of government.

Over the centuries renowned authorities have continually issued warnings to our political leaders and the American public

---

3. In 1963 Joseph Valachi publicly revealed the inner workings of what he called "this second government," known to its members as La Cosa Nostra, It is also referred to in Ed Reid's book *The Grim Reapers* (1969), p. 22.
4. *Deskbook on Organized Crime*, p.

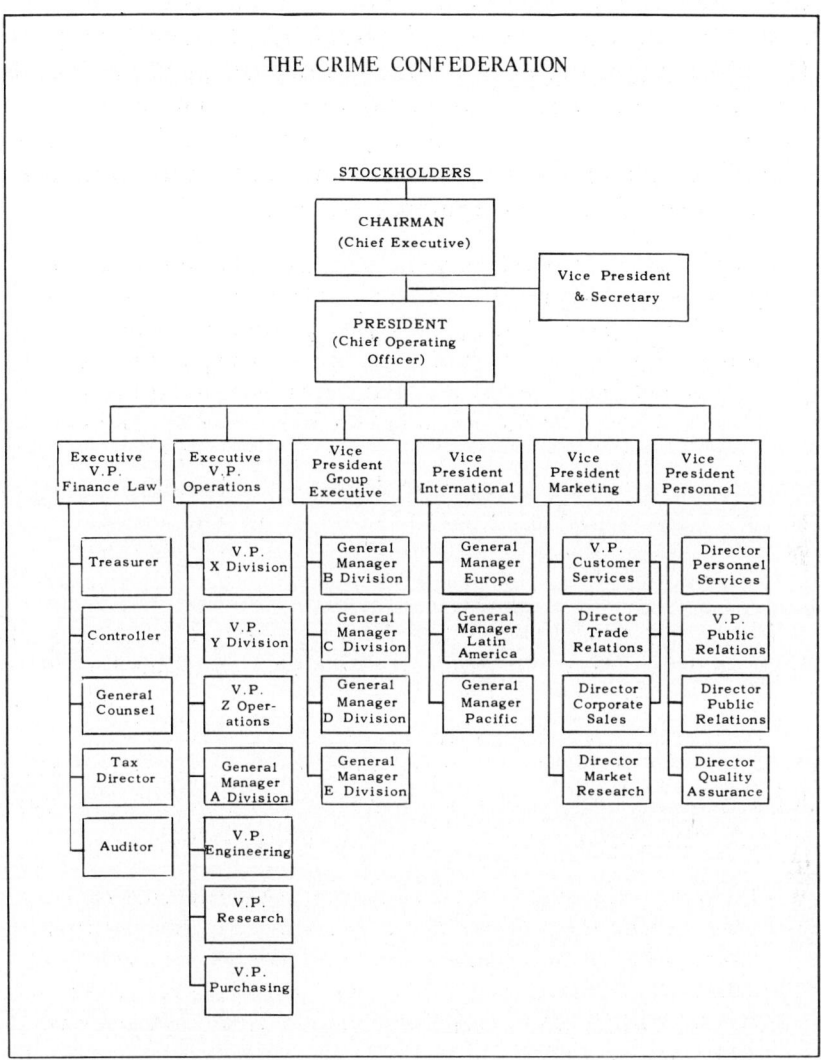

Figure 4-1. The organizational structure of a legitimate business and the division of responsibility, delegation of authority, and coordination of activities within a company. (From Salerno and Tompkins: *Crime Confederation*. New York, Doubleday, 1969, p. 84)

that there is a force within our country known as the Mafia, the Mob, the Syndicate, the Outfit, the Confederation, the Black Hand, an Organization, a Criminal Cartel, a Conspiracy, a Cult, a Brotherhood, and today these organizations have become best known as La Cosa Nostra or simply — "Organized Crime." (5) In May, 1965, a term was defined by a group of forty of the nation's most renowned law enforcement authorities:

> The product of a self-perpetuating criminal conspiracy to wring exorbitant profits from our society by any means — fair and foul, legal and illegal. Despite personnel changes, the conspiratorial entity continues. It is a malignant parasite which fattens on human weakness. It survives on fear and corruption. By one or another means, it obtains a high degree of immunity from the law. It is totalitarian in its organization. A way of life, it imposes rigid discipline on underlings who do the dirty work while the top men of organized crime are generally insulated from the criminal act and the consequent danger of prosecution. (6)

The existence of this organization was suspected as long ago as 1890, when a New Orleans Grand Jury concluded that an organization called "Mafia" existed. This acknowledgment came about from an investigation into the brutal slaying of New Orleans Police Chief Peter Hennessey, who was investigating two murders which occurred over contracts for the handling of cargo on the New Orleans docks. The Grand Jury stated:

> The range of our research has developed the existence of the secret organization styled "Mafia." The evidence comes from several sources fully competent in themselves to attest the truth, while the fact is supported by the long record of blood-curdling crimes, it being almost impossible to discover the perpetrators or to secure witnesses. (7)

---

5. Research has provided the following names as being applied to organized crime: Peter Maas "The Story Behind the Crime Hearings," *Saturday Evening Post* (November 23, 1963), pp. 21-23; Sandy Smith, "The Crime Cartel," *Life* (September 1, 1967), pp. 15-24; Peter Maas, *The Valachi Papers* (New York: Bantam Books, 1969), p. 1.

6. Ralph Salerno and John Tompkins, *The Crime Confederation* (New York: Doubleday, 1969), p. 313.

7. Ed Reid, *The Grim Reapers* (Chicago: Henry Regency Co., 1969), p. 8.

In 1915, a Chicago Crime Commission concluded that there was a loosely organized, interstate band of professional criminals. The Bureau of Narcotics and Dangerous Drugs considers the 1957 Apalachin Mafia meeting as but one of several dating back to 1928. (8) It was, however, a breakthrough for law enforcement in its struggle to make politicians realize that there was such a thing as a "Criminal Cartel" within this country; it was this meeting and numerous other reports by both private and governmental investigations that bolstered the evidence pointing toward the existence of an organized underworld beyond crescendo proportions — evidence now ignored by only the naive, the uninformed, or by those paid to look the other way. (9) President Nixon has in fact observed:

> Today, organized crime has deeply penetrated broad segments of American life. In our great cities, it is operating prosperous criminal cartels. In our suburban areas and smaller cities, it is expanding its corrosive influence. . . . It quietly continues to infiltrate and corrupt organized labor. It is increasing its enormous holdings and influence in the world of legitimate business. (10)

It has been further concluded by other authoritative sources that:

> Organized crime is a society that seeks to operate outside the controls of the American people and their governments. It

---

8. Organized crime as it is known today began to develop on December 5, 1928 when 23 top Mafia leaders met in Cleveland, Ohio. Their next meeting took place in 1931 at Atlantic City, New Jersey. It was here that organized crime set its policies and plans into a finalized form, while the FBI and other agencies were making public statements that the Syndicate had been defeated by the defeat of Capone. The next meeting took place in 1957 at Apalachin, New York, where more than 50 top leaders of the Mafia had gathered to divide up the territory of the late Albert Anastasia but were surprised by the arrest from law enforcement officers. The last known public gathering of Mafia members was held in a Queens New York restaurant in 1966. It is believed that this meeting was called to settle unfinished business from the 1957 Apalachin meeting.

9. Reports stating that there was an organized criminal cartel dates back to the twelve separate reports filed by the Wickensham Commission during 1929-1931; Chicago Crime Commission Report, 1942; Kefauver's Commission reports, 1950-1951; and the present McClellan Commission report. Prior to the reports of the McClellan Commission and the forceful tactics by the late Robert F. Kennedy, then Attorney General of the United States, organized crime was considered to be a local problem and not nationally oriented.

10. *Deskbook on Organized Crime*, p. 3.

involves thousands of criminals, working within structures as complex as those of any large corporation, subject to laws more rigidly enforced than those of legitimate governments. Its actions are not impulsive but rather the result of intricate conspiracies, carried on over whole fields of activity in order to amass hugh profits. The core of organized crime activity is the supplying of illegal goods and services . . . but organized crime is also extensively and deeply involved in legitimate business and in labor unions . . . (11)

But the real and most dangerous threat of organized crime is not just the dealing in illicit goods and services. The danger arises because of the vast profits acquired from the sale of illicit goods and services which are being invested in legitimate enterprise, both in the business sphere and the governmental sphere. "It is when criminal syndicates start to undermine basic economic and political traditions and institutions, real trouble begins, and the real trouble has begun in the United States." (12)

The past history of the Mafia is clouded with mythology and legend. (13) Some theorists hypothesize that its birth began as an underground resistance movement against one of the invaders who oppressed Sicily in the ninth century. It was a time when all of the inhabitants of this sun-drenched island were trodden under the despotic dictatorship of a cruel and harsh ruler from France. (14) We are told that the Mafia during this period created an image of Robin Hood; it would take from the rulers by bribery, threats, arson, murder, and extortion, then divide its ill-gotten gains among the poor and subservient peasants. After many decades of this rule, the French were finally thrust from Italy and

---

11. *Ibid.*, pp. 3-4.
12. *Ibid.*, p. 4.
13. As Salerno and Tompkins indicate in the footnote on page 108 of their text, "The beginnings of the Mafia itself are lost in antiquity, though it probably started as an underground resistance movement against one of the invaders — Romans, Arabs, Norman, Spaniards, Neapolitan Bourbons, and Northern Italians — that have oppressed Sicily since the ninth century. The origin of the word Mafia is similarly vague. It has been identified as a Piedmontese word for gang, an Italian neologism for bravado, and a word coined in the thirteenth century from the initial letters of the phrase 'Morte alla Francia Italia anela' (Death to France Italy cries). The most likely explanation is that mafia means 'place of refuge' in Arabic, a reference to dispossessed farmers who fled to the hills rather than become serfs."
14. *Ibid.*, p. 109.

Sicily. Peace reigned throughout the land; now the Mafiosi found that they would have to return to honest toil, a task which they were neither willing nor prepared to accept. The Mafia had found its way of life so profitable that it adopted the same methods and techniques which were fostered by its captors. Its victims, now instead of despotic rulers, were the shopkeepers, the farmers, and townspeople of the small villages and islands that it had previously protected and supported. Everyone was forced to pay tribute to the Mafia or suffer the consequences of total destruction of their property or their very lives.

It was not until the end of the nineteenth century and the beginning of the twentieth century that the influence of the Mafia began to take hold within the boundaries of the United States. This was brought about by two major factors which occurred during this period. First was the immigration of Italians into the United States who were escaping the fascist methods employed by Benito Mussolini, dictator in Italy. (15) Under the direction of Mussolini, a complete purge was instigated in Italy and Sicily to rid the country of the Mafia influence and domination. By use of fascist methods — arrest without warrant, confessions extracted by torture, imprisonment without trial — many of the Mafia members were jailed, and by the late 1920's the government had reduced the open activities of the organization to its lowest level. However, many shrewd Mafiosi saw what was in the future and joined the fascist movement so they could infiltrate the government itself. Even those who went to jail were able to survive the trials and tribulations encountered during this period. Through the aid of those Mafiosi who had obtained government positions, the convicted were usually able to continue controlling their gangs from within the prison. Most important, though, were those nimble and enterprising Mafia members who escaped by immigrating to the United States, mostly as illegal aliens. In 1925, the United States worsened this problem, by curtailing the immigration of Italians into this country by placing a restrictive quota upon their admittance. This contributed to the illegal entry of Mafiosi into the country, as did Italian laws that placed a

---

15. *Ibid.*, p. 276.

person suspected of involvement with the Mafia on a blacklist and would not allow them out of Italy. (16) Prior to this time, Italian immigrants who came to the country were different from other American ethnic groups — they tended to settle into areas where they could set up their own communal groupings. This cultured an ideal social structure for the rise of the Mafia terrorist movement in America.

In Sicily the Mafia is a tight-knit collection of gangsters preying on the peasants. So great is the power of the Mafia that when they commit a murder against one of their people it is accepted with no more than a shrug of the shoulder, a few tears and the sign of the cross. (17) There is also a tradition in Sicily, centuries old, that when a young man wishes to marry a girl who is unwilling to become his wife, he must abduct her, carry her off to the hills, and rape her. Then the crude and primitive justice of the Mafia takes over. The girl must marry her abductor to protect her honor. To refuse would endanger the life and property of her family and, furthermore, no other Sicilian would dare marry her. (18) On one occasion where a girl was taken by a Mafioso member against her wishes, she decided not to follow the Sicilian tradition. As an inducement to make her change her mind, her father's farm equipment was mysteriously destroyed. His vegetable plants were uprooted. Animals were let loose to trample and eat his oat fields at night. Five hundred of his grapevines were mysteriously slashed at their bases. "I didn't dare complain," the father said. "They would have destroyed our house if I had." (19) Thus one can fully realize the ease with which the Mafia continues its hold upon Italian peasant immigrants inside the United States.

Second, a major factor which added to the influence and power of the Mafia in America was the passage of the Volstead Enforcement Act or Prohibition. This act prohibited the manufacturing, distribution, and use of any form of distilled spirits. These two ingredients came together in the "roaring

---

16. *Ibid.*, pp. 276-77.
17. "A Mother's Pain," *Newsweek* (May 2, 1960), p. 41.
18. "Justice for Francia," *Newsweek* (January 2, 1967), p. 37.
19. *Ibid.*

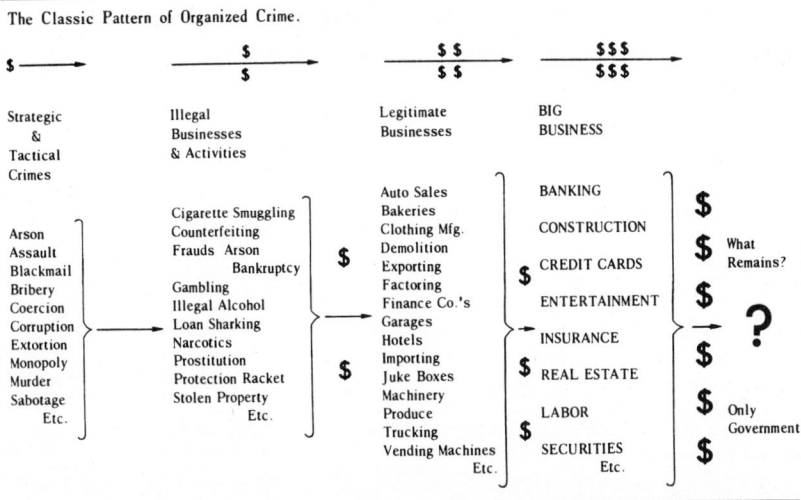

Figure 4-2. The flow of money from the criminal activities of organized crime into legitimate business sphere. Once the money has entered this field, the rake-off and skimming process of the organized crime cartel is channeled into either unidentified financial institutions inside of the United States or to foreign financial institutions (From Salerno and Tompkins: *Crime Confederation*. New York, Doubleday, 1969, pp. 230-231.)

twenties" — prohibition and a group of men already well-schooled in organized criminal activities. The Mafia observed that prohibition laws were not being enforced, and that the majority of the people did not want them enforced. The results were natural. The illegal alcohol business was organized and run with the zest and bravado of men who suddenly found themselves living in a country where respect for individual liberty worked in their favor. (20)

Parenthetically, the long-standing affinity of Jewish gangsters for Italian and Sicilian gangsters was cemented during this period. The Jews had also fled from oppressive European governments. The two groups had a common bond which went beyond their mutual interest in the profitability of prohibition.

---

20. Salerno and Tompkins, pp. 277-279.

However, prohibition helped to foster organized crime by combining the major criminal factions of ethnic groups — Italians, Jews, Welsh, Irish, and other separate groups into a central controlled organization. (21) Prohibition also provided the organization with its first real source of big money. Until this time, prostitution, gambling, extortion, and other criminal activities had not generated much capital even on their largest scale. (22) With illegal liquor being a multi-million dollar industry, it furnished the capital needed to expand its operations into other illegal activities, but primarily to penetrate legitimate businesses as a front for its continued operations. It also opened the way for corruption of politicians and police on a large scale. It began the Syndicate connections with politics and demoralized many law enforcement groups to a point from which they never fully recovered. (23)

Mass evasion of the Volstead act put the average citizen in touch with criminals, resulting in tolerance and eventually admiration, even to the point of romantic approval of the mobsters. It permanently undermined the respect for law and order and the people charged with enforcing it. Ever since prohibition the manin the street has accepted the idea that policemen can be bought.

The manufacture and distribution of illegal liquor in the United States and the illegal entry of foreign-made liquor gave the men who were organizing crime experience in the administration and control of multi-billion dollar, worldwide business, with thousands of employees and long payrolls. Men who had never before managed anything bigger than a family farm or a local gang got on-the-job training which turned them into leaders with developed executive qualities. (24)

With the repeal of the Volstead Act and the death or arrest of the notorious gangsters that plagued the nation during the roaring twenties, the public and most law enforcement men rejoiced that the Syndicate had finally been smashed. But little did they realize that this was not the end of the organization so destined to become

---

21. *Ibid.*
22. *Ibid.*
23. *Ibid.*
24. *Ibid.*

the greatest cancer of our society.

A new era began. It was from these very roots that the crime leaders realized that they could no longer operate under the methods and techniques of the past. They now began to cast aside their former traits — flashy automobiles, operation of pretentious clubs, and the wearing of fancy, glaring clothing which had previously symbolized their particular breed. They now adopted the atmosphere of the ordinary, distinguished businessman and became prominent civic leaders. Next, organization leaders devised plans for a tremendous conspiracy — to create the greatest worldwide criminal cartel ever to exist within the geographical boundaries of a nation. They formalized the most unique organizational structure that has ever been developed before or since. Even though it sometimes resembled the operational structure of a large legitimate corporation (25), it was so complex that it created a very distinctive buffer between each layer of operation and made it virtually impossible to identify the boss or bosses of the system. (26) This new organization was designed to handle every known type of criminal enterprise from murder, blackmail, extortion, and importation of narcotics to the "ten-cent bet place" on a street corner. From the profits of these activities, money channels into every imaginable form of legitimate business in our industrial and commercial complex, even to the hot dog stand on the corner of the street. (27)

As this criminal cartel expanded into every mode of American life, only a limited number of men in this country ever suspected that this organization existed or that it was formed for the express purpose of controlling all crime in the United States. These few, essentially law enforcement officials, educators, and newsmen, tried to warn the public and governmental officials of this impending danger, but were pooh poohed as "alarmists." (28)

---

25. This is an ordinary organizational chart of a legitimate corporation showing the division of responsibility, delegation of authority, and coordination of activities in a company. Charts, of course, show only the formal corporate structure; they do not reveal the de facto relationships that may be even more important.
26. Task Force Report: Organized Crime. The President's Commission on Law Enforcement and Administration of Justice.
27. Salerno and Tompkins, pp. 230-31.
28. *Ibid.*, pp. 282, 287.

Even as late as 1959, the director of the FBI believed that there could not exist a criminal cartel in this country. He stressed Communist subversion as the major threat to the nation. (29) So while men of this caliber were taking a complacent attitude, Mafia leaders managed to cover their tracks and organizational abilities to the finest details while at the same time they knitted together the world's most powerful and well-organized criminal cartel. They had managed to bring under their control everything from the Harlem ghetto, where a resident bets a dime a day on the numbers racket, to the weekend playboy who pays out fifty dollars for a woman companion for the evening.

Even though there was no overt action taken against the Mafia, all of their activities did not go unnoticed. It had been observed by the public and those who have attempted to deter its gradual success. Mafia leaders were seen hosting parties attended by political leaders, lawmakers, judges, and other influential figures in the world of politics. Here the mobsters cemented contracts with politicians who would pass laws or fail to pass laws in order to favor organized crime. In turn, this enabled candidates for political office to gain support either by financial contributions or by being assured of sufficient votes to win an election. The Mafia leaders were assured that their help would not be overlooked and that they would be able to continue operating without interference of any kind. With this political influence, the Mafia leaders decided to broaden their scope of power from the criminal cartel to one of legitimate businesses where its opportunity from detection was assured. This was the beginning of a second government. There was no further need for extensive expansion of criminal activities but only to utilize the profits from these activities to foster their future plans.

Many experts believe that the Cosa Nostra (formerly the Mafia) found that milking legitimate business was so profitable that it pulled more than half of its 60 billion dollar bankroll out of the traditional "dirty" operations in order to get its hooks into "clean" businesses — banks, real estate development, land investment firms, entertainment media, luxury hotels, and small

---

29. Reid, pp. 200, 278, 300, and 306.

businesses of all types. (30)

In this new endeavor of expanding and intensifying their activities, the mob's methods ranged from highly sophisticated stock manipulations, involving tens of millions of dollars, all the way down to the most basic extortion and violence and even use of their ultimate weapon — murder. To accomplish this design, Cosa Nostra used and is still using major infiltration techniques: bankruptcy fraud (scam and bust out), dummy association (protection), usury (shylocking), loan manipulation, labor involvement (racketeering), hijacking (insurance frauds), real estate coups, stock thefts, monopoly, reverse monopoly, investment steering, simple extortion, illegal cartels, and inplant gambling. (31)

Everybody pays the high cost of the Cosa Nostra's ticket from the darkness of the underworld to the daylight of pretended respectability. The cost can be measured in dollars and cents and in human misery. The cost can also be measured in higher taxes. If the Cosa Nostra paid taxes on the millions it makes, every citizen's tax bill would be reduced. Profits can be measured in the thousands of needless bankruptcies resulting from scam operations, in which the mob takes over a successful business, quickly milks it dry of every drop of stock, assets and credits, leaving behind a bankrupt company and a stack of unpaid bills. It can be measured in higher insurance rates for everybody — the rates go up a little every year because of Cosa Nostra — arranged stock pilfering and hijacking frauds. It can be measured in lower wages for tens of thousands of workers who are trapped in sweetheart contracts between Cosa Nostra controlled unions and Cosa Nostra controlled companies. And it can be measured in higher price tags on all kinds of consumer goods — a one-cent increase in the cost of a loaf of bread because of syndicate-controlled trucking monopoly, or a ten-dollar increase in the cost of a new car because of payroll padding by a subcontractor. (32)

---

30. Donald Singleton, "How orgainized Crime Takes over Business," *The American Legion Magazine* (April, 1970), p. 15.
31. *Ibid.*
32. *Ibid.*

As a result of the overall Cosa Nostra operations, investigators estimate that the syndicate's annual intake is at least 60 billion dollars. Sixty billion dollars is almost incomprehensible to most people. Reduced to more understandable terms, 60 billion dollars is more than the total combined yearly sales of General Motors, Ford Motors, General Electric, International Business Machines, United States Steel, and DuPont. (33) But this does not produce an accurate picture of the Cosa Nostra's worth, because the Cosa Nostra's money is "freer" than the money taken in by legitimate corporations. The mob pays very little, if any, taxes; it does not adhere to antitrust laws; it answers to no stockholders; it has no internal labor problems; and perhaps most important of all, during periods of recession and "tight" money, it has almost limitless source of capital funds from its criminal loan-sharking and gambling operations to expand its legitimate business operations, especially increasing plant assets and equipment. Because of its alarming growth, business organizations and government agencies have begun working hand-in-hand in an effort to plan an attack on their common enemy organized crime. (34)

Now the reader can understand some of the plans and designs of this powerful and destructive organization, determined to control and subvert by any means possible the government and people of the United States. Therefore consider the operational structure that affords maximum efficiency. Investigators today have identified between 3,000 and 5,000 individuals as members of the Cosa Nostra (LCN). Some authorities estimate he overall manpower at 3,000; others consider the 5,000 figure as merely the visible tip of a very deep iceberg. LCN members represent the inner core of organized crime. However, this inner core (LCN members), works in concert with othe nonmember criminals or syndicates. By including this latter group of nonmember LCN-affiliated racketeers and taking into account their control of political machines, labor unions, businesses, and other types of organizations, the manpower leverage of this nation's criminal conglomerate is estimated at several hundred thousand strong. (35)

---

33. *Ibid.*
34. *Deskbook on Organized Crime*, pp., 4-5.
35. *Ibid.*, p. 5.

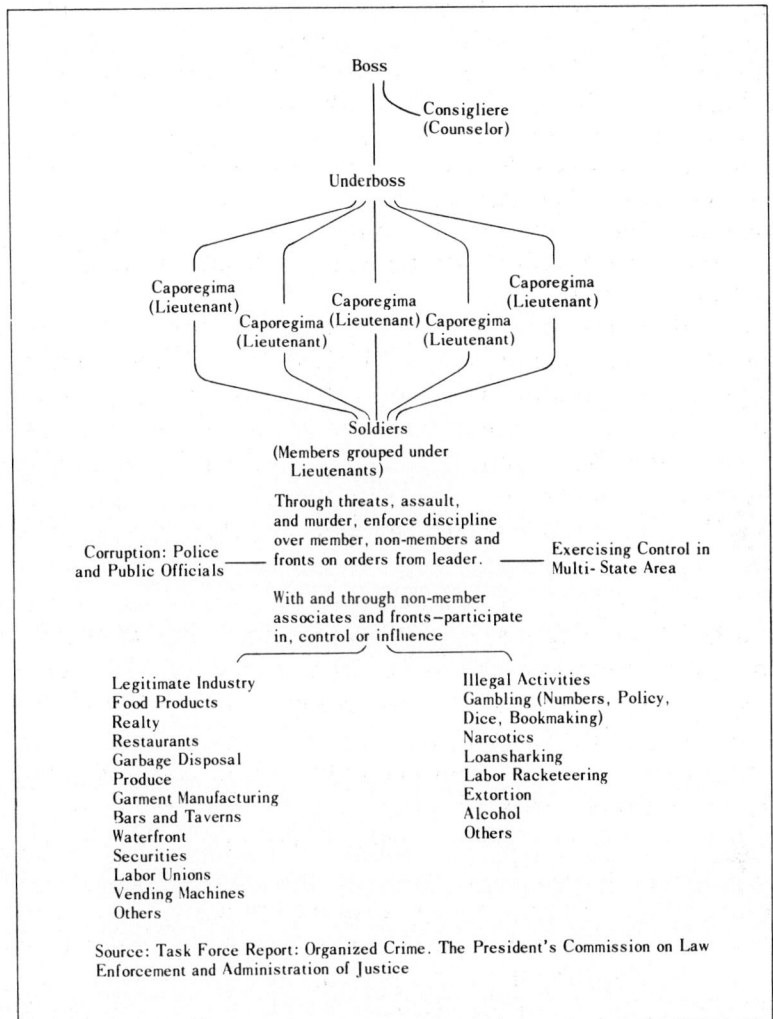

Figure 4-3. Since organized crime does not have or maintain an organizational per se, investigators of organized crime have compiled sufficient documentation to formulate a chart outlining the basic structure of its organization which identifies its chain of command like that of a typical Mafia family.

LCN members belong to basic operating units or "families," of which there are currently twenty-four within the United States. The "president" of each family unit is the Boss, whose dual responsibility is to maintain order and maximize profits. His authority within his family is almost absolute; he may be overruled only by the "Commission," which is usually comprised of twelve members, selected from the bosses of the more powerful families. The Commission is the ultimate authority on organizational and jurisdictional disputes; it serves as a combination legislature, supreme court, board of directors, and arbitration panel.

Each Boss has access to a *consigliere* or counselor, a staff man who often is an elder member of the family and whose advice and judgment are sought and respected. On the same level as the consigliere is an Underboss, who acts as buffer or insulator between the Boss and the rest of the family. He collects information for the Boss, relays messages and instructions from him. The position of the Underboss is analogous to that of an executive vice-president.

Directly below the Underboss are the *caporegimes* or lieutenants, analogous to plant supervisors or sales managers. They serve either as buffers between top men and lower level personnel or as chiefs of various operational areas of the family. Typically, each lieutenant has one or more associates carrying orders, information, and money to the soldiers or "buttonmen" who are attached to his sphere of operation and are the front-line managers of the criminal cartel. They may operate various enterprises; partnerships between one another or between themselves and higher-ups are common practice.

Soldiers employ a large number of street-level personnel who are not family members. They bear the "nitty-gritty" of the criminal enterprise by performing such tasks as taking bets, driving trucks, or working in legitimate businesses.

Though there are no written rules, standards, or procedures, except the unwritten role of *"Omerta,"* (36) these matters are understood and govern the relationship among themselves as

---

36. *Omerta* — a word utilized by the Mafia to mean in general terms, "Golden silence" or "Talk and you die." For the modern Mafia, terror, not the concept denoted by the time-honored word, has achieved a simplicity of operation which continues to create something even more time-honored than a word: profit. (Reid, p. 7).

well as other family members. Enforcers are assigned to each family to maintain organizational integrity among its members by utilizing force or murder. Thus organized crime is a confederation of families, with each family so structured that the loss of even its leader will not destroy its continuity in operations. (37)

Since organized crime now considers the business sphere of American life as its major industry, we can now see how it has advanced with this era of sophistication, automation, and computerization. Today's activities within the field of business mandate an individual to accumulate expertise, based upon technical knowledge and skill, to handle the operations of these expanding enterprises. Therefore, observers of this phenomenon speculate that bosses of organized crime realize that they are not equipped personally to handle the problems of business and finance and therefore are sending their sons to universities to learn business administration or related skills. Perhaps this need to attract additional expertise will lead to increasingly decentralized decision making within families and, in time, result in blurring the lines between members and nonmembers. (38)

Not only does the LCN need individuals which have expertise but also those with ability to handle and control the incredible financial resources of organized crime which supplies more than enough capital to penetrate and exploit legitimate business and provide an abundant slush fund for crime's lobby of corruption in such a way that it will continue to reap their ultimate goal — profit.

The ability and finesse of Cosa Nostra to manage this lobby fund is considered its critical weapon of political power and control. Through payoffs to legislators, mayors, judges, police, and other officials, the underworld is able to operate under a political umbrella of official inaction or even encouragement. This is a must in their industry, as it is axiomatic that where organized crime flourishes, so also does public corruption. This lobbying is directed at federal, state, and local officials and other agencies of government. The objective is to neutralize law

---

37. *Deskbook of Organized Crime*, p. 6.
38. *Ibid.*

enforcement by having their hands tied by a paid politician. As the President's Commission on Law Enforcement and Administration of Justice commented, "What can the public do if no one investigates the investigators, and the political figures are neutralized by their alliance with organized crime? Anyone reporting corrupt activities may merely be telling his story to the corrupted. . . " (39)

So important is political power to organized crime that each family designates a member to act as a corrupter. Among the fruits of the corrupters' efforts are judges who hand suspended sentences to major racketeers even though found guilty by juries, (40) anticrime legislation bottled up in committee, (41) police who look the other way, (42) a trial judge conspiring with a prosecutor to obstruct justice, (43) officials awarding lucrative contracts to LCN businesses, (44) and the appointment of Mafia associates within political offices, (45) while in the field of industry and commercial enterprises the corrupter is utilized to take control of such businesses as Murray Packing Company, New York; (46) R. N. Landon Construction Company, White Plains, New York; (47) and Kennedy International Airport, New York. (48) There are literally hundreds of citable known incidents of the Mafia's involvement in every sphere of business, but these should be sufficient to emphasize the dangers of organized crime in America.

If organized crime is so ubiquitous, why is it not more visible or

---

39. *Deskbook on Organized Crime*, p. 7.
40. John L. McClellan, *"Weak Link in Our War On the Mafia,"* Reader's Digest (March, 1970), pp. 56-59.
41. "Opposition is Assured for Any Crime Bill," *Omaha World Herald* (March 1, 1970), p. 20.
42. Salerno and Tompkins, p. 246 (Cites stories of police payoff).
43. McClellan, p. 61.
44. Sandy Smith, "The Mob Finds a Patsy in a Mayor's Circle," *Saturday Evening Post* (January 5, 1968), pp. 44-50. (Story of James L. Marcus, former Commissioner of Water, Gas and Electricity, New York, N.Y.).
45. Christopher S. Wren and Margaret English, "Murder New Jersey Style," *Look* (March 10, 1970), pp. 43-47.
46. Salerno and Tompkins, pp. 235-36; Singleton, p. 16.
47. Singleton, p. 17.
48. John N. Mitchell, "Mob Controls Big Airport," *Omaha World Herald* (January 24, 1970), p. 2; Singleton, p. 19.

more apparent? Because of this nebulous quality, some would have us believe that LCN is a myth, a figment of overactive imagination. Unfortunately, the skeptics seem more concerned with scoring debating points than examining reality.

Reality reveals that organized crime labors hard at keeping itself out of the public eye. The status quo is valued, for rocking the boat will elicit unwarranted attention by citizens, the press, and police. Criminal operations thereby suffer. This is why each family has an enforcer who minimizes bloody internal flare-ups by meting out discipline; this is why the corrupter is so valuable; this is why the organized underworld mounts public relations campaigns to throw the public off guard; this is why underworld higher-ups generally lead unostentatious lives and attempt to

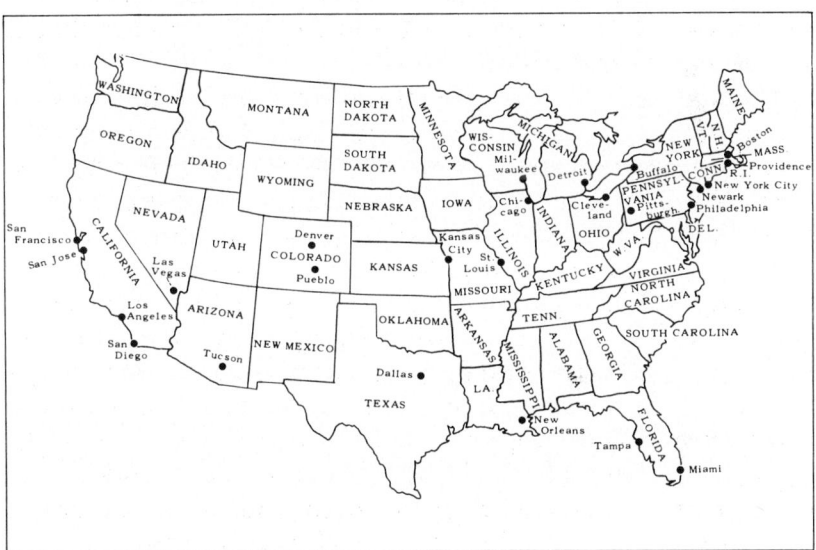

Figure 4-4. This is a map compiled by investigators and presented to the President's Commission on Organized Crime showing and identifying the exact locations of major cities within the United States where the core elements of the Mafia are located and operating. Because of political involvement, the Commission was not allowed to furnish this map for public scrutiny. (From Salerno and Tompkins: *Crime Confederation*. New York, Doubleday, 1969, p. 321.)

assume a mantle of respectability through their business connections or other means; this is why the underworld kingpins like to hear the public and officials say that they do not believe in the existence of organized crime.

Actually, the criminal confederation is so pervasive that it is highly probable that most U.S. adults have contributed, knowingly and unknowingly, to the coffers of crime by donating to charities or foundations established by the underworld; patronizing hotels, restaurants, or dry clearning establishments operated by LCN; purchasing automobile insurance from racketeer insurers; using vending machines installed by a syndicate; voting for a politician secretly obligated to organized crime; renting an apartment or conducting business in a building owned by a mob-controlled real estate concern; wagering with the local bookie, who may be a nice guy but none-the-less is at the end of a string pulled by organized crime.

Those who doubt the presence of organized crime in their communities should ask themselves, "Has anyone ever looked?" Just as the discovery of oil usually requires considerable drilling, unearthing organized crime involves diligent digging. Skeptics should ask themselves, "Have local police established units to investigate organized crime?" "How does the local bookie service his many accounts or how does he obtain 'the line' or odds?" or "How does he receive race results so quickly that no one can past post him?" or "How is he the recipient of a massive nationwide flow of information?" "How does merchandise written off as inventory shrinkage appear in retail outlets thousands of miles away?" They should ask themselves many such questions and their answers will reveal the wide-ranging operation of criminal cartel deeply embedded in the fabric of American life. (49)

Now is the time for all Americans, ordinary citizens, businessmen, and politicians to open their eyes and observe what has been occurring and listen to the warnings of dedicated men who are expounding the rise of organized crime within the United States. In a speech very recently before the United States Senate, John McClellan, Chairman of the Sub-committee on

---

49. *Deskbook on Organized Crime*, p. 7.

Criminal Laws and Procedures, said:

> Legitimate business is another area into which organized crime has begun most recently and widely to extend its influence. In most cities, it now dominates the fields of jukeboxes and vending machine distirbution. Laundry services, liquor and beer distribution, nightclubs, food wholesaling, record manufacturing, the garment industry, and a host of other legitimate lines of endeavor have been invaded and taken over. The Special Committee to Investigate Organized Crime in Interstate Commerce, under the leadership of Senator Estes Kefauver, noted in 1952 that the following industries had been invaded: advertising, amusement, appliances, automobile, baking, ballrooms, bowling alleys, banking, basketball, boxing, cigarette distribution, coal, communications, construction, drug stores, electrical equipment, florists, food, football, garment, gas, hotels, import-export, insurance, jukebox, laundry, liquor, loan, news service, newspapers, oil, paper products, radio, real estate, restaurants, scrap shipping, steel surplus, television, theaters, and transportation. (50)

Today we hear shouts — Robbery! Rape! Murder! — and many other cries considered prime evils of an orderly society. Yet have we realized or looked at what may be behind this surge of crime in order to gain insight into why it might exist? As if organized crime, in its own unique ways, did not generate enough problems for business and society, consider the correlation between the astounding economic and political successes of the criminal confederation and the explosive surfacing of street crime in recent years. Though the organized underworld certainly is not responsible for all street crime, LCN makes a substantial contribution, directly or indirectly, to such violence. One of the strongest statements in this regard was made by the Director of the National Council on Crime and Delinquency: "Almost every bit of crime has some link to organized crime." (51)

Strangely enough, organized crime's indirect link to street crime is the most serious. The "shining" record of the underworld serves as a powerful magnet by attracting numerous fence-sitters

---

50. *Ibid.*
51. "The Conglomerate of Crime," *Time* (August 22, 1969), pp. 17-27.

to a life of crime. As a consultant to the President's Commission observed:

> For good or for ill, the law and its failure teach. People know when crime pays. Kids in the slums see the cop on the beat take money. They know the pusher seldom gets caught, and his wholesaler is virtually never touched. They learn this lesson better than any middle class values taught in the schools from which they drop out. This impliction of the failure of our legal system to hold those who openly flaunt our laws accountable undermines the entire system. Not only is crime not deterred, it is indirectly promoted. (52)

Another crime authority reports that a group of youths in a large city "once told me that they saw life in their community as racket figures with public officials running the world." (53) Also the President's Commission concluded that "Cosa Nostra leaders and their racketeering allies preach a sermon all too many Americans heed: The government is for sale; lawlessness is the road to wealth; honesty is a pitfall and morality a trap for suckers." (54)

In short, all too often the LCN has demonstrated that crime pays and pays handsomely. Even lower echelon Nostra personnel can be millionaires. This fact is not lost upon today's youth. As one observer commented, "Racketeers are often the heroes of the young persons in deprived areas." (55)

More directly bearing on street crime is the recruitment activity of LCN. According to testimony, racketeers have been known to train youths in lower-level crimes as preparation for entry into the ranks of the criminal elite. LCN sponsors burglaries and hijackings — even bank robberies. (56) Another LCN contribution to everyday crime is theft-to-order operations. This involves old-fashioned cattle rustling in order to supply meat for syndicate restaurants, and hijacking valuable merchandise to supply racketeer controlled retailing operations. Attorney

---

52. *Deskbook on Organized Crime*, p. 13.
53. *Ibid.*
54. *Ibid.*
55. *Ibid.*
56. *Ibid.*, p. 14.

General Mitchell has said, "When you read of housebreakings, shoplifting and industrial thefts, you should realize that organized crime provides a major network for the disposal of stolen goods." (57)

Now that we have dealt with the aspects of organized crime and are able to understand the inner workings, final purpose and goals within the American society, we can consider what each and every American can do to assist in the ultimate defeat of organized crime. First, we must look at organized crime from the standpoint that it can be defeated, but a successful war against it requires that we recognize crime as an enemy of society. We must anticipate that organized crime is as dedicated to eventual and ultimate control of our country through subversive and forcible tactics as certain Communists are in their design for world domination. Second, we must make it known to each and every person in the United States that Cosa Nostra and organized crime do exist. Third, we must understand that organized crime will not disappear by itself and armies of police alone will not solve the problem.

Americans must take the initiative and exert some overt action against the crime threat. To correct the conditions in which organized crime thrives, citizens must stop, knowingly or unknowingly, cooperating with criminals. This may mean uncomfortable changes in behavior for many people. We will have to stop buying smuggled, tax-free cigarettes. We will have to seek legal outlets for our gambling instincts. We will have to stop betting with the bookmakers and lottery operators. Businessmen will have to give up services of "labor consultants" who earn their fees by victimizing workers. We will have to come forth and give evidence without fear of reprisal and testify to our knowledge of organized criminal activities. We will have to give full faith and support to law enforcement officials who have dedicated themselves to the general welfare and protection of every citizen's life and property. We will have to force the complacent politicians to take an interest in the citizen and support of the laws that will curtail organized crime. The citizen will have to be

---

57. *Ibid.*

willing to sacrifice some of the rights he feels he deserves under the constitution, such as liberalization of statutes involving wiretapping and eavesdropping and broader rights of search and seizure.

Is it not better to sacrifice some of these privileges to be protected or later become subjected to the complete control and domination of an organization which will enslave society? Do we have the courage for this kind of individual moral, political, and intellectual honesty? The ultimate choice belongs to the citizen. What are we going to do? Will it be apathy or action? If we choose apathy, organized crime will continue to grow. If we take action, organized crime will fail. If we decide on action, it must be in the right direction and swift, for the syndicates are alert and will marshal their political and public relations muscle in an attempt to defeat the new threat. If organized crime is successful in this countermove and manages to brand all our attempts to fight crime as unfair, un-American and unconstitutional, crime will win, growing faster and stronger than ever before to become not just a major factor in the American way of life, but the way of life. Victory is not at all certain, even if we choose wisely, but no war against a determined enemy was ever a sure thing. Losing would be no disgrace. The only disgrace would be not to fight.

The majority of the law enforcement agencies within the United States have begun to realize that there is a major threat to the American way of life from organized crime, and they have begun to fight it. In the last decade, the nation's Law Enforcement agencies have mounted an increasingly vigorous assault against the estimated 5,000 Cosa Nostra who dominate organized crime in America. Yet, despite some significant successes in prosecution, President Nixon told Congress in April 1970 that "we have not substantially impeded the growth and power of organized syndicates. Not a single one of the twenty-four Cosa Nostra families has been destroyed. They are more firmly entrenched than ever before." (58)

Why is this, and what has caused this ineffective fight against organized crime? This disheartening routing by the enemy is due

---

58. McClellan, pp. 56-59.

in significant part to the shocking judicial leniency in sentencing convicted Mafiosi leaders. Consider the following instances:

Chicago: Rocco Potenzo, right hand man of Mafis Ross Sam "Momo" Ciancana. Internal Revenue agents arrested Potenzo for feloniously operating without Federal liquor licenses under the names of front men. Maximum sentence could have been fifteen years in jail and a $10,000 fine. Upon conviction, Potenzo was fined $1,000 by the judge trying the case and given no jail time.

Pennsylvania: Walter Joseph Plopi, Mafia corrupter charged and convicted of bribery to operate a gambling establishment. Maximum sentence was a year in jail. Plopi was convicted and fined $250. He was given back the $300 bribe money so when he walked out of court he was $50 richer than when he walked in.

California: Jimmy "The Weasel" Fratianno, West Coast Enforcer for the Mafia. Charged with swindling truck drivers working on a Federal contract hauling dirt for the interstate highway project. Convicted in court of sixteen counts of conspiracy and filing false statements which could have netted him eighty years in prison, he was only fined $10,000, no jail time.

New York: Anthony Corallo, a Capo of one of the five New York Mafia families. He had been convicted twice by the same judge for bribery and loansharking. Sentenced to pull a little over five years out of a total ten years he could have received.

New England: Louis Taglianetti, a soldier in Patriarca crime family. Convicted of income tax evasion where he could have received a five-year sentence. However, he only received seven months. Ironically, for the ordinary citizen committing the same offense the sentence averaged ten months.

New York: John Lomnardozzi, brother of a Capo in New York's Gambino Mafia family. Charged with four separate felony counts. Convicted on all four counts. Sentenced to five years in jail when he could have received twenty-eight years.

New England: Jerry Angiulo, Underboss in Patriarca Family who controls the Boston Syndicate. Charged with assault of a Federal officer where he could have received three years. Sentenced to thirty days in jail.

These are but a few of the many cases where judges have meted out very minimal sentences because they are allowed by state statutes to exercise their own discretion in handing out sentences upon conviction. (59) It is this type of action by judges throughout the United States that has caused the National Crime Commission in 1967 to make the following statement: "There must be some kind of supervision over those trial judges who, because of corruption, political considerations or lack of knowledge tend to mete out light sentences in cases involving organized crime management personnel." (60)

Because of the power and influence that the Cosa Nostra has established over its four decades of operations within the United States and the leniency that it has received from our legal system, there are recommendations being presented to Congress for adoption in order to prevent the continued expansion of organized crime. Such recommenations are being presented by Senators Sam J. Ervin (D., N.C.), James B. Allen (D., Ala.), Roman L. Hruska (R., Nebr.), and John L. McClellan (D. Ark.) under the Organized Crime Control Act of 1970. This bill includes the following provisions:

(Senate Bill #30)

> This bill provides for both prosecutor appeals and special sentences for habitual offenders and members of organized criminal conspiracies. Under its provisions, the trial judge would, after a presentence hearing at which the offender would have the right to call witnesses, cross-examine the government's witnesses and be informed of the substance of any information the judge might rely on. Upon finding that the offender had two prior felony convictions or had committed a felony as a part of a conspiracy with three or more others to engage in a pattern of criminal conduct, the judge could order a sentence up to thirty years. (61)

This is, in fact, the cornerstone of the federal government's mounting campaign against organized crime. President Nixon has given his support to this bill by stating:

> Through large-scale target investigations, we believe we can obtain prosecutions that will imprison the leaders, paralyze the

---

59. McClellan, pp. 56-59.
60. *Ibid.*, p. 57.
61. MCClellan, p. 61.

Organized Crime 77

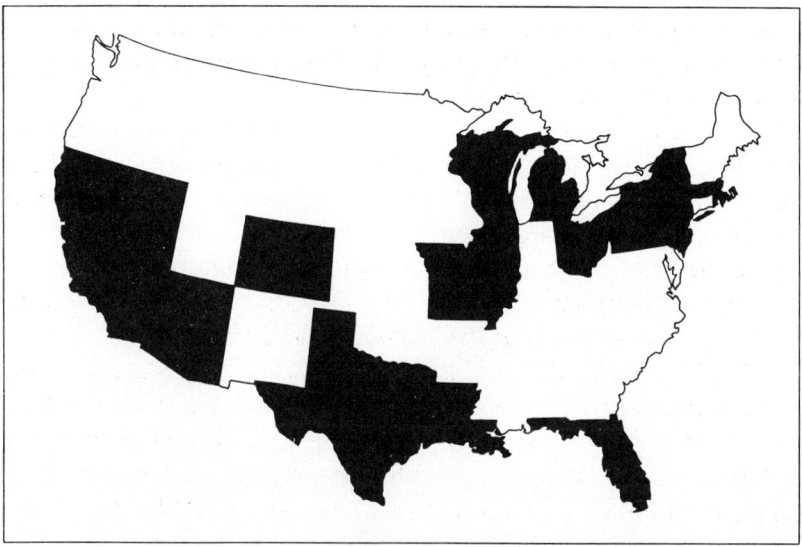

Figure 4-5. Since the map as presented in Figure 4-4 was not acceptable for public scrutiny, the Commission prepared a compromise version of this map. Instead of showing the exact location of the core elements of the Mafia, this map shows the general areas within the United States where the Mafia has penetrated and is maintaining its area of operations. (From Salerno and Tompkins: *Crime Confederation*. New York, Doubleday, 1969, p. 323.)

administrators, frighten the street workers and eventually, paralyze the whole organized-crime syndicate in any one particular city. This strategy can succeed— but only if the court record of the past ten years can be reversed. (62)

To combat the elements of organized crime, perhaps some steps of immediate action are necessary.

First: More active involvement by local law enforcement agencies to organize an effective Intelligence section within their departments which will accumulate and document vital information concerning any alleged or actual operations of organized crime should be the rule.

---

62. *Ibid.*

Second: Federal and state laws should be established to organize a specialized Criminal Investigative Agency in each area of the United States with compulsory standards and training in the area of organized crime.

Third: All information obtained from investigative agencies regarding organized crime should be by law forwarded to the Law Enforcement Intelligence Unit for correlation and overall statistics of organized crime.

Fourth: A comprehensive computerized Data System on all known or suspected persons engaged in organized criminal activities should be established and maintained.

Fifth: A liaison with the Crime Prevention and Control section of the Chamber of Commerce of the United States should be coordinated and maintained in order that known organized criminal leaders, associates and their methods of operations can be disseminated to the businesses for their protection from infiltration of organized crime.

Sixth: There must be instruction incorporated into our academic structure in the high schools, colleges, and universities. In high school, in civic and government classes students must be made aware that organized crime does exist and affects every mode of our society. In colleges, and universities. In high school, in civic and government classes students must be made aware that organized crime does exist and affects every mode of our society. In colleges and universities a specialized course could be adopted under the title of "Organized Crime," to be taught to business, law enforcement, public administration, psychology, and sociology majors as well as to students in other related fields. This course could cover the origin and development of the Mafia, its development and penetration into the United States, its methods and techniques employed to subvert and corrupt the business sphere and law enforcement and politicians within the United States, its sociological and psychological effects upon the American society and the ways and means to combat the further penetration of organized crime into our way of life. Only through comprehensive educational achievements can one understand the complexity of organized crime and its ultimate effects within our democratic society. It is with the younger generation that the hope of defeating organized crime exists.

There are many other possible solutions, but these must be worked out through the complete cooperation of all entities: businessmen, politicians, law enforcement officials, and most of all, the citizens.

CHAPTER 5

TEAM POLICING ORGANIZATION: A THEORETICAL MODEL

John P. Kenney

TEAM policing is based on a phenomena of accepting the premise that all personnel have a contribution to make to the policy and operational decision-making process. It presupposes that all personnel have a major contribution to make to the operation of the department, are capable and willing to make that contribution, and that there will be acceptance of the contribution. It is a continuing process whereby involvement of all personnel takes place, a continuous input of ideas, suggestions and constructive criticism is fostered, and new ideas and concepts are ingested into the system. Management personnel assume responsibility for broad policy making, planning of operational activities, for dealing with substantive issues regarding personnel, operations, budget and unusual situations and community relations. Operational personnel become concerned with routine day-to-day operations and implementation of broad policy guidelines laid down by the management team.

Team policing suggests that all personnel will be removed from a nice neat "box" which prescribes jobs, tasks and duties. All personnel will be perceived as having a major contribution to make to the success of the organization, and capabilities will be maximized. It is recognition that each person in the organization has talent, develops an expertise, has a basic know-how and a quality of leadership and an ability to contribute to the total operation of the department. Capitalizing on the talents of all persons in the organization is the key to success.

Can a police department match these lofty concepts? A break from tradition is required. The structures of the traditional and orthodox concepts of organization are being challenged. The giving up of command authority — not responsibility — are the

NOTE: Reprinted from *Police* magazine, August, 1972.

first of the hallowed myths of organizational relationships which follow. Collegial decision-making replaces orders by administrative *fiat*. Operational activities involves the maximizing of the expertise of the individual members of the organization, the development of a system whereby the most capable (not necessarily the highest ranked) officer is called upon to decide and handle specific situations.

Superior-subordinate relationships dealing with concepts of command and supervision are questioned. Perhaps it is better to approach activities from a basis dealing with programs, that is, investigation, traffic, repression, juvenile and community relations as a foundational basis of departmental goals and objectves. The emphasis is placed upon work to be done rather than upon the bureaucratic rewtionships of "who is responsible to whom." The dealing with specific situations replaces emphasis on command relationships. Elaborating on this issue, program goals become the principal focus of operations. Personnel work as a team in dealing with problems and situations rather than being concerned with the chain of command. Organizational relationships focus on adaptation of the capabilities of individuals to deal with specific situations, be they management or operational, rather than on the rank of individuals.

Team policing is not necessarily a new concept in organization; rather, it incorporates many features of current approaches to police organization and integrates a broad range of ideas from recently developed organization and management theory. Team building has long been essential for police operations, but for the most part has taken place outside of the existing formal structure except in the smaller departments where a team approach has been required from a practical standpoint. Writings in organizational theory recount that team building innovations in structure will work.

A brief review of present approaches to organizing police departments is in order. The *traditional model* which emerged in the 1930's emphasized a specialized unit for each functional operation. The structure was adopted by both large and small departments. The *modified model* appeared in the 1940's and still predominates. It called for a consolidation of like functional activities into major departmental units leading to the three divisional structures of field operations, services and investigation. In the past decade the model has been amplified by consolidating the staff activities of personnel, planning, budgeting and training into the office of chief of police, often referred to as "administration."

The *Vollmer model* was developed by the late August Vollmer, Chief of Police in Berkeley from 1905 to 1932. It is identical in structure to the modified model, however, the relationships between the field operations and investigations divisions is quite different. Under the modified model the field operations division is specialized for traffic and patrol and the investigation responsibility of the patrol officer is limited to the preliminary investigation. The follow-up investigation is a responsibility of the detectives and juvenile officers in the investigation division. The Vollmer model establishes the uniformed field officer as a "criminologist" responsible for the performance of *all* police activities on his assigned beat *including traffic enforcement, accident and offense investigations.* The traffic, detectives and juvenile units provide support and assistance to the field officers on a preplanned basis. Only in the investigation and processing of specified cases predetermined by policy decisions would any of the units other than patrol have full responsibility.

The *small department model* provides for a generalist approach to police operations with a minimal specialization. The department is divided into three shifts which from a practical standpoint are self-contained. All situations requiring police attention must be handled by personnel on duty. Personnel on each shift work as a team. In fact, the department as a whole consists of one major team.

The *large department model* is unique in that it reflects all the features of a large organization. Organization can be defined for the large department as ". . . the pattern of ways in which a large number of people, of a size too great to have intimate face-to-face contact and engaged in a complexity of tasks which relate themselves to each other in a conscious systematic establishment and accomplishment of mutually agreed purposes." (1)

---

1. John M. Pfiffner and Frank P. Sherwood, *Administrative Organization* (Englewood Cliffs, Prentice-Hall, 1960), p. 30.

However the large departments have not been too different in their approach to structures than departments following the modified model. The difference is that the larger departments are decentralized into precinct or district stations and that there exists a higher degree of specialization. A multiplicity of specialized units prevail at headquarters and precinct or station unit relationships are complex. Basically, the larger departments have centralized support and staff functions.

The police structural models which have been described are arbitrary and primarily descriptive for the purpose of better understanding police organizations. They reflect the concepts of formal organization theory developed in the first half of the 20th century. A brief description of formal organization theory follows.

The key features of traditional formal organization theory are applied to the police in *Municipal Police Administration*, published by the International City Managers' Association, and in O. W. Wilson's *Police Administration*. (2) Basically, the organization is hierarchical and authoritarian, emphasizing command, control and communications through channels. Workers are viewed as automatons with organization based on jobs and tasks, and the position as the basic unit. Every employee is placed in a "nice, neat box." Workers are expected to adjust to the job, behavioral patterns of individuals are to be ignored, and leaders' and supervisors' orders are not to be questioned. Rules, regulations, policies and procedures become sacrosanct and unquestionable.

The advent of the human relations approach to organization theory in the 1930's recognized man as a social as well as a physical being. The approach introduced the ideas and the concepts that man was motivated by other than economic rewards, that group behavior influenced organizational relationships and that specialization does not necessarily become the most efficient form of the division of labor. The human relations approach was based on the assumption that the most

---

2. O. W. Wilson, *Police Administration*, 2nd ed. (New York, McGraw-Hill, 1963); *Municipal Police Administration*, 6th ed. (Chicago, International City Manager's Association, (1969).

satisfying organization is the most efficient. (3) In it workers are happy, and the organization is one big happy family. The informal nature of organization is considered as important as the formal.

Informal organization refers to the social relations that develop among people in the organization which are above and beyond those formally prescribed, or which have evolved as a consequence of the interaction between workers and the pressure of interpersonal relationships which follow from formal or prescribed relationships. Informal organization introduces the complex factors of human behavior which work on the formal organization, and which reflect the nature of interpersonal relationships with a recognition of outside pressures, including personal preferences, interaction patterns, individual capacities, power struggles and communication. It brings into perspective the relationships between specialist and operational personnel, recognizes that there are decision and power centers other than those formally prescribed, and that channels of internal communication are often quite different than outlined formally. The socio-psychological behavioral features of man are thus recognized as an important feature of organization influencing the relationships between individuals, groups, and formally established units. Such relationships are in addition to and supplemental to organizational patterns designed by management which, in essence, is formal organization.

The literature on informal organization has in general provided a means for analyzing organizations. Informal organization is viewed separate from formal organization with the "ideal" being that the two meld perfectly together. The fact that the "ideal" seldom exists has not deterred the separatist approach to analysis. The formal organization is generally deemed to be the principal determinant of relationships, and although informal factors may predominate, formal organization is usually allotted credence.

That the police view of organization gives credence to formal organization is generally accepted. However, police

---

3. Amatai Etzione, *Modern Organizations* (Englewood Cliffs, Prentice-Hall, 1968), Chapter 6.

organizations have felt the influence of the human relations approach, and where there exists a formal police organization there also exists an informal organization. The nature of police organizations are highly susceptible to external and internal pressures because they primarily revolve around people interacting in face to face relationships, both within and outside of the organization.

A new body of organizational theory referred to as "the structuralists' approach" has emerged in the past decade. Basically, it suggests that formal and informal structures may be logically melded together, realistically accommodating the features of both orthodox formal organization and the human relations informal organization. (4) Robert T. Golembiewski, the more recent of the structuralists, introduced the colleague model of staff-line relationships, which does not prescribe a particular pattern of behavior, but implies a continuous bargaining situation with respect to the decision making process, resulting in the fluidity of organizational relationships. The model, in effect, discards the classical models and molds the conepts of the human relations approach into a new theory of formal organization. The design of the colleague structure calls for organizing around sub-units focusing on pro-gram activities traditionally referred to as line with integration of essential sustaining (staff) activities into each sub-unit. (5)

Essentially the colleague model is based on a team approach to organization. Relationships are circular rather than hierarchical. The top level of organization reflects an assemblage of top management personnel, each with particular expertise in a functional or program area, working together to provide direction to the organization. The lower levels of an organization are discrete sub-assemblies for the performance of specific programs. Essential expertise is included in each lower level team.

The *team policing model* incorporates the characteristic role features of Golembiewski's colleague model which provide that in some situations staff units or personnel may be dominant over line, and in other situations line units or personnel may be

---
4. *Ibid.*, pp. 21, 41-44, 47-49.
5. Robert T. Golembiewski, *Organizing Men and Power: Patterns of Behavior and Line and Staff Models* (Chicago, Rand McNally, 1967), p. 7.

dominant over staff; however, the most suitable characteristic role for the model is acceptance of the concept of consensus about alternation of roles. (6) Traditionally, the police emphasis on team activities has accentuated the dominance of the line units or personnel. Only occasionally does one find the line in a subservient position to staff. Basically, reference here is to a recognition that units and personnel other than those directly charged with program (line) operations may often be in a better position to make appropriate decisions than the line unit or personnel.

The Vollmer model varied in the approach by identifying the field uniformed unit and personnel as the *line,* making the traffic and investigation units and personnel, *staff,* along with the other traditional staff activities such as personnel, training and planning. However, the interrelationships of the line and staff personnel under the Vollmer model implied a concensus about alternating roles between the investigators, traffic, and services personnel and the uniformed field officer.

The emergence of the office of chief police incorporating the administrative staff activities into the chief's office suggests movement toward the "alter ego model" in which the staff unit personnel assist the chief in his exercise of command, a middle ground between the orthodox organizational models and the colleague model. (7) Staff personnel become much more intimately involved in the decision process often dominating line activities.

Movement toward the team policing model suggests changes in perception about line and staff and the introduction of new terminology which is more descriptive of line and staff concepts. The traditional view of staff as advisory and aiding and assisting without "authority," and line as having sole responsibility for operations, is too delimiting. Rather, an abandonment of the traditional line-staff relationships in favor of a distinction between "program" and "sustaining" units acting within a network of power is in order. Briefly, programs refer to the functions and policies related to what is to be done — whereas sustaining activities deal more with procedures and how

---

6. *Ibid.,* p. 9.
7. *Ibid.,* p. 10.

something is to be done. A team approach to the meeting of agency goals and objectives is suggested, in which "programs" and "sustaining" activities are reflected in a grid or "network of authority." (8)

Police programs have traditionally been perceived along functional lines. That is, the patrol unit performs the patrol function, the traffic unit the traffic function, the investigations unit the investigation function, and so on. Sustaining activities are reflected in separate functional units. The fact that in actual operation the sustaining and program functions are intertwined is often overlooked. The tendency is toward overspecialization. However, an analysis of informal relationships which pertain in many departments, suggests that team efforts do prevail but are not officially recognized.

The Vollmer organizational model does in fact recognize a team approach to police organization. In a sense, the programs are identified in terms of field unit responsibilities; to wit: that primarily all operational police work is a responsibility of the field unit. Thus, the patrol, traffic, investigation and services program are the field unit's responsibility. Sustaining (staff) activities are designed to support the field operations. This includes the follow-up investigation function for both juveniles and adults as well as traffic support activities.

However, conceptualization of programs in discrete terms has been weak in most police departments. As indicated, the emphasis has been on vertical program subdivisions rather than horizontal integration. More specifically, for example, an investigative program has been viewed in terms of the preliminary investigation considered a patrol unit program function, and follow-up investigation an investigation unit program function. Although the Vollmer model does not differentiate on such terms, the program issue is clouded.

What appears to be needed is a statement of the police agency role followed by a clarification of goals and objectives. If the police role is perceived as maintenance of ordered liberty which requires performance of coercive and non-coercive activities and

---

8. *Ibid.*, pp. 46-57. see also O. Glenn Stahl, "The Network of Authority." *Public Administration Review*, Vol. XVIII (Winter, 1958), pp. ii-iv; and Stahl, "More on the Network of Authority," *Public Administration Review*, Vol. xx (Winter, 1969), pp. 35-37.

the protection of personal liberties and civil rights, a basis is provided for the establishment of goals and objectives. Coercive activities include criminal, traffic, regulatory and juvenile law enforcement; keeping the peace and intelligence gathering. Non-coercive activities include social service, crime prevention, participation in the development of an environment of order and stability, and the provision of services.

With the establishment of goals and objectives departmental programs follow logically. For example, an investigation program is essential for achievement of law enforcement goals and objectives; a community relations program becomes essential for achievement of crime prevention and participation in the development of an environment of order and stability. A program may be perceived differently by different departments, but programs can be operationally defined, an important process in changing structure.

Clarification of sustaining activities and their relationship to programs is necessary. Orthodox organizational models reflect sustaining activities in terms of functional units. Thus, the personnel and training functions are perceived as a responsibility of a singular unit. Records management is perceived as a function of the records unit. Integration of the sustaining activities with program operations and goals suggests a broader perception. For example, a career development activity (a personnel function) is not a singular function of the personnel unit. All units, of necessity, must be involved. This is also true of training. Likewise, records management may be integrated into program operations to provide a more meaningful support for programs, a most feasible operation with the advent of automatic data processing.

Thus, in developing a team policing organizational model, it is in order to perceive program and sustaining activities as integrated and intertwined. However, this does not just happen. Continuous planning is the key to success, including a continuous monitoring of all activities for control and coordination purposes. Planning does not just take place as a function of a planning unit. To be successful, all segments of the organization should be involved. True, basic guidelines must be developed by sustaining personnel, and "staff" work is necessary for data processing and preparation of reports, directives and procedures. Basically, long-range planning is a function of top management, and day-to-day operational planning a responsibility of operational personnel. However, the most successful planning both of a long range and operational nature takes place when all concerned personnel are involved, or at least are aware of what is taking place. Long-range plans, of necessity, must be resolved into operational plans, and often operation plans require or lead to the development of long-range plans. (Note: See Golembiewski's discussion of substantive vs. technical issues.) (9)

Although there may be no one best way to structure for the team policing model, a circular arrangement for the top management team and the operational teams is suggested. The circular nature of the structure suggests that continuous bargaining relationships will prevail between the members of each team with all members intimately involved in the decision-making process. The top management team will be primarily concerned with the policy decisions, and the operational teams with the operations decisions.

First, a look at the top management team. Normally, the team will consist of the chief of police and the top command personnel of a department. The command personnel will not have the traditional command responsibility but will bring to the team the "expertise" of their function specialty which will be utilized in planning, directing, coordinating and controlling an integrated operation. In essence, the team will be constituted as a "board of directors" with a collegial responsibility for overall management of the affairs of the department.

The chief of police is the "chairman" of the top management team. He may be perceived as the hub of the circle surrounded by other team members. His function is to provide leadership for the team as well as the department as a whole. The "buck" stops with him, but more importantly he is responsible for creating a management environment in which the top management team members may tackle and resolve major departmental issues. It is up to him to provide a proper balance in the resolution of issues to assure that no one program is overemphasized, and that the

---

9. *Ibid.*, 119-120, 131-133, 159.

operation of the department proceeds in a reasonably smooth fashion.

The other members of the top management team will be responsible for designated program areas for which their background of education and experience reasonably provide them with an expertise. Using the orthodox organization's command officers as examples, the commander of the investigation division would bring to the team expertise in investigation and juvenile programs; the commander of the operations division, expertise in patrol and traffic programs; the commander of the services division, expertise in records and property management, communications and custody; and the head of the management services division, expertise in personnel, training, planning and budget. Each in a sense would become the "director" of their individual program area. One "director," more than likely the expert in operations in a medium-sized department, would become "director of operations" with responsibility for coordinating and directing the work of the operations teams. Departmental size would dictate the number of personnel in the team and program areas of responsibility for each team member. Necessary support personnel would be provided to perform "staff" work.

How would the team function? Each member of the team would be responsible for inputting into the planning and policy decision making process program requirements for his area of "expertise." Each input would be evaluated by the team as a whole, vis-a-vis all other inputs. The ultimate team decision with respect to each input would assure that implementation provides for a balanced operation. It is presupposed that there is a continuous flow of information on all operations and activities to the top management team.

Although the "director of operations" would have primary responsibility for coordinating and directing operational teams, all other directors would engage in a continuous process of monitoring the operation of their program areas. This would be done by review of information and by inspections. In essence, the top management "circle" would revolve for the purposes of a continuous evaluation and integration of all programs to assure a proper balance in operations.

The question arises, would not the dominant "director" usurp leadership of the team leading to an imbalance in program emphasis? This could happen; however, the role of the chief of police is to minimize such a tendency, and since there is collective responsibility for the whole operation the other "directors" would probably join together to assure a reasonable balance in program development and direction.

The operations teams are responsible for program implementation. The number of operations teams, their personnel complement and responsibilities would vary depending upon departmental size, planning and agency requirements. For the most part, teams with overall program responsibilities are suggested, however, specialists teams may be required on a continuing basis or to meet specific needs depending on agency size and problems.

The basic operational team will consist of a manager and personnel with the necessary expertise to implement program requirements as designated by the top-management team. The manager will be responsible for organizing the team and planning its operation with involvement of all team members. It should be emphasized that the manager and his team members are delegated full responsibility and authority for operations.

The responsibility of the basic operational team under one concept would consist of the performance of substantially all program and sustaining activities essential for fulfilling the police role in the community and acheiveing departmental goals and objectives. In effect each team will be self-contained with respect to performing all operational functions. The field operational personnel will consist of generalist patrolmen capable of performing the basic traditional field tasks including traffic enforcement and accident investigation. Personnel traditionally performing investigation duties including juvenile will become an integral part of the field team. Thus the field personnel will have the capability to handle all routine operations and major investigations. Preplanning calls for development of a case assignment system whereby the expertise of the most capable officer on duty will be assigned to handle each case. Routine cases will be handled by the generalist officer. The officer in charge of each case will, in effect, supervise the investigation of that case.

One may ask what about supervision? The team approach suggests that basic supervision will be accomplished through a system of peer control. However, the model suggests that a "lead officer" approach could be used to supplant the traditional first line supervisor, which calls for a clearly defined superior/subordinate relationship. A clear delineation of the superior/subordinate relationship does not appear necessary when all personnel become a collegial body equally responsible for the success or failure of operations. Furthermore, careful preplanning of relationships in which all personnel participate in the decision-making process can eliminate confusion and tension situations. In addition, a system can be preplanned for meeting emergency situations requiring precise leadership and supervision.

Sustaining personnel performing records, communications, property, crime laboratory and custodial functions will be an integral part of the operations team responsible for supporting the field operations. They too, will function under the general direction and in cooperation with the team manager. Again reliance is on the most capable or qualified person to give direction on the performance of work related to his field of endeavor.

As indicated, the number of basic operational teams will depend on departmental size and needs. One approach could be to determine total departmental program workload, then divide the department into two teams, each responsible for a twelve-hour period, seven days a week throughout the year. Development of personnel and scheduling of assignments would be a responsibility of each team. Preplanning should take care of overlapping responsibilities.

Another approach might be to follow the traditional three-shift pattern with appropriate distribution of personnel to meet shift loads. This appears to be somewhat cumbersome since there would be unequal teams, but it may be the best approach under certain circumstances.

Inevitably there will be certain activities which may be incompatible for the basic operation team structure. Narcotics, vice and intelligence activities are probably better performed by use of a specialist team. The same could be true of warrant service, forged document investigations, and other types of activities which are somewhat incompatible with the basic team operation.

In the larger department with substations or precincts, a number of structural relationships may be feasible. One approach could be for headquarters to consist of the top management team, and to provide specialist support through a number of specialist teams. The substations or precincts could use the approach of having a "minor" top management team and then constitute several basic operational teams to provide twenty-four hour coverage of designated *areas,* workload to be relatively equal. Sustaining activities could be performed for all basic operational teams by a station team. Careful preplanning for designation of responsibilities and interteam relationships would be required.

What about such sustaining activities as recruit and inservice training, budget preparation, and purchasing? Again, specialist teams under the general direction of one of the top management directors may be the answer. Each department will have to decide. However, it must be remembered that insofar as is feasible the sustaining functions should be performed as an integral part of the activities of each operational team.

The team policing organization model is a drastic breach with tradition. However, it does provide an "ideal" to be strived for which can reduce the rigidity and the tension building features of current approaches to organization. It provides a means for involving the "new breed" of police officer who brings to the department talents and potential capabilities superior to his predecessor. It makes possible a continuous input of ideas and observations about the community, the operations and agency relationships which have been severely restricted and which are becoming extremely vital for meeting the dynamic and changing demands of society on the police. Admittedly, many problems are posed in changing over to adoption of the model. Serious questioning of many current practices must take place and a number of "myths" challenged. However, the end result may be a more viable, meaningful and dynamic organization.

CHAPTER 6

POLICE PERSONNEL ADMINISTRATION: LATERAL ENTRY

William H. Hewitt

CONCEPT OF LATERAL ENTRY

POLICE personnel administration is, without a doubt, an enigma wrapped in a mystery. Joshua Pratt was appointed the first police constable in America, for Plymouth, on January 1, 1634. (1) Today, after years of law enforcement history one would expect this country to have a progressive, professional approach to police personnel administration. Nothing could be further from the truth. Uniformity in the selection, recruitment, and training of police officers in the United States is, for all practical purposes, non-existent. Although we do possess some flexibility in the recruitment of manpower, there is far too much rigidity in our present closed-career police personnel (civil service) systems when it comes to the selection of staff, management or supervisory personnel. The key to this dilemma is an increase in the application of the *lateral entry* (L/E), mobility concept.

Law enforcement administrators must face the fact that it is timely and in the best interest of their profession to create conditions which will enable police officers of all ranks to transfer from one force to another, either at the same rank or to accept a promotion without personal loss. Today such L/E between police forces is very rare. The factors of this rarity appear directly related to:

1) tradition, which speaks against such a practice;
2) reluctance of personnel to move; and
3) by far the greatest problem, the fact that men transferring

---
NOTE: Reprinted from *Police*, (January-February, 1971; March-April, 1971; and May-June, 1971).
1. Raymond B. Fosdick, *American Police Systems* (New York, Century, 1920), p. 58.

laterally must surrender pension rights and accept the conditions of service governing the new department.

To encourage the L/E concept, tradition must be broken before men will be motivated to move. Both the state and the federal government must encourage lateral movement of personnel by standardizing conditions of service, including actuarially sound pension programs which a man could take with him. Otherwise, the mobility concept is stillborn.

Lateral Entry

There has been very little written in public administration and police administration literature relative to the concept of lateral entry or mobility. The concept, however, is not new. American business and industry and the military have employed it for many years. Open competition to secure the best men for the position and dollars that a firm has to spend, is sound personnel administration. Professor George Eastman defines lateral entry as: "The appointment to a position in any rank of a person who is not, at the time of appointment, a regular member of the appointing department; usually considered to apply to positions above patrolman." (2) In commenting on the subject of lateral entry, Doctor Eastman stated:

> The practice of lateral entry between patrolman and chief has been and is used frequently, although lateral entry to the position of chief of police is becoming increasingly common. Results have not always been satisfactory, but where great care in recruiting and selecting is exercised, results have been outstanding. (Lateral entry precedents will be discussed in more detail later.) Lateral entry will become common as more police administrators attain professional status. (3)

This, then, is the concept of lateral entry. Why isn't it a common personnel administration practice? Why are we not putting the best man in the vacant position for the dollar we have

---

2. George D. Eastman, *An Analysis of Words and Terms Relevant and Important to the Study and Teaching of Police Organization and Management in the American Municipal Police Service and Recommended Definitions.* Doctoral Thesis (East Lansing, Michigan State University, 1965), pp. 46-47.
3. *Ibid.*

to spend? Why wasn't this concept adopted over a century ago? To answer these questions we have to turn to history, civil service and, especially the "spoils system."

CIVIL SERVICE

It is often said by chief police executives that police administration has come of age. This is, however, not the case. Contemporary police administration embraces many activities. However, none are more critical than the area of police personnel administration. *An organization is no better than the personnel serving it.* The quality of personnel selected will always be in direct proportion to the service rendered the community.

O. W. Wilson, former Superintendent of the Chicago Police Department, commenting on the importance of professional police personnel administration, stated:

> Police service is rendered by individual policemen on a person-to-person basis. Its quality, therefore, is determined by the individual men who provide it, and obviously cannot be raised above the quality of service rendered by the individual members in the aggregate. If police service is to be of high caliber, the members must have suitable qualifications, and they must be directed and controlled. The simple statement that the management of personnel is the most important of all police administrative tasks seems to be an entirely inadequate expression of such a tremendously important fact. (4)

Spoils System

Professor Austin F. MacDonald, University of California, describes very aptly the civil service system we in the twentieth century have inherited.

> The concept of public offices as prizes to be distributed among the faithful proved particularly intriguing. "To the victor belong the spoils of the enemy," declared Senator William Marcy in 1832. Since that time his name has been linked with the spoils system, but he only expressed the sentiment of his day.

---

4. Richard H. Blum, *police Selection* (Springfield, Thomas, 1964), p. 3, citing O. W. Wilson in an address delivered before the IACP in Los Angeles, September 25, 1952.

Virtually in every city, the triumph of the opposition at the polls was the signal for a complete turnover in the municipal working force, from the mayor to the janitor of the City Hall. Incompetents and numbskulls were similarly dismissed to make way for other incompetents and numbskulls who happened to have cast their lot with the winning faction.

Commenting further on costliness of the spoils system, Professor MacDonald says:

This unfortunate attitude toward public office proved particularly disastrous because during the 30's and 40's of the last century, the cities of the United States were beginning to undertake for the first time enterprises requiring a considerable degree of administrative ability and technical skill. Under the spoils system they could secure neither, and yet the work had to be carried on. The streets of most municipalities were lighted with oil lamps, and in a few gas had to be introduced as an illuminant. The first steps were taken to supply the cities with adequate water supplies and professional police protection. The development of these services was irritatingly slow and far from satisfactory, but that they developed at all is surprising. Had it not been for the rapid growth of cities and the increasing complexity of city life, making necessary some solution of the new city problems, municipal administration would inevitably have remained dormant in the grip of the spoilsmen. (5)

Municipal personnel administration sank to its lowest level during the two or three decades following the Civil War. Inefficiency, flagrant corruption, and total public apathy were rampant. This was the era of the "Boss" Tweed Ring in New York. During the period between 1865 and 1890, cities were more prosperous than ever before. They were multiplying at a rapid rate. Property values doubled while the services required to operate these cities spiraled.

Municipal functions previously believed to be the sole responsibility of private individuals, were now regarded as within the sphere of government. Water, fire protection, sewers, garbage disposal, and police were transferred, in many communities, from private to governmental control. Our cities employed more people and spent more and more money. Corruption, graft,

---

5. Austin F. MacDonald, *American City Government and Administration*, 6th ed. (New York, Crowell, 1956), p. 37.

debauchery, and maladministration increased in a near direct proportion to this growth. With the spoils greater, the spoilsmen became more active. Because effective and professional municipal leadership was lacking, the citizens in most communities accepted the situation with little or no protest. But the prevailing atmosphere fostered revolt. Soon, in community after community, political leaders were defeated at the polls. In 1871 and 1881 respectively, the Tweed Ring of New York was beaten and the Philadelphia Gas Ring was driven from power. As Professor MacDonald states:

> The reformers were similarly successful elsewhere. Yet their triumph was short-lived. If they carried one election, they were virtually certain to lose the next. If they succeeded in arousing popular interest during an election campaign, that interest dwindled to the zero point soon after election day. "Government by indignation" proved no match for government by vested interest. Within five years after the reformed victory of 1871 in New York, Tammany was back in the saddle, slightly more responsive to the public, but holding as firmly as ever the reigns of government. (6)

Reform Movement

It is not the purpose of commissions, boards of inquiry, surveys, and governmental inquiries to immediately remove those who practice corruption and inefficient police administration, but, rather, to encourage reform. But, in our civil service system, reform was long coming. The public soon tired of paying large salaries to incompetent public officials. The theory, "Just because a man lived within the community or within a particular subdivision that he should be given sole preference" soon gave way to an egalitarian system of personnel selection. "They were questioning the soundness of the old maxim — To the victors belong the spoils — and suggesting in its place a new precept — To the competent belongs the jobs. . . ." (7) New York State, in 1884, was the first state to establish by law a merit system for the selection of its public employees. Soon after, many cities

---
6. *Ibid.*, p. 42
7. *Ibid.*, 43

across the country fell into line and began to adopt one merit system or another.

It is axiomatic that without a professional law enforcement machine democracy could not function. In cities of more than 100,000 inhabitants, 92 percent of the people are protected by some form of civil service regulation. The overall effectiveness and quality of these programs varies greatly from community to community. Some receive strict enforcement, others do not. In some communities the civil service program applies to all public servants. In other communities it does not. Municipal administration is a field for the expert; it is not to be the "Christmas grab bag" for the henchmen of a political boss. The taxpayers deserve the best for each dollar spent. The concept that the taxpayers of a municipal corporation have the right to demand the same quality of service from their corporation as the stockholders of a business corporation demand from top management must not be subverted.

> In many municipalities the civic renaissance has carried into office men of unquestioned integrity and ability, whose work compares favorably with the work of highly trained, highly paid business executives. City employees are commonly chosen by a system of competitive examinations, though in some cities the civil service laws are regularly evaded and appointments are still made on a partisan basis. The boss is still the dominant figure in municipal politics, but he is a very different type of person from the boss of fifty years ago. Today he makes an earnest bid for popular favor. He is as sensitive to criticism as a prima donna — in Walter Lippman's colorful phrase. (8)

Civil service reform today is far from complete. Many cities with long established civil service commissions still ignore the spirit of the law and find ways to reward party workers with public office. In some municipalities the merit system applies only to certain offices and certain departments. A considerable number of cities, chiefly the smaller ones, have never accepted the merit principle and, quite frankly, make appointments on a political basis. William Marcy's famous utterance, "To the victor belong the spoils of the enemy," was recently paraphrased by the mayor of a New England city. "I believe in good government for

---

8. *Ibid.*, p. 45.

everyone," he said, "but my friends get the gravy." To raise the standards of municipal administration, the "gravy" must come out of government. The spoils system must give way to the merit principle. The philosophy that "any man is good enough for any office" must be buried along with the witch and the dodo. (9)

Standards, not panaceas, are needed to streamline and professionalize our law enforcement personnel system. It was Socrates who said more than two thousand years ago: "No one undertakes a trade he has not learned, even the meanest; yet everyone thinks himself sufficiently qualified for the hardest of all trades — that of government." These words are most apropos to municipal personnel administration in these United States during the nineteenth and early twentieth centuries.

> We cannot escape history, said Abraham Lincoln. It is Lincoln who . . . occupies an unusual place in the history of the spoils system. In his first administration he made the most thoroughgoing sweep of the government service that had been seen. It was almost total. In the higher ranks, 1,457 out of 1,639 were replaced, and subordinate employees were changed in proportion. Lincoln used patronage to gain vital support for the Civil War from the large number of factions that existed in the Republican party. When elected to his second term, however, he flatly refused to make changes. (10)

Career Service

The fifty states, 3,043 counties, 17,997 municipalities, 17,144 townships, and 18,323 special districts each have their own unique history. This is a grand total of 56,507 units of government. (11) Several items are of particular interest: (12)

    1) There is no uniformity in public personnel administration.

    2) There are units of government, at all levels, at all stages of personnel development — from the most primitive to the most

---

9. *Ibid.*, p. 127.
10. *Municipal Personnel Administration*, 6th ed. (Chicago, International City Managers' Association, 1960), pp. 5-6.
11. *Municipal Year Book, 1965* (Chicago, International City Managers' Association, 1965), p. 12.
12. *Municipal Personnel Administration, op. cit.*, pp. 14-16.

sophisticated.

3) History tells us there has always been a reciprocal influence between the local, state, and national personnel systems.

4) Almost three quarters of the states, in the decade from 1948 to 1958, followed the federal government's two Hoover Commissions with their own "little Hoover" commissions. A major focus of these investigations was personnel administration.

5) State and local units of government developed and pioneered many personnel techniques prior to gaining acceptance in the federal government. An example is the "position classification" system developed by the Chicago Civil Service Commission during the period 1905 to 1912. By 1920 the concept spread to five states and eleven major cities. The federal government followed suit in 1923 with its Classification Act of 1923 for the Washington service. In 1940 with the Ramspeck Act the law was extended to the federal field service.

6) Twenty-two states have civil service programs for substantially all state employees.

7) Five states have civil service for grant-in-aid employees.

8) Thirteen states have merit system councils to administer the minimum program required under Social Security. Nine states have extended the jurisdiction ofhhssvuncils to limited groups of other state employees.

9) For 40 percent of the total state employment there is no organized system of recruiting and appointing; employees are normally excluded from classification plans; uniform compensation standards are absent and many additional essentials of an efficient personnel system are absent.

10) The number of cities with civil service systems ranged from none in 1883, to one hundred in 1903, to 867 in 1940.

11) "In 1941, of 1,072 cities reporting, 22 percent had civil service programs covering substantially all employees; 29 percent had civil service programs covering limited groups of employees (usually fire and/or police personnel): and 49 percent had no civil service programs. In 1958, with 1,032 cities reporting, the percentages were, respectively: 41 percent; 30.4 percent; and 28.5 percent." (13)

There is little information on personnel administration in most of our rural local governments. Counties in the states of

---

13. *Ibid.*, p. 15.

California and New York enjoy the best record in public personnel administration. However, only approximately 10 percent of the counties in America possess formal public personnel systems. "The spoils system reigned almost unchallenged in most county governments — which may account in part for the designation of the counties as the 'dark continent of American politics'. (14)

In sixteen states, the township still serves as a unit of local government. In addition, the United States is dotted with many thousands of special districts. Collectively they employ a third of a million persons. There is no evidence to indicate that any significant portion of these agencies possess a formal, professional personnel program. (15)

Development of an Open Career Police Service

In terms of recruitment and training procedures there is almost no connective tissue between the members of federal law enforcement agencies and the 30 state law enforcement agencies, (16) between a particular state agency and the hundreds of city, county, village, and town departments within the state. There is, in some states, the umbrella of a state civil service statute over all these separate units, seeming to establish an integration of all the civil servants in the states under uniform general rules. But the integration is formal rather than real, and it does not touch the most significant aspects of the civil service officer's work and life.

There is, for example, very little circulation or interchange between police departments by way of transfer or promotion. The career bridge rarely spans the broad gulf between the hundreds of separate governmental jurisdictions. There are many roadblocks which hamper the L/E concept.

> The rules and statutes, indeed, usually attach penalties to or prohibitions against circulation — such as local residence requirements, promotion barriers, cumbersome transfer procedures, the loss of pension and retirement benefits. The rules are set heavily against circulation, a fact which is

---

14. *Ibid.*, p. 16.
15. *Ibid.*
16. Hawaii does not have a state law enforcement agency.

emphasized not only by the presence of these barriers but also by the absence of personnel procedures to overcome them. To these conditions, adverse to mobility between bureaucracies, must be added a stronger version of the seemingly universal habit of organized groups to prefer promotion from within rather than the recruitment of "new blood" at the intermediate and higher levels. A bureaucrat from another governmental jurisdiction is as much "a stranger" to a civil service group as is a nonbureaucrat. (17)

The politician, however, can aspire to move both vertically and horizontally, however he chooses. Compared with the narrow compartmentalized arenas of the police civil servant this provides an interesting contrast — one which defies logic. The barriers to mobility between law enforcement agencies are in sharp contrast also to the L/E which characterizes most non-governmental (business and industry) careers in the United States.

A major premise underlying civil service recruitment methods in the United States, according to Doctor Wallace S. Sayre, City College of New York:

> ... is that there are in the labor market many more qualified candidates for the public service than there are jobs. It is this premise which supports the structure of recruitment practice, ranging from the minimum publicity of forthcoming examinations through all the intricate procedural steps between candidacy and appointment.
>
> This premise of a surplus of highly qualified candidates, all of them eager and persevering in their determination to enter the public service, is obviously unrealistic in a full employment economy. It is difficult to understand how the premise ever became embedded in civil service recruitment doctrine in the United States, especially since it has never been valid here except in a few situations on limited occasions in our history. Perhaps the premise had its origin in the excess of patronage applications over available patronage jobs. If so, the fallacy lies in the equation of marginally qualified (or unqualified) patronage seekers with highly qualified career aspirants for the public service. The premise also perhaps gained accidental but temporary support with the depression decade of the 1930's,

---

17. Wallace S. Sayre, "The Recruitment and Training of Bureaucrats in the United States," *Annals Academy Political and Social Science* (March, 1954), pp. 39-40.

when a deficit in private employment opportunities coincided with the attractions of meaningful careers in an expanding and dynamic government.

Whatever its origin, it is clear that the premise is not a realistic one for the recruitment problems, of the public service, as a whole and most of the time, in the United States. A more realistic premise would be that civil service recruitment processes must be shaped to meet the problems of a scarcity of highly qualified candidates for the public service, in a competitive labor market where the public service is rarely the most favorite employer. Such a premise would require drastic revision of established civil service recruitment practices. (18)

Another goal for developing a law enforcement career service is to facilitate happy personal relationships with political leaders. The solution to this rests in greater mobility of executives in the career service.

This might well be achieved by borrowing some features of the system used in assigning, compensating, and advancing military officers. If men now in the three or four highest civil service grades did not have their rank and status so tied down to an individual assignment and if it were part of a pattern for them to be moved about from one executive position to another from time to time without loss of rank, it would not only provide the government with broader-gauged executives and reduce the risks currently involved in movement from agency to agency, but would also provide the machinery that would facilitate reshuffling of executives when necessary at times of change in administration. Such a plan would obviously entail some kind of pool or corps concepts. Career people above a certail level would be placed in a special category automatically, or selectively as the result of leading certain criteria as to training and personal qualifications. They would be compensated on the basis of rank rather than current duties, available for reassignment where needed and protected from loss of job or status under the vicissitudes of program or organization and under changes in political leadership. (19)

This idea has exciting possibilities in providing a way to

---

18. *Ibid.*, pp. 42-43.
19. O. Glenn Stahl, "Security of Tenure — Career or Sinecure?" *The Annals* (March, 1954), p. 54.

preserve tenure at high levels and to provide a more flexible means of utilizing career-executive manpower.

History has demonstrated that promotion from within *does not* produce the quality needed among key administrative, professional and technical (APT) personnel. Those covered by civil service have less formal education than those who are exempt.

The average police executive has considerably less varied experience than his counterpart in private business. More than 95 percent of our police executives have worked for one unit of government. Career-development programs are nonexistent. There are virtually no opportunities for excellent advanced training of APT personnel who have the potential to assume broader responsibilities. Many law enforcement agencies are too small to provide an adequate challenge for satisfying careers. America has no National Police College and one is urgently needed.

The principle of "merit" — that officers should be selected and promoted only on the basis of proved competence and accomplishment — must be observed in any enterprise faced with great changes and public responsibilities. Modern police personnel administration can build a merit system based on ability, performance on the job, and capacity for growth. There are no facts anywhere to support the proposition that examinations alone should be used as promotion criteria.

Personnel experts are able to establish well-defined criteria of merit. Appointment and promotion, for example, should not depend upon military service, union membership, political allegiance, or seniority without evidence of ability.

When patronage and spoils still prevail, or threaten, a means can and should be devised to safeguard law enforcement personnel from arbitrary or discriminatory treatment, but without depriving the chief executive of the essential authority to hire, promote, discipline, and dismiss personnel.

Another career-development area which offers promise, and in which we are acutely interested, is that of establishing a degree of career mobility and interchange of personnel between federal, state, and local law enforcement agencies. The federal civil service has recently taken a positive step in this direction by giving federal agencies authority to grant employees leave without pay in order for them to accept employment in a state or local government post. The federal government has opened the doors for state and local government employees to accept federal employment on a temporary basis. Many obstacles remain, however, to the complete attainment of career mobility between jurisdictions, but this is an important step forward.

The federal government has taken other steps to encourage greater career mobility — more interchange of personnel between headquarters and field stations and between different agencies.

> The Municipal Manpower Commission's report, in calling for greater facilitated mobility and in citing action taken in this direction by some state and local governments, urges that: "... upon these precedents new and more effective devices must be built." (20)

John W. Macy, Chairman, U.S. Civil Service Commission, continues to point out:

> Civil service, as a human institution subject to human failings, will never achieve perfection and must be constantly changed and improved to make it an increasingly responsive instrument of the people. As has been said about democracy as a form of government, it may be said likewise that civil service is the worst system until you contemplate the alternatives. (21)
>
> Mobility is not an unmixed blessing. Frequently an agency cannot afford to lose talent which it has recruited and nurtured. Neither can government afford to stagnate and hinder the free movement of public servants seeking greater opportunities. All too often, fringe benefits, such as longevity bonuses and retirement, serve as millstones around the necks of officers seeking to change employment to another law enforcement agency.
>
> In an attempt to solve this problem, the State of Michigan has introduced a "reciprocal retirement system" in which, it is expected, most public employees will participate. This will promote a freer interchange of professional career personnel.

---

20. John W. Macy Jr., "How Should We Implement a Program to Obtain an Adequate Public Service?" *The Annals* (August, 1963) p. 74.
21. *Ibid.*

There is precedent for such practice and it certainly seems worthy of study to extend the concept on a reciprocal basis among the states. For those concerned with quality in the police service and how to integrate some of the other fringe benefits, which have been provided by public employment, into a more rational system that would not hinder mobility is certainly worthy of imaginative and creative thought.

In 1961 at the Public Personnel Association Conference in Denver, under the authorship of Jay F. Atwood, research was conducted on the interchange, L/E and mobility concept to determine how many states had positive legislation dealing with this problem. This study should be reviewed by all those interested in promoting mobility. In summary, the study points out: (22)

1. States where specific legislation permits employee participation in interchange programs:
   A. By detail from state — 1
   B. By leave of absence and appointment — 3
2. States where laws or regulations are broad enough to permit employee participation in interchange programs:
   A. By detail from state — 11
   B. By leave of absence and appointment — 34
3. States where laws, regulations, or other administrative authority allows use of nonresident federal employees:
   A. By detail to state — 33
   B. On leave of absence and appointment by state — 41
4. States where employee benefits and/or rights would be suspended or lost by interchange program:
   A. Retirement — 35
      1) Suspended — 29
      2) Lost — 6
   B. Seniority — 24
      1) Suspended — 19
      2) Lost — 4
      3) Determination made by individual department — 1
   C. Leave — 40
      1) Suspended — 35
      2) Lost — 5

---

22. Jay F. Atwood, "Interchange of Public Personnel: Progress, Problems and Prospects," Public Personnel Association, *Personnel Report #631* (1961), pp. 22-29.

D. Group Insurance — 25
   1) Suspended — 8
   2) Lost — 14
   3) Special arrangement — 3

Under an interchange arrangement the employees involved return to their home agencies at the end of the interchange period and the basic employer-employee relationship is not disturbed. However, under the L/E concept the employee leaving does not return. It is extremely difficult to separate interchange and L/E. Both concepts are intended to achieve almost identical objectives. (23)

If we are ever going to see more "L/E" and "mobility" we must concomitantly encourage more interchange. This will surely develop an open law enforcement career service. Some of the problems and advantages of an interchange program as listed in Mr. Atwood's study are: (24)

Advantages
1) Enhances mobility of professional, administrative, and technical personnel.
2) Mitigates "inbreeding" tendencies.
3) Increases opportunities for maximum individual development and service.
4) Encourages sharing of experiences and the search for solutions to common problems.
5) Provides a way to meet short-term emergency needs for a particular skill.
6) Improves relations and creates a climate for cooperation between those within and without the public service.

Problems
1) Limited participation by public jurisdictions because of legal or policy obstacles, or both.
2) Suspension or loss of employee rights and benefits.
3) Possible loss of promotional and other career opportunities.
4) Payment of travel, moving, and other expenses and allowances.
5) Fear of having better employees "Pirated."

---
23. Generally, personnel who participate in an interchange arrangement are administrative or management, professional and technical (APT) employees.
24. Atwood, *op. cit.*, pp. 4-16.

6) Inability to perform official acts.
7) Disruption of work operations.

In summing up the advantages and problems of an exchange program, Doctor William J. Ronan, former Secretary to the Governor of New York, had the following to say:

> Despite the conviction on the part of most leaders in public personnel management that these employment interchanges are both useful and important, there is relatively little interchange. There are technical and housekeeping obstacles, but the biggest hurdle has been inertia on the part of management. Interchange as an abstraction is fine, but if it means disrupting the routines of personnel management, it all too often has been avoided. What is needed is a genuine desire on the part of management to effect a workable program of exchange. (25)

To elucidate:

> I would like to see provision made for interchange of managerial and some professional personnel with other governmental jurisdictions. Such exchanges of high quality employees can be invaluable in stimulating new ideas, in maintaining understanding among organizations, and in developing employees, and should be viewed as an essential characteristic of a broadened career development program. Career strength is gained, not lost, through the entry of outside talent at all levels. (26)

It logically follows that as public personnel administration continues its transition from a "job-centered" to an "employee-centered" approach, police personnel interchange and L/E will achieve added stature, greater consideration and, therefore, increased usage.

Whatever the possibilities of interchange of personnel among police jurisdictions, the basic kind of mobility required is that which leads to the development of career generalists within the police service. Only through the achievement of a career corps of

---

25. *Ibid.*, p. 9, citing William J. Ronan, "Personnel Opinions," *Public Personnel Review*, Vol. 22 (October, 1961), p. 276.
26. *Ibid.*, p. 16, citing John W. Macy, Jr., "Merit System Revisited," *Looking Ahead*, Vol. 9 (September, 1961), p. 4.

professional executives with a sound education, with a variety of experience, and with a government-wide perspective, can law enforcement hope to cope with its tasks. This calls for a planned projection of personnel requirements spanning a period of several years, rather than reliance upon borrowed talent in time of emergency. Unfortunately, the myth of the Minute Men dies hard. Organized planning of assignments for persons of first-rate ability to provide for the kind of variety of experience which the career generalist needs is, of course, a must.

The promises for progress, for obtaining the greater measure the prime ingredients of the improvement of law enforcement, for capable and trained police manpower, are doomed by the environment in which these metropolitan governments now operate.

There are three reasons for this contention. First, the police manpower problem will not be solved until there is an increased appreciation of the present situation. Perception on the part of the councils, the mayors, and city managers and local personnel directors is all too often absent.

Second, law enforcement personnel problems will not be resolved until we surmount — and this is an old chestnut — the problem of low prestige of the police service — probably lower than that of either its federal or state counterpart. And this low esteem of police employment held by Americans is a deteriorating handicap to the recruitment and retention of the best talent our society offers.

The third element in the milieu which darkens the promise for progress is the expansion that has given the metropolitan area the importance in American life it now enjoys, for that growth has concurrently tended to destroy the leadership that the metropolis urgently needs. The extension of the community over an ever-widening area has meant there are no leaders for the entire metropolitan police service, but rather only for the older towns and neighborhoods, each with its own particular interest. There is a multitude of overlapping local police departments, each with provincial leaders. But there are no leaders for the metropolis or megalopolis. The birth of new pressure groups and a conflict of values has tended to fragment the power of earlier spokesmen.

Law enforcement can no longer sit back and wait for high-quality applicants to come seeking career opportunities in the police service. It must actively recruit them. Some units of government have demonstrated cognizance of this fact. California has pioneered among the states in nationwide police recruiting. Many states and cities have now followed suit.

An important element in our quest for quality is our egalitarian system based on opportunity. This has not always been one of the basic principles of the merit system; and, therefore, it has not enjoyed enough positive attention. Quality talent is a very scant commodity, and, entirely independent from questions of justice and fair play, no serious talent search — whether it be for the best recruit or the best employee to promote — can overlook or bar any latent source of qualified candidates. The sooner law enforcement bodies, as employers, put this truth into action, the sooner we will begin to view a substantial upgrading in the quality of our police forces.

Law enforcement, in its quest for quality, must concentrate on the colleges and universities. Here is the most productive source of immediate manpower for the most urgently needed categories: supervisor and staff, trainees, lab personnel and technicians. High schools, which have been neglected most, are very fertile fields in which to sow the seeds of interest in law enforcement careers. A plan to intensify recruitment at the high school level — not so much in an effort to recruit as an effort to arouse an awareness, develop a better image of law enforcement and what it offers those who prepare for careers in it — should be promulgated.

The police community must work with educators in communicating opportunities to our youth. Police executives must recruit on college and university campuses. Additional information and education about law enforcement as a career should be a part of the high school guidance counselor's program. The very limited coverage of this subject in textbooks should be augmented by the availability of special study units, films, filmstrips, audio tapes, and other visual aids.

To attract, we must offer adequate salaries. Too often our least expensive help has turned out to be our *most* expensive help.

The point that must be made is that we cannot afford not to pay ample wages. Pay, however, has rarely enjoyed first place among the employment conditions which the better employee-applicant is seeking; more likely such aspects as "interesting and important work" and "opportunity for advancement" are sought. Therefore, these factors must be stressed in recruiting youth and staff material.

The Municipal Manpower Commission reports that some state and municipal governments have been attacking the salary problem, but it still ranks as the leading dissatisfaction listed by municipal executives.

This political problem must be solved jurisdiction by jurisdiction. Otherwise, each applicable community will have to settle for the highest possible degree of mediocrity.

Attracting quality APT personnel is only the first step toward obtaining an adequate police service, assuming all other measures have been taken to make the career system attractive. Of equal importance is what is done with this talent after appointment.

L/E RECRUITMENT

The following serves as a preface to data on recruitment as it relates to the L/E, mobility concept.

The terms employed here are defined by some of the nation's leading public administration authorities.

The term "recruitment" is a term which has been given many definitions. Professor George Eastman, in his doctoral thesis, defines recruitment as ". . . the process by which potential employees are brought to the initial point of the selection process." (27) Webster says, however, ". . . recruitment is an act of offering inducement to qualified personnel to enter a particular job or profession." (28) Professor A. C. Germann defines recruitment as ". . . the process by which potential employees are attracted to the agency, strongly influenced by the philosophy of personnel management adopted by the agency." (29)

---

27. Eastman, *op. cit.*, p. 95.
28. *Ibid.*, p. 95, as cited in Eastman's Thesis.
29. A. C. Germann, *Police Personnel Management* (Springfield, Thomas, 1958), p. 27.

In his evaluation of the term recruitment, Professor Eastman goes on to say: "What is the purpose of the three principal hiring procedures, recruitment, selection, and placement? This statement properly establishes that the process of recruitment is different from the process of selection, and precedes in implementation. Coppock and Coppock confuse this concept and sequence. They say, 'Generally speaking you will do well to plan the selection program to attract men who will not only be successful policemen . . . but who have the qualifications and the characteristics of successful higher level officers.' They later say, however, 'The use of proper techniques for attracting the best candidates possible is known as "positive recruiting".' " (30) Professor Germann in his treatise *Police Personnel Management* states: "Effective recruitment must involve itself with: 1) increasing the prestige value of a police service career; 2) eliminating the unrealistic pre-employment residence requirement; 3) utilizing every productive device available to attract qualified manpower; 4) conducting continuing research to determine the best techniques and sources." (31) To elucidate, Professor Eastman then concludes his comments on recruiting by saying: "Recruiting must be applied to a broad base, extending whenever possible to anyone of United States citizenship regardless of present residence. Recruitment needs to be aggressive, using possible ethical means to reach prospective applicants." (32)

LATERAL ENTRY (MOBILITY)

Introduction

Government, at all levels, is the major employer of manpower in the United States. All levels of government encounter strong competition from the private sector for APT personnel. The National Manpower Council has stated that ". . . the number and diversity of governmental units, the types of personnel they

---

30. Robert Coppock and Barbara Bl Coppock, *How to Recruit and Select Policemen and Firemen* (Chicago, Public Personnel Association, 1958), pp. 1-3, as cited in Eastman's Thesis.
31. Germann, *op. cit.*, p. 27.
32. Eastman, *op. cit.*, p. 96.

employ, the nature of the labor markets in which they compete for workers, and the differences in pay, fringe benefits, and working conditions they offer, all warn against general statements about the abilities of federal, state and local governments to secure the manpower they require." (33)

The dynamic changes which occur continually in most modern law enforcement organizations require both a wide source of applicants and freedom in the selection of persons to fill responsible positions. Frequently, these positions involve requirements not anticipated when present personnel of the organization were hired.

Today's police department requires outstanding persons; it cannot be handled acceptably by second-rate men and women. The nation cannot afford either mediocrity or severe shortages in the police service. The police community must have access to a substantial proportion of our talented, highly educated, trained, and creative men and women.

The current concern about the movement of career police personnel within and between jurisdictions is a vital element of the larger and urgent objective — the best possible staffing of a rapidly expanding police service. A society in which the accent is on change cannot afford and will not long tolerate a static police and civil service.

Professor James R. Watson of Princeton University speaking of competence stated:

> Community and urban leaders who wish to take full advantage of federal grants and services and still maintain local initiative and responsibility must be able to staff programs with well-trained, dedicated and motivated men and women. If the local jurisdictions do not give personnel management a positive concern, the federal aid will be drastically affected in one of two ways: either the federal agencies will move in and perform all services directly, or the grants will be restricted or withheld until the jurisdictions can demonstrate staff competence for effective implementation. (34)

---

33. National Manpower Council, *Government and Manpower* (New York, Columbia University Press, 1964).
34. James R. Watson, *State Personnel Systems and Mobility Problems*. An address delivered before the American Society of Personnel Administrators National Conference on Mobility in the Public Service (1966), pp. 1-2.

In other words, the traditional debates on federalism may today turn more on the competence of local personnel than on any other single factor. That the above-mentioned developments will require increased public employee mobility there can be no doubt. The big question is whether or not the public leaders, including personnel management technicians, program administrators and politicians can produce the standards, flexibility, and other elements to make mobility a positive force, rather than create a situation of increased confusion and instability. The movement of men and women between jobs, jurisdictions, etc., cannot be completely smooth and systematic. However, enough is at stake to expect that some system, some new planning, some new techniques, may result in a valuable type of systematized flexiblity. (35)

Some Definitions

As used here, Lateral Entry (or L/E as a convenient symbol) means the appointment of APT personnel at compensation levels above normal entrance planes from outside existing local, state, and federal governmental organizations. In other words, L/E is the intake of personnel on an inter-agency, inter-state, inter-city, or inter-government basis, as well as intake from business, education and the professions. (36)

It has been stated that "seldom in the history of man have so many written so much, so hopefully, to so little effect." While perhaps subject to some criticism on the grounds of hyperbole, the statement stands as a fair summation of "the state of the art" when discussing mobility in the public service from the point of view of the local units of government. (37)

The concept of police mobility, on the other hand, is offered as

---

35. *Ibid.*
36. Sam N. Wolk, *Lateral Entry Into the Public Service* (Washington, D.C., U.S. Civil Service Commission, 1966), p. 3.
37. "Local units of government" is a term used here to designate primarily municipal corporations and counties (particularly urban counties), but a term which also connotes the entire spectrum of villages, towns, townships, rural counties, school districts and both single purpose and multi-purpose regional or metropolitan government entities in the United States, as cited in P. J. Conklin, *Mobility in the Public Service: A Look at the "State of the Art" at the Local Level* (1966), p. 1. (No other data available.)

both a limitation to its purview and a suggestion for inclusion in any discussion leading to the formulation of a national plan of action. Mobility is also understood primarily here as "A personnel action in which an individual serves away from his permanent office for a period not exceeding two years; in which a local unit of government is involved as point of origin, as receiving unit, or both; and in which the individual returns to the point of origin with the intention of resuming his permanent employment there." (38)

Additional definitions of police personnel mobility would include all long-term or permanent interchanges, as well as special purpose and very short term interchanges. In terms of the theoretical justifications for a program of national action, however, the distinctions between various orders of temporary versus permanent interchanges may be crucial to the setting and the attainment of the objectives of the individual involved, the unit of origin, the receiving unit, and to the mode of effectuation of the interchange. (39)

Conklin suggests that,

> . . . the observations carry special significance in mobility discussions involving local units of government, since it might not be amiss to label as "piracy" much of the one way mobility which obtains today between units or levels of government, and between (local) units of government and the private sector. The available skimpy data — hardly yet evidence — suggest that most of the flow affecting local units of government is one-way. The same data suggest that the terms of the equations analogous to this flow may be hypothesized as: from poorer to richer; from smaller to larger; from rural to urban; from lower to higher; and perhaps, from amateur to professional. (40)

Extent of Use

Professor A. C. Germann discussing L/E stated:

The police service of America should either adopt a policy of

---
38. *Ibid.*
39. Jay F. Atwood, "Interchange of Public Personnel: Progress, Problems and Prospects," Public Personnel Association, *Personnel Report #631* (1963), pp. 2-4, 14.
40. Conklin, *op. cit.*, p. 2.

lateral entrance, or remove some of the bars to rapid advancement — if a superior type of personnel is to be recruited and utilized to the fullest extent. (41)

Also on the subject of L/E, Professor V. A. Leonard, in his treatise on "Police Organization and Management," has the following to say:

> The city of Seattle, on a consultant's recommendation, (Leonard) amended its charter and in 1946 held a national open competitive examination for the position of chief of police.... The outstanding record of the Seattle Police Department (under the new chief's administration) more than vindicated the decision of the people of that city to select their police chief executive by open competitive examination. (42)

In addition to the aforementioned police executive who has succeeded under the concept of lateral entry, this writer, acting as a consultant to the Chester Township and Russell Township Police Departments in Geauga County, Ohio, employed the L/E concept and recruited for all ranks on a nationwide open competitive examination basis. This proved highly successful, and both Departments are enjoying excellent office. This is the first known experience with lateral entry into the police arena in the State of Ohio.

Additional individuals who have been appointed to positions as police administrators via the L/E concept are as follows:

> O. W. Wilson, Chicago, Illinois (Former Superintendent.)
>
> F. Wilson Purdy, Former Commissioner Pennsylvania State Police, former Chief of Police, St. Petersburg, Florida, and currently Director of Public Safety, Dade County, Florida.
>
> George D. Eastman, Head, New York Port of Authority Police (now a Professor).
>
> Bernard L. Garmire, Tucson, Arizona and now of Miami, Florida.
>
> Howard R. Leary, former Commissioner, New York City, N.Y.P.D.
>
> James Bale, Sheridan, Wyoming, and Sierra Madre, California.

---

41. Germann, *op. cit.*, p. 118.
42. V. A. Leonard, *Police Organization and Management* (Brooklyn, Foun. Pr., 1969), p. 58.

Police Personnel Administration: Lateral Entry 119

Ivan A. Robinson, Downey California.
Fred Stoeker, Wilmette, Illinois.
Vincent Broderick, Former Commissioner, N.Y.P.D.
Roy Ashworth, Head, New York Port of Authority Police.
J. Edgar Hoover, Former Director, Federal Bureau of Investigation.
Clarence Kelley, Kansas City, Missouri, now Director, FBI.
James Kelley, Commissioner, Nassau County, New York (now retired).
Edmund MacNamara, Commissioner of Police, Boston, Massachussets.
Samuel Chapman, Multnomah County, Portland, Oregon.
Roy Holliday, Fort Collins, Colorado.
Richard Mitchell, Russell Township, Ohio.
Maurice Layfield, Chester Township, Ohio.
Theodore B. Peacock, Kansas City, Kansas.
Orson F. Myers, Independence, Missouri.
Arthur Cornelius, New York State Police (now retired).
John L. Barry, Commissioner, Suffolk County Police Department, New York.
John P. Finnerty, Deputy Commissioner, Suffolk County Police Department, New York.
William H. Hewitt, former Director of Public Safety, State College, Pennsylvania.
John Spreen, former Commissioner of Police, Detroit, Michigan.
George O'Connor, new Director of Public Safety, Cleveland, Ohio.
(Many others too numerous to list).

Obviously, the above list is not all inclusive, but is used to illustrate that the idea is not one of "all talk and no action" but, rather, a concept recognized as inevitable and being practiced by progressive units of government. Lateral entry should not be practiced for the sake of lateral entry. It should be used only when and where necessary. The following letter from the City Manager of Modesto, California, John C. Keefe, makes this point very clear.

> It is our policy, in the city of Modesto, to promote when we believe it serves the best interests of the City. It is the responsibility of the City Manager to make this determination

and, in the case of the Police Department, he makes the decision with the advice of the chief and the higher ranking officers in the Department.

When it is our determination that we do not have qualified candidates in the Department for the position that becomes vacant, we advertise nationally to fill the position. It is my belief that we should not advertise an open examination unless we have made the determination that we really consider it to be open.

The last examination we held for captain, the second highest ranking position in the Police Department, was an open exam. We did not believe we had qualified men in our department because our eligible men were too young and inexperienced. Since then we have held one promotional exam for lower ranking positions in the Department because it was our belief that our own personnel were qualified to fill the positions.

... Our rule is flexible and we do what we think is best, with the thought in mind that we promote when we believe this best serves the City's interests.

Doctor Richard H. Blum in his treatise *Police Selection,* offers two alternatives to the dilemma of recruiting and attracting executive type police officials for the nation's law enforcement agencies.

One is to provide lower level standards for recruitment, but to make eligibility for promotional examination dependent upon further educational achievement. This system, practiced in some European nations, would, for example, allow a high school graduate to enter the department and to rise as high as sergeant, but in order to become an inspector or lieutenant he would have to complete junior college, and to become captain, director, or chief, he would have to finish college. For such a system to work, the department would have to encourage off-duty studies. Some departments do just this; Berkeley, for example, subsidizes an officer's education at the near-by school of Criminology at the University of California. Other departments are resistant; assignment policies are made more difficult by having to adjust assignments to class times and there can be a loss of working time as men take time off to study or attend special school events. These hazards can be too much for some departments. In addition, some administrators, themselves lacking formal education, may feel uneasy about their subordinates becoming educated. The administrator feels threatened and, disguising his own lack of self-confidence, attacks schooling as "ivory tower" or a "frill." (43)

As to the other alternative, Doctor Blum had the following to say:

> The other alternative to the dilemma is lateral recruitment to command positions. This method also used in Europe, allows non-police personnel to enter police service as lieutenants, captains, and chiefs. It defies the seniority system and the democratic notion that every man has equal opportunity to rise from the ranks. Lateral entrance is based upon the achievement of special educational levels; ordinarily degrees in law, public administration, or criminology. It does provide highly trained and socially respected persons to fill the most responsible administrative posts. It does not rule out promotion from below, for the system can declare that anyone is eligible who has completed the educational and experience requirements. Nevertheless in a society such as ours where at least the hope for equality of opportunity is fostered, the lateral system faces strong opposition. (44)

There is very little information on staffing the "middle range" law enforcement dilemma. Police literature contains short references here and there. No major police studies have been conducted about the problem of L/E. There is no significant data dealing with the current status of this employment feature for any police agency, be it federal, state or local. Nor do we have material detailing any notable successes in any jurisdiction. We hear of scattered returns, from various units of government, concerning some interchange programs, job rotation, special training programs; but nowhere do we see a real program for taking positive action in recruiting APT personnel in positions above entrance levels.

On the private sector, Mr. Wolk, U.S. Civil Service Commission, notes it has its problems also.

> Our novels about business and our tracts against business are

---

43. Richard H. Blum, *Police Selection* (Springfield, Thomas, 1964), p. 59.
44. *Ibid.*

full of cliches about conformism and conservatism. But these are clearly not the true characteristics of private enterprise. The head of a firm is more often than not a man of extraordinary aggression. In conformity with other stereotypes, he is often cocky, self-confident, loud, domineering, sometimes even a tyrannical egomaniac.

How does one recruit these dynamic, aggressive, self-confident characters from a system which cannot tolerate them in its lower echelons? That is a general business problem. The career ladder is not designed to produce candidates for the presidency. That is one reason why so many presidents come into the firm from outside. Bright young men from business school or elsewhere are shunted in midcareer into specialized roles where there is need for them. As they head up the path of the career maze, some get bottled up, some get into places where many are needed at lower levels and few above, and a few get into places where few are needed at lower levels but where the demand above is enormous, and where therefore the recruitment base is inadequate. (45)

As Mr. Wolk goes on to point out, a study of foreign civil service systems, such as those in England, France, Japan, and Denmark, indicates that they are "closed" systems. They present a cradle-to-grave employment picture showing very little opportunity for the outsider. We have several such systems in this country. The symptoms of a closed system are mediocrity, sterility, isolation, and insulation or self-protection. On the other hand, migration and mobility can be an effective mechanism for matching people and jobs over space and time; they can be important to an individual's career development. (46)

Our communities, of inevitable and fast change, which the police must serve, make mobility a real, if not always a desirable, fact of life. One of the greatest challenges to this inescapable concept of L/E is to assure career planning and development that will be salutary to both the employee and the employer-police organization.

Transformation is upon us whether we like it or not; and the

---

45. Ithiel deSola Pool, "The Head of the Company: conceptions of Role and Identity," *Behavioral Science,* Vol. 9, No. 2 (April, 1964), pp. 154-55, as cited in Wolk, *op. cit.,* pp. 2-3.
46. Wolk, *op. cit.,* p. 3.

rate of speed of metamorphosis is compounding. One need only look around to observe numerous evidences of reformation which are having a tremendous influence on the mobility and development of our individual careers. For example, there are the knowledge explosion, technological revolution, transportation progress, new businesses, new products, population explosion, new countries, new markets, new occupations, and social rights pressures.

Since mobility and L/E is, and promises to be in the future, a way of life, law enforcement must give serious thought to the factors affecting this relatively new concept and more particularly to the influence that it will have upon sound career planning and development.

Advantages of L/E

Facetiously, Mr. Wolk states:

> Why worry about bringing in people at intermediate or senior levels? A few maybe. But not too many. We do have to think of our own, our young people, or people who have been here a long time, our seniority system, and besides it's too much trouble! The debates could be endless. There may be some inconvenience, both to individuals and government units, but there are also some advantages. (47)

Some of the advantages of L/E are:

1) Attracts APT personnel — especially for the small department. People who are mobile and thereby have a wide range of experience and contacts may also be innovators. Also important is the fact that rare skills may be attracted to the organization.

2) Provides for a fresh point of view (invigoration) — intake of people with different experiences and insights can minimize "organization arteriosclerosis" and introduces variety, change, and receptivity to new ideas. The creative person generally is one who "has been around."

3) Saves on training time — experienced APT persons need

---

47. *Ibid.*, only be given orientation to the new environmen p. 4. The advantages and disadvantages listed are generally those of Wolk.

only be given orientation to the new environment. Professional development for the individual is enhanced because of new environments, associates, and insights. Experience and methods of operation are frequently transferred with the executive or manager.

4) Bolsters management and technical strength — new talent provides organization with ability to keep the current staff highly productive in order to compete with outsiders for promotions and other rewards. Internal competition sparks new ideas and broadens individual perspective.

5) Disturbs the "status quo" — particularly in a coasting or fading department showing signs of reduced effectiveness. Avoids the "we've always done it this way" approach.

6) Provides management with a better yardstick for evaluating executive performance — persons with differing experiences can produce a staff balance and a variety of insights into complex problems. A competitive system for new hires at middle ranges forces management to compare the present group with the outsiders.

7) Creates a better understanding of law enforcement affairs — this could be a most important reason for having an effective system of L/E. The taxpaying citizens who depreciate or are ignorant of police service ought to have the opportunity to learn through actual experience.

8) Offers personal advantages to the individual — ease of mobility between police jurisdictions, or to and from government, may stimulate self-development, avoid production plateaus, develop risk-takers, provide career stimulation, illustrate how L/E can be a two-way street, and provide the attraction of greater possible rewards (the hope of upward movement).

There are also certain advantages for the police community as a whole to enjoy from the L/E concept:

1) Provides a broader use from which to choose its key staff personnel.

2) Law enforcement can provide more meaningful, broader academic education for potential top management personnel.

3) Permits the police community to shift and interchange key APT personnel to locations and organizations where their particular talents are needed.

Regardless of the advantages that could be listed in favor of L/E, there must be critical study given to the future of police personnel administration and the future concept of careers. Professor Stahl summarizes this relationship as follows:

> We are beginning to see the end of single channel, single occupation, single organization, single location careers for all but the most routine functions. Just as in the thirties we concluded that there was no career without movement upward, so in a few years we will not regard a lifetime experience as a career without movement outward. (48)

Disadvantages of L/E

Why is it so formidable to move into the police service at levels requiring experience, maturity, and talent? Current personnel practices of law enforcement prevent acquisition of new blood at intermediate levels by rigid regulations, archaic civil service regulations, and promotion from within on the basis of tenure rather than merit, thus pushing mediocre quality upward. Seniority systems, private pension plans, and severance pay plans have a very important role in affecting APT personnel mobility. There is no documentation as to whether these factors have notably impeded L/E.

In recruiting quality APT personnel, and especially for easy entry at intermediate levels, law enforcement is under handicaps (politically determined in many instances) that are generally not found in the private sector. Following are listed many of the inhibiting factors which must be recognized if the dilemma is to be overcome: (49)

> 1) *Promotion from within* — quite often is a defense mechanism for those who are already there — a reliance on seniority. Frequently such promotions are made on an unorganized basis or because individuals are close at hand when vacancies occur. Rigid adherence to promotion from within leads to agency provincialism, limited understanding and appreciation of broad problems of police service, and a narrow outlook, imagination, and usefulness. It may also interfere with

---

48. O. Glenn Stahl: *A Developing Concept of Careers.* An address delivered at the Public Personnel Association's 1965 International Conference, as cited in Wolk, *op. cit.*, p. 6.
49. Wolk, *op. cit.*, pp. 7-12.

the introduction of newly required specialized knowledge at the higher supervisory levels.

2) *Residence requirements* — serve to restrict recruitment activities to small labor markets, or even artificial labor markets. State constitutions sometimes require employees to be qualified voters.

3) *Qualification standards* — quite often are established as rigid requirements without regard to the realities of the labor market, or include restrictions based on education or sex. Also, rigid, unrealistic standards tend to regard the insider and penalize the outsider. Narrowly developed standards tend to prevent movement across occupational lines.

4) *Veteran preference* — is held by many to be disruptive to sound personnel systems and a source of inefficiency. It restricts appointing official in freedom of choice for initial appointment and, in some systems, in promotion selections. It is strongly supported by lobbies and will probably continue to prevail.

5) *Lack of career planning* — career pipelines may be twenty or thirty years long, but in times of change or stress may not produce enough or the right kind of leaders. Planning for careers could as easily be outlined at the intermediate level as well as the trainee level.

6) *Fear of favoritism* — keeps the outsider out because he may be someone's friend and would create internal problems. The principles of merit need not and should not be sacrificed at any level.

7) *Retirement rights* — differences in pension plans mean that the longer a person stays under one plan, the harder it is to make a break. A breakthrough concerning transfer of pension credits could be one of the most significant factors for increasing effective L/E.

8) *Mobility* — more career APT police people need to change traditional work habits, especially those who aspire to be career generalists. They need to move as freely as possible between all sectors of law enforcement to get the variety of experience and the stretching of perspective.

9) *Pay* — police departments are all too frequently weak competitors in money as well as other terms for personnel in high demand. Wide variations in salary scales among local, state, and federal agencies cause talented people to gravitate to the higher paying professions. More flexibility in pay systems is

needed to attract talent from business and industry.

10) *Low prestige* — police employment has traditionally ranked low on the status symbol scale. There are many well-known reasons for this fact. The federal government has, for some time now, called attention to the challenges and excitement of police work. So have a few states, counties, and cities. But there is no coordinated effort to improve the image of law enforcement.

11) *Opportunities for advancement* — lack of job satisfaction, tied in with inadequate or narrow opportunities to advance and develop, reduces ability of law enforcement to secure and retain experienced APT manpower. Many municipal departments are too small to provide "elbow room," unless staff members can progress from one small organization to another.

12) *Diversity of employment systems* — emphasis on rigid safeguards to prevent the return to the spoils system, assuming that there is an ample supply of talent, indicates that police personnel philosophy is not aimed at recruiting personnel of high ability. Remnants of patronage, rigid applications of conventional civil service practices, and traditional systems of job classification and pay, limit the ability of law enforcement to react quickly and effectively to changing labor market conditions and personnel needs brought about by a technological society.

13) *Conflict of interest statutes* — there is some feeling that such legislation is out of tune with present-day government and current APT affect on recruitment in the police service. The Second Hoover Commission stated that such laws are "a significant obstacle to bringing competent men into political service." It is also said that these laws are ambiguous, invite evasion, are ignored, and do not prevent the abuse of public office.

14) *Limited funds for personnel departments* — inadequate allocation of money and manpower to the personnel office or recruiting programs means a weak recruitment effort. It is most typical of state and local levels. Few states allocate even as much as one percent of their budget to these functions. It makes for a passive approach rather than a positive program.

15) *Inadequate information on job opportunities* — few police jurisdictions advertise specific job vacancies; most do

not. Many treat recruitment the same regardless of level or occupation. There is a lack of imagination in recruiting literature and the manner of distributing it. There are no central sources of information.

16) *Age, sex, and color* — discrimination of any type has no place in a modern personnel system. But it exists, especially at state and local levels. Age barriers are significant in the placement of experienced APT personnel at intermediate levels.

17) *Recruiting programs* — there is a noticeable lack of well-planned, forward-looking programs to secure competent APT manpower. Inadequate supervisory participation exists, especially in recruiting professionals, where the right kind of background can more readily excite enthusiasm among applicants. Coordinated recruitment plans or programs among law enforcement organizations are unheard of.

18) *Inconvenience* — this is mostly personal rather than organizational. It includes such matters as: (a) insecurity, or the reluctance to trade a permanent job (tenure) for the unknown; (b) abuse, or the reluctance to have a reputation opened to public scrutiny, and (c) timing, or inability to make a move because of fear of missing promotions at current assignment.

19) *Background investigation* — the speed in which conducted and the quality of a background investigation will vary immensely from department to department. The receiving department may have to rely on another department 3,000 miles away to conduct the investigation. Agencies must depend upon each other for very careful and proficient investigations. Teamwork is essential if a formal L/E program is to be launched successfully. The police community must understand that all agencies comprise the team of law and order.

On the subject of background investigations, Doctor Blum notes:

> At present the variations in the quality of investigations point up the remarkably different standards of performance and administration from one department to another. At the present time, there may be no solution for these inequalities, but we must over the long run make sure that interdependent agencies provide each other with the best in work and cooperation. If less effective departments do not improve and if national voluntary coordination is not enhanced, there will inevitably be many who will demand that national standards be developed and

enforced through federal law. There will also be many who will view a national or federal police as the best answer to present local inadequacies. Indeed, since these latter suggestions have already been forthcoming, it is incumbent upon us to consider the advantages and disadvantages which federal standards or a national police would impose. (50)

Faults of the Present Police Career Service

The machinery for recruiting in our police establishments is not adapted to the variety and numbers required. It has proved to be too slow and cumbersome. As a result, there have been far too many vacancies pending the establishment of regular civil service lists. Police administrators too often fail to get the right man for the job or the right job for the man. Not enough time and effort are being spend on recruiting our best young men and women for junior APT posts. To enable us to recruit more ably with the L/E concept, a comprehensive pay administration policy for the entire top level APT staff positions in our police departments is long overdue. Pay structure in our law enforcement agencies not only varies from one police agency to another, but it can also be found to vary within departments.

Different salary ceilings and salary structures must be established if we are to recruit APT personnel under the L/E concept. Many of these specialists today are leaving law enforcement for service in private business.

The responsibilities of police administration in the various departments are today so great that danger to the welfare and security of the country, as well as immense financial losses, can result from incompetence at the top executive level. Efficient executives can eliminate cumbersome and wasteful forms of management.

Many able men, while willing to serve the police community at lower salaries than are available to them in private employment, cannot be obtained, or retained, in the police service at present levels. Law enforcement salaries in the higher levels do not have to be fully comparable with those in private life, but they do have

---

50. Blum, *op. cit.*, p. 168.

to go considerably further than at present in relieving able men from financial worries if law enforcement is to maintain or improve the quality of its executives. The root of this problem is at the door of the mayor or the governor, depending upon which unit of government we are discussing. The executive branch has not done an adequate job in developing career promotion programs for law enforcement.

The executive branch, for example, has not clearly identified the opportunities which exist for persons who are interested in pursuing an APT career in the police department. In addition, it has not developed adequate programs for insuring that career personnel are moved into administrative positions at various levels on the basis of merit.

The legislative bodies of our units of local and state governments must raise the present salary ceiling for career employees. This would put the police community in a competitive position with business and industry. The chief executive of these units of local and state government should direct the police departments to work out programs designed to facilitate the promotion of career employees, and the Civil Service Commission should enforce these directives. The chief executive of these units of local and state government should direct the police departments to work out programs designed to facilitate the promotion of career employees, and the Civil Service Commission should enforce these directives. The chief executive of these units of local and state government, and the legislative bodies, should place the Civil Service Commission in a position where it can spend more of its time and resources on developing a program to facilitate transfer of competent career personnel — particularly in the APT executive areas — from one agency to another.

"Each honest calling, each walk of life, has its own elite, its own aristocracy, based upon excellence of performance." (51) This statement is apropos if we are going to develop an elite and professional police administration in America. The concept of L/E will certainly promote this philosophy. Recruiting, training, and developing leadership and middle management

---

51. James B. Conant, *Excellence: Can We Be Equal and Excellent Too?* (New York, Harper-Row, 1961), p. 75.

competence for the law enforcement community is one of the most formidable problems facing the present generation.

What about the qualifications of this man we are recruiting under the L/E or mobility concept? There still appears to be no unanimous agreement among the nation's leading police administrators on either what the chief police executive's job really is or the qualities he should possess to fill it successfully. Little has been accomplished in the nature of research, and it is doubtful whether any generalizations can be drawn that will apply to all circumstances. On this subject, Professor Stahl states:

> At this point in work on the subject we can safely conclude that the government executives must be men and women of the broadest education practicable, endowed with keen intellect and insight, possessed of human sympathy and understanding, equal to the most critical demands on the integrity, and gifted with the persistence and patience necessary to achieve action — to say nothing of having a generous sense of humor. (52)

Most of America's contemporary and modern organizations plan to fill top level posts five, ten, and twenty years ahead. On this subject Professor Stahl states:

> Executive ability is such an important asset that any sizable enterprise should know what its executive retirement and turnover rate is likely to be, appraised to what extent existing staff can replace this loss, determine at what point reinforcement by recruitment from the outside is necessary, and plan for a minimum intake each year of college-caliber people in junior levels to build up a reservoir of potential capacity to draw upon in the future. Not enough governmental organizations are being this deliberate in planning for their future executive needs. This approach is an essential ingredient of any serious effort at long-range executive development. (53)

It was Ordway Tead, in his work *The Art of Administration,* who stated:

> For nothing less than the cultivation of whole men is what our kind of society is dedicated to. Nothing less than this, therefore, has to be shared as a responsibility by administrators who

---
52. O. Glenn Stahl, *Public Personnel Administration* (New York, Harper & Row, 1962), p. 298.
53. *Ibid.*

themselves have become wholesome enough to know their labors combined the creative demands both of self and of society. (54)

When a man elects to employ the L/E or mobility concept and chooses a new organization in which to serve, he is interested not only in that organization but in his own career. "The term career is an old one. It has been widely used to denote the *progression* of an individual in a field of work throughout the employable years of his life . . . it usually implies some degree of success. Career is a pleasant term." (55)

Professor Stahl in commenting further on L/E concepts even extends this concept and philosophy beyond inter-agency; that is, inter-police agency. He states:

> In recent years increasing attention has been given to the concepts of careers that even bridge the gaps among public service jurisdictions and between the public service and private employment. In commenting on the federal service, for example, the Sixth American Assembly concluded that "a closed, self-contained system is not in the American tradition." Government employment, it stated, "should be open to interchange with the other fields of American life — business, trade unions, universities, the professions, state and local governments." Of benefit to all these groups as well as to the United States government, such exchanges were viewed as especially desirable to meet emergency needs and "to improve relations between those in and out of government." Thus, the monolithic career, identified with one institution of government, may be less emphasized in the future than in the past. A fine example, of course, of a kind of career which involves movement from one jurisdiction to another is that of a city manager, for which the whole advancement tradition has been one of progression from small municipalities to larger and more important ones. (56)

When one advocates the L/E or mobility concept in police personnel administration, he is concomitantly advocating and

---

54. Ordway Tead, *The Art of Administration* (New York, McGraw-Hill, 1951), p. 208, as cited in Stahl, *op. cit.*, p. 129.
55. Stahl, *op. cit.*, p. 131.
56. *Ibid.*, p. 132.

promoting what is also commonly known as the "open type" career system. As this term implies, it permits entrance at any grade level (by rank or position) in the police service. Such entrance, of course, is still governed by whatever qualification requirements and competition that particular jurisdiction prescribes for each level. In the open system, opportunities for advancement are still afforded through the natural advantage that insiders have when vacancies are to be filled, but infusion of new blood at middle and upper levels is not precluded. (57) As Henry Wadsworth Longfellow once stated: "Lives of great men all remind us we can make our lives sublime; and, departing, leave behind us footprints on the sands of time."

On the subject of L/E, Felix Nigro states:

> American society is highly mobile — ... and the frontier history of our country extols the virtues of free movement from place to place and from job to job. The prevailing belief is that the government stands to gain by frequent interchange of private and public personnel and that it would be undemocratic to cut off entry into and service after the entrance grades. This thinking is so strong that all recent proposals for achieving the career service stress the need for fairly frequent *"lateral entry,"* by which is meant allowing some mature and experienced persons to be brought in from the outside to fill openings in the higher jobs. (58)

Australian recruitment resembles that of the United States rather than that of England. (59) Commenting on Australia, Nigro notes:

> In the history of Australia, much the same individualistic, frontier, and egalitarian outlook which has been so characteristic of American life is to be noted. Class divisions, similar to those in England, have never existed in this commonwealth. Practical achievement, as against academic attainment, has been greatly admired. As in America, the mobility which permits the common man to rise to positions of prominence, including those in the public service, has been

---

57. *Ibid.*, p. 136.
58. Felix A. Nigro, *Public Personnel Administration* (New York, Holt, 1959), p. 142.
59. Solomon Encel, "Recruitment of University Graduates to the Commonwealth Public Service," *Public Administration*, Vol. XXXII (Summer, 1954), pp. 217-228.

deemed essential. Thus it is not surprising that the closed career system does not exist in Australia, for no governmental institution can thrive when transplanted to an environment which is not friendly to it.

Yes in both Australia and the United States there is growing opinion in favor of *career systems which draw upon university-trained recruits, with enough "lateral entry" to provide a comfortably reinvigorated, fresh outlook, and which assure that administrative positions are filled by generalists instead of specialists.* Encel in his article cited above comes to the conclusion: "Though the staff associations may persist in their refusal to admit the fact, differential (meaning university) recruitment is inevitable in a large and complex bureaucratic machine. This 'spectre' can never be exorcised, so at least let it be materialized without destroying the valuable features of the egalitarian tradition which has dominated Australia for two generations." A similar statement of objectives could be phrased for the United States: To achieve a career service which is adapted to American tradition. (60)

Nigro feels that government service is not a career in the United States — a deep source of preoccupation to those aware of the importance of public administration. (61)

Metropolitan Dilemma

Commenting on the expanding and "vertical city" metropolis of the mid-twentieth century, Doctor Samuel Humes, Executive Secretary, Metropolitan Washington Council of Governments, had the following noteworthy observations:

> The problem of metropolitan areas is not transportation or water as such. It lies in finding a responsible area-wide, yet locally acceptable, means of developing programs to meet common needs. And the apparent dilemma, shared by large urban areas throughout the world, between interdependence and independence must be resolved.
>
> The rapid growth of metropolitan communities is one of the principal manifestations of the age in which we live. In 1960, U.S. metropolitan areas, for example, accounted for more than

---

60. Nigro, *op. cit.*, p. 144, citing Encel, *op. cit.*, p. 227.
61. *Ibid.*, p. 145.

63 percent of the population, 75 percent of the nation's economic activity and 70 percent of local government revenue and expenses. More important, they are the nuclei of American economic, social and political life, dominating large regions, including rural and semi-rural, as well as heavily urbanized areas. Interdependence, bigness and heterogeneity are three principal characteristics of a metropolitan area: the trademarks of a modern regional economic system.

As interdependence, bigness and heterogeneity characterize the metropolis, littleness and independence distinguish its component parts. The size of the metropolis magnifies local needs, and its heterogeneity and interdependence necessitate an area-wide approach to their solution. The littleness of the governments within a metropolis together with their homogeneity and independence frustrates such an approach. As the population migrates outwards, a new kind of locality has been produced, inhabited largely by people of the same class, income, age group and race. The local governments serve to promote a sense of separate identity, community consciousness and independence for their inhabitants. Localities develop their own legal boundaries and political processes. Local autonomy provides a means whereby the various minorities, both in the wealthy suburbs and underprivileged core may participate in political life and thus protect themselves from those whose standards and ways of life they do not share. The multiplicity of independent governments has increased rapidly, and of the 212 metropolitan areas, 79 are multicounty, 27 inter-state, a few international in nature, and all have a multitude of special purpose authorities. It is difficult to develop the necessary confidence and communication, let alone consensus and commitment among so many local governments. The problem is magnified when conflicting state laws and even constitutional requirements must be met. *Ironically, the very presence of so many governments prevents government providing the services expected.*

Local governments in metropolitan areas have, for the most part, too little area and population, too little power, revenue, organization and leadership to cope adequately with the forces creating metropolitan needs. The root of their failure has been the lack of representative, responsible areawide general purpose institutions capable of developing concerted programs of action. Without these, they have no means of identifying needs, preparing workable regional plans, agreeing on common policies, arousing public interest and support, determining the allocation of available resources, establishing priorities and promoting programs of action. Man's proverbial propensity to wait for the roof to leak before fixing it applies to cities as well.

The delimma facing local governments is how to organize institutions capable of developing the concerted program necessary for an independent metropolitan area without sacrificing the independence of the localities. Only by resolving this satisfactorily will they be able to close the gap between the demands on local governments and the services they provide. (62)

The Peace Officers Research Association of California (PORAC), in 1960-1961, conducted a survey of L/E in the State of California. A summary of that study follows:

A survey was conducted of all the Police Departments, the California Highway Patrol, and the Sheriffs' Departments in California. Communications were directed to 368 law enforcement agencies and replies were received from 292. This survey revealed the fact that seventy-two law enforcement agencies had charter provisions or departmental rules which permitted sworn personnel of their departments to take a leave of absence for employment with another law enforcement agency within the State. The maximum period of time allowed among these seventy-two law enforcement agencies varied grossly. The variance was from a maximum of a day leave of absence allowable in one of the departments, in contrast to several departments which indicated that there was no maximum to the time allowed members of their departments who were granted a leave of absence for employment with another law enforcement agency in California.

If the survey that was conducted brought any one fact to the forefront, that fact would be that there is much variation throughout the State in all of the various law enforcement agencies in their individual regulations pertaining to the recruitment, selection of personnel, physical requirements, education requirements, training, promotional practices,

---

62. Samuel Humes, "The Metropolitan Dilemma: Interdependence and Independence," *Local Government Throughout the World*, Vol. IV, No. 4 (July-September, 1965), pp. 71-2.

salaries, retirement programs, and all of the other factors with which you and I are familiar.

In 1958 at our Sixth Annual Conference at Long Beach a resolution was adopted directing the Retirement Committee to investigate the feasibility of the establishment of a state-wide retirement plan for all law enforcement officers in California.

At our Seventh Annual Conference in Oakland in 1959, the Retirement Committee reported that "the fundamental objective underlying the resolution is sound and worthwhile, and that until such time when the Peace Officers of California can freely move from one political jurisdiction to another in response to better employment opportunities, it will be impossible to obtain an optimum utilization of their training and abilities to the advantage of both the members themselves and the state as a whole.

To make maximum mobility possible, it would be necessary to have a state-wide retirement system covering all peace officers and making possible transferability from job to job without loss of hard-earned pension rights.

The 1960 project of the Legal Research Committee as set forth at the Spring Meeting of the Board of Directors was to investigate the legal aspects of the feasibility of a California peace officer being able to transfer from one law enforcement agency to another within the State.

The project adopted by this year's Professionalization Committee will be to probe into as many aspects as possible to determine the feasibility of a California Peace Officer being able to transfer from one law enforcement agency to another within the State. The transition to be made without any reduction in grade, loss of retirement credits already earned, or the loss of any of the generally recognized "civil service" or "merit system" benefits — unless done so with the approval of the officer making the transfer.

The general idea as set forth is not original. Some law enforcement agencies in other parts of the world have had similar programs in effect for many years. Within the State of California there are professions and trades wherein such transfers are made from one political subdivision or district to another with complete satisfaction to all parties concerned. The most common being among the school teachers and nurses. Not infrequent is the transfer of highly skilled and experienced administrators in government.

Reasons why a law enforcement officer would want to transfer from one agency to another would probably be for the same basic reasons that individuals in other professions and trades transfer. The most common are found to be:

1. for health purposes;
2. to accept a promotion;
3. to further one's education; or
4. to change residence for purpose of enjoying one's off-duty time more.

Not to be overlooked is the fact that the employer in many instances profits from such transfers due to the fact that he does not always have qualified personnel within his organization to step into certain vacancies as they occur in certain technical and administrative positions. Or, because of the size of his organization, he could acquire a better qualified person for the position if allowed to make the selection from without his organization or political subdivision.

MOBILITY CONCEPT

Mobility, A Training Device

The mobility concept can be employed quite effectively as a training and development process for APT employees, and particularly so for lower and middle level managers. "Personnel administrators should seriously consider adopting a policy which includes frequent job changes, although not necessarily ones involving geographic moves, for middle and lower level managers." (63)

Most will agree that a system of internal job rotation for newly hired professionals, spread out over the first year or two, can be very effective in APT personnel career development. A variety of assignments, within the profession, help both the individual and management to find the job satisfactory to both parties. Actual geographic L/E, or mobility, has been used most effectively in

---

63. Edward E. Lawler, "How Long Should a Manager Stay in the Same Job?" *Personnel Administration* (September-October, 1964).

Police Personnel Administration: Lateral Entry

giving the new employee a more conceptual view of the work and mission to be accomplished within the organization and the police as a whole.

Factors Which Affect Mobility

The size and geographical dispersion of a police department have much to do with the usefulness of L/E in career planning and development. Obviously, an agency with 7,000 employees in twenty locations has many more mobile, rotational training assignment opportunities than the department of only one hundred officers in one location. Nevertheless, a small department may desire, after utilizing its own internal rotational possibilities, to work out an agreement of rotational assignments with another law enforcement agency. Proper safeguards, such as prohibitions against proselyting, etc., could be agreed upon, man-for-man swaps could be arranged, and effective broadening training could be provided.

The Committee for Economic Development, in its report entitled *Improving Executive Management in the Federal Government*, stated that both government and business could benefit from an increased interchange of people. In fact, the Committee's etude went on to say that mobility between federal agencies and those of state and local governments was highly recommended. Also, the study indicated that it might well be rewarding to explore the possibilities for systematic interchanges with the best of these to mutual advantage.

Studies made of federal executives by Paul T. David and Ross Pollock (64) showed that in the past there had been little or no mobility or interchange of managers between agencies. The older establishments possessed a strong sense of their separate identity, and they seldom sought to recruit executives by transfer from elsewhere in the government. In fact, these agencies resisted the proselyting of their better employees at mid-career points by other agencies.

Doctor O. Glenn Stahl, president of the Public Personnel

---

64. Paul T. David and Ross Pollock, *Executives for Government* (Washington, D.C., Brookings, 1957), pp. 63-66.

Association, provided some pertinent remarks on the feasibility of L/E in his address before the Public Personnel Association's International Conference on Public Personnel Administration, Milwaukee, Wisconsin. He stated:

> There will be increasing diversification in a worker's lifetime. ...Instead of regarding shift and movement as aberrations, we will see them as normal features of progress. Not only no man, but no career, will be an island.
>
> Furthermore, education will become a way of life instead of just preparation for it. . . . During the employed years, the professional or managerial careerist will be expected to spend a major share of time in continuing education . . . he will not only be paid for it; it will be foolhardy for the employer not to insist on it. Here, then, is a further dimension to mobility.
>
> Another expectation is that careers will be more responsive to planning. Manpower research is beginning to come into its own. The advent of computers is making the storing and analysis of complex data more feasible than we dared dream a decade ago. Diversification and continuing education will not only happen by chance to future careers; they will be the product of purposeful and deliberate design — based on regularly updated facts about needs and supply.

John A. Kouwenhoven has stated:

> Our history is the process of motion into and out of cities; of westering and the counter-process of return; of motion up and down the social ladder — a long, complex, and sometimes terrifying rapid sequence of consecutive change. And it is this sequence, and the attitudes and habits and forms which it has bred to which the term "America" really refers. (65)

Psychological Factors in Mobility

There are two schools of thought regarding the question of police APT mobility and L/E. The first holds that turnover of personnel is bad for the department, and thus the success of its personnel program can be judged by its turnover rate. A contrary viewpoint states that it is not in the best interest of either the

---

65. John A. Kouwenhoven, "What's American About America," *Harper's* (July, 1956).

officer or the department for any employee to stay in one job too long, and that maximum efficiency results from rotating personnel from one job to another to keep them from becoming stale.

A corresponding conflict of opinions pertains to the proper source of APT candidates for jobs. Current civil service career services are based on the premise that the best possible candidates should be selected at the entrance level and from then on the jobs should be filled from within the organization. This is the closed system. Outside recruiting is considered to be a violation of the career principle and destructive to morale. An opposing position emphasizes the need to broaden the base of recruitment to get the best qualified candidate for vacancies. Therefore, the police career service will tend to become ingrown and concerned more with the preservation of the status quo than with innovation. If the organization is to remain viable, new blood must be injected continuously into it.

The notion that law enforcement L/E might be a good idea is a relatively new concept. For the most part police have stayed in one job throughout their career. In many societies, the occupations available to individuals are determined at birth, and it is very difficult and often impossible to make a change. It is only in recent years that L/E has been viewed as a "possibly" desirable policy. Even today there are comparatively few occupations for which mobility is the rule. This is true for high as well as low prestige occupations. Doctors, lawyers, accountants, small businessmen, and even politicians may be doing very nearly the same thing at the end of their careers as they did at the beginning.

In this section an attempt will be made to explore some of the implications of the conflicting points of view concerning police L/E. Relevant research findings will be studied in the behavioral sciences, and based on this foundation will suggest some of the variables which must be considered when establishing sound police personnel policies with respect to law enforcement mobility.

L/E appears to be desirable in some cases, and for other situations stability seems to be needed. It takes careful analysis to determine the dynamics of each situation and the optimum strategy for achieving organizational goals. For example, Regis H. Walther studied the relationship between the number of previous jobs held by an applicant and the quality of his performance after he had been appointed to a Foreign Service job. The results indicated that it was better to select candidates for routine clerical jobs who had stayed with previous jobs for long periods of time, while for higher level work, including responsible clerical work, the number of previous jobs did not appear to be important. It was concluded from this study that the important consideration is the reason for changing jobs and not the number of jobs held in the past. Job changes for persons working at routine jobs can be motivated primarily by dislike of the work. Such an individual can be expected to be a poor risk for further routine work since he will have a low level of commitment. Job changes can also be motivated by the attraction of more desirable work, and in such cases, the number of previous job changes cannot be used to predict commitment to a new job. This finding is consistent with the observation that changing jobs is more common among the most and least competent members of the labor force. Position stability is more common for those in between. The job-hopper never settles down, and operates on the fringes of social responsibility and respectability. His shifting of jobs is considered to be a vice, and contrary both to his own interests and those of society. At the other extreme the individual who is in great demand is encouraged and sometimes forced to shift from job to job. In his case L/E and mobility is regarded as a sign of a satisfactory developing career. (66)

Walther points out another apparent contradiction, a conflict between the requirements of modern technology and the needs of human beings who do the work. As our society grows more complex, the role of law enforcement becomes more complicated, requiring longer periods of training to acquire the needed knowledge and skills. In professional APT areas in particular, such as the natural sciences, law, and medicine, competence in the work class for a lifetime specialization within a narrow field may

---

66. Regis H. Walther, *Psychological Factors in Mobility* (Washington, D.C., Center for Behavioral Sciences, George Washington University, 1966). A nonpublished address delivered before the American Society of ersonnel Administrators.

be most necessary. The resultant longer periods of preparation and greater specialization in work argues for limiting job rotation. But this is only part of the story. There is extensive research which shows that variety, novelty, and some type of challenge are important needs for man. Research has shown that when jobs become routine, the monotony and loss in satisfaction from the work will affect productivity adversely. (67)

Being more productive and satisfied with one's work is not all. There is evidence that persons who are exposed to a stimulating environment retain their mental abilities longer than those who are not. Changing positions and facing new challenges helps to keep the individual alert and adaptive to different circumstances. Available research data suggest that up to a certain point, the longer a person stays in a job the more reliable and technically competent his performance becomes. If, however, he stays beyond this point and his work becomes tedious and *lacking in challenge,* he will tend to lose his enthusiasm and his ability to adapt to changing phenomenon. (68)

> In many respects a more important consideration than the effect on the individual is the effect of group processes on job mobility. Work is always performed within both formal and informal group contexts, and what happens within this work group has been found to be decisively important. Recent research starting with the Western Electric studies at the Hawthorne Plant has shown the importance of group cohesiveness and the influence that informal group values and norms have on organizational effectiveness. It has been found that the most effective performance occurs when the goals of management are endorsed by the informal values and norms of the work group. The most ineffective performance occurs when the informal work group goals are antagonistic to those of management. This line of inquiry suggests that management gets the best results when it builds cohesive work groups with high morale based on an endorsement of management goals.
>
> As a specific example of research leading to these conclusions, the work done by the Institute for Social Research at the University of Michigan has led to the conclusion that American

---

67. *Ibid.*
68. *Ibid.*

management will make full use of the potential capacity of its human resources only when each person in the organization is a member of one or more well-knit, effectively functioning work groups that have high skills of interaction and high performance goals. If every organization were made up of cohesive and effectively functioning teams, it would result in greatly increased productivity and substantially greater satisfaction than now exists.

Other research indicates that the less change there is in a group's membership, the higher the group's morale will be. A corollary finding is that the more compatible the members of a group are in norms, skills, personality, status, etc., and the more the procedures of the group are accepted and understood, the more effective and satisfying will be the performance of the group. These findings suggest that the best results are obtained when stable work groups are created which, through the interaction of its members, will come to share values and norms resulting in the maximum cooperation and minimum conflict.

Group cohesiveness, however, is achieved at a price. There is evidence that the longer the life of the group under the same leadership the less open and free the communication within the group, which tends to make the group less efficient in the solution of new problems. A related observation of large scale organizations is that there is a tendency as organizations get older for them to turn away, at least partially, from their original goals. Practically every serious observer of large-scale organizations has noted instances of this tendency toward "goal displacement" which typically occurs through putting means in the place of ends, and procedures in the place of goals. It should also be noted that goal displacement can arise when personal goals replace organizational goals. As Berlson and Steiner in their book *Human Behavior: An Inventory of Scientific Findings* suggest, "this is sometimes viewed as the central dilemma of organizational life — in order to get some things done, you have to organize others to do them; as soon as you do, they want to get into the act of deciding what is to be done and how." There is a tendency for people to want to do things in ways which are most comfortable for them and give them the most satisfaction. It can therefore be expected that as organizations get older there may be a gradual shift away from the behaviors which are needed to accomplish organizational objectives toward behaviors which are personally satisfying to the members of the organization. (69)

Mr. Walther concludes noting that first, the rotation of personnel among work groups is probably one of the best ways to limit the dysfunctional effects of culturally induced blind spots. The person from outside the work group coming into a situation often sees very clearly what the insiders may have overlooked or taken for granted. For example, the Department of State now rotates its Foreign Service officers to keep them from becoming too closely identified with the country to which they are assigned.

Second, worker mobility, as related to performance, is a complex problem requiring a delicate balance between counteracting forces. Work habits and group behavior become more reliable but less adaptive as tenure in the job increases. Position satisfaction reaches the maximum when the employee has fully mastered the job and then, after this point is reached, starts to decrease because of boredom due to lack of challenge. If a person is kept in a slot for too short a period, he fails to learn it; if he is kept in it for too long a period, he starts losing his capacity to grow.

Third, the optimal period for service in a particular position varies over a wide range depending on the level of the job and its context. For some very routine tasks, a few weeks or months may be long enough for rotation to add interest and stimulation. For other jobs it may take many years to acquire the knowledge and practice of the skills needed to perform well; for example, crime lab specialist, personnel administration, staff specialist.

Fourth, work must, therefore, be organized so that positions are staffed by individuals with sufficient experience in a particular type of work to be able to perform competently. Effective personnel administration requires a skillful balancing of the need for immediate efficiency and the need for developing the potential of personnel; between the organization's need for reliability of performance and the individual's need for novelty and stimulation, and between the need for group cohesiveness and high morale and the need for creative, resourceful and novel

---

69. *Ibid.*

solutions to problems.

The Senate Committee on Post Office and Civil Service stated tersely in a decade old report:

> There is reason to doubt the value of any such program as that now under consideration by the Civil Service Commission which is designed to merely regard a select few who by one means or another have been selected as the cream of the crop. It is believed that the harvest will be more bountiful if the seed is selected with greater care and the crop is cultivated during the entire growing season. (70)

RECOMMENDATIONS

One cannot help but note the great need in law enforcement for highly qualified APT personnel. Under the present "closed" civil service system the police community is not getting the desired APT manpower. Therefore, it is suggested that there immediately be:

1. Positive recruitment of APT personnel in American colleges and universities. These personnel to be brought in to law enforcement for a brief training period and then given, gradually, increased responsibilities. The military junior officer concept is the intent with this recommendation.

2. Positive recruitment, nationwide, for APT manpower from the entire police community. This will surely develop a sound law enforcement career service.

3. Financial assistance to those desiring to move, laterally, by the receiving unit of government. This is currently done by the Federal government.

4. Demand upon all American citizens for quality APT personnel to serve in their police agencies.

5. Cancellation of any Federal funds and assistance to any law enforcement agency not engaging in positive L/E recruitment.

6. Activation of six-month, one-year, two-year, and even longer if necessary, interchange programs with other police agencies and universities.

---

70. Senate Committee on Post Office and Civil Service, *Administration of the Civil Service System*, 85th Congress, 1st Session (Washington, D.C., U.S. Government Printing Office, 1957) p. 16.

7. Development of promotion programs to encourage L/E by quicker promotions for those possessing one, two, or special academic degrees. This will most certainly enhance L/E.

8. Abolition of all traditional, provincial, archaic barriers to an "open" civil service career program.

The national implementation of the L/E concept will develop, almost immediately, an unimagined, untapped, labor market for the nation's police community.

Major Policy Considerations

May we now approach the problem of policy formulation and an action program with respect to L/E. In light of the foregoing discussion, what are the alternatives which, if brought together in some suitable way, might form the basis for the development of a more positive approach to police mobility?

At least eight conceptions seem to merit attention here. There may be others, but certainly these all appear to be of major relevance to the policy issue involved. It should be emphasized that the largely administrative matters discussed here are no substitute for a total national law enforcement APT manpower policy which also must be based on economic and fiscal considerations. (71)

1. *An enterprising and positive police labor market policy.* Police personnel administration has moved through three stages in recent decades; from an essentially negative and restrictive concept of the personnel function prior to the middle thirties, to what then became known as "positive police personnel management" in the fifties, and now what has become known as "manpower management." Under the latter concept police personnel management has become a much more unified system, especially as applied to the internal management of police departments. As an aspect of full manpower management, most law enforcement agencies have stepped up their recruiting efforts, especially since competition for scarce manpower became evident during and after World War II. Nevertheless, with respect to the

---

71. National Manpower Council, *Manpower Policies for a Democratic Society* (New York, Columbia University Press, 1965).

management of manpower resources available to the police community, but not yet part of government, we are still functioning largely in terms of nineteenth century notions. We extend our publicity and even send out interviewers on behalf of the department, but as for where the manpower is, its condition and mobility, and its availability, police administration has assumed little or no responsibility.

Any national labor market policy must be initiated with government, not only because our more than 100,000 governmental units employ well over 10 percent of our civilian labor force with an annual wage bill of more than $70 billion, but also because only government has the encompassing structure and authority suited to such a purpose. By an "enterprising and positive police labor market policy" is meant, not restriction of occupation and forced labor by public edict, but simply a general and at least moderately coordinated effort to provide for both employers and potential employees the police labor market information necessary for all concerned to function in a rational way. Other possible components of such a policy follow.

2. *Manpower market research and information.* A number of gaps in our knowledge have already been mentioned; many of these are suitable for investigation by the personnel of both governments and our institutions of higher learning. But in addition, a revision in our approach to the preparation of job market information is badly needed. This is a formidable undertaking in a nation as large as ours, and it will require a much better statistical, reporting, and predicting effort than has thus far been conceived of, much less carried through. The U.S. Department of Labor has also proposed to move more in the direction suggested here; The U.S. Civil Service Commission's 1964 publication entitled *Federal Workforce Outlook: 1965-1968*, is an example — though a drop in the bucket — of what will be required.

Americans pride themselves on a "free" labor market, but such a market becomes in fact severely restrictive if the information required for rational movement is unduly restricted and limited to hearsay from relatives, newspaper columns, professional newsletters, and post office bulletins. From an administrative point of view what is involved is an enormous cooperative effort for public information of a detailed nature concerning law enforcement labor markets. This will be costly, but nothing compared to the costs of under- and ill-utilization of manpower on the scale now occurring, *for the most expensive help is the inexpensive help,* in the end. Such an information program could also be coordinated with a stepped-up effort to improve the image of the police service, for this can best be realized through improving the image of particular aspects of the police function. Many prospective law enforcement employees could not care less about the image of the police community in general, but they do care about the pay, prerequisites and working conditions.

The police service has generally been at a disadvantage in the labor market because of lack of public knowledge of opportunities for police service, and therefore, should benefit from such a program.

3. *A medium for disseminating job information.* Many proposals have already been made on this subject, most of them involving better use of the public employment services. It is highly recommended that we engage in much more of a cooperative effort, utilizing public personnel agencies and most of the existing means of disseminating job information such as professional associations, newspapers and the like. The U.S. Civil Service Commission has had a few centers where some job information is available, not about examinations but about jobs actually open and waiting. There is no easy blueprint, but it should be possible to develop, fairly quickly, a cooperative and much more efficient medium.

4. *A program of potential employee assistance in moving.* Here the reference is not to such things as severance pay, though that is relevant, but rather to the provision of special travel and transfer grants for those willing and able to relocate. In Sweden, geographical mobility has long been stimulated by such grants, payable directly to the worker, provided he is either unemployed or about to be, and providing the employment situation is such that a move is necessary or desirable. Sweden also provides family allowances for workers with double housekeeping costs due to any shortage of housing.

This would be difficult for single police agencies to attempt alone, but could easily be done on a national scale, with benefits to all.

5. *More realistic relating of program to manpower.* Program budgeting has become fashionable in many governmental units, and many budgets attempt to relate program and manpower required. Police Departments have some flexibility as to what programs they undertake or expand in any given year. At least short-run adjustments can often be made in programs where manpower is temporarily scarce.

But also many more departments need to project their manpower requirements with considerably more precision. This would assist legislative bodies and city councils as well as police administrators. It would also do much to improve the general caliber of police labor market information.

6. *Promotion of a national career concept.* In light of the mobility of American manpower and the shifting needs of law enforcement, our career concepts seem unduly restrictive. There are large numbers of persons who are able and willing to operate in more than one organizational setting.

In terms of legal and administrative barriers to such a concept, governments rather than private enterprise are the chief culprits despite the fact that most governments must depend on a vast amount of L/E from private enterprise if they are to fill their manpower needs. Our Constitution provides for the free movement of goods and information, and unquestionably, people may travel freely. But, oddly, there is not full occupational and job freedom.

This is primarily because of such controls as residence restrictions and the non-vesting of pension rights. A recent study of *Pensions and Employee Mobility in the Public Service,* supported by the Twentieth Century Fund, came to the conclusion that pensions were not really a barrier. But the subjects studied were exclusively from the professional and scientific group. That pensions are not effective barriers to this type of personnel is not impressive with respect to others less fortunate in job offers and less conditioned to movement.

In and among governments we are still treating occupational

mobility more as a privilege than as a real civil right. If we are to have "freedom from want" as Franklin D. Roosevelt proposed, it would seem even more appropriate to treat free occupational movement, rather than merely freedom to travel for pleasure, as a full civil right. This is especially a problem at the state and local levels. Sooner or later, this kind of barrier, which has long been attacked on efficiency grounds, may also be attacked on civil rights grounds.

Most of the other action possibilities outlined there would lend support to a broader concept of careers. But barriers must also be reduced and other aspects of police personnel management dealt with so that new barriers are avoided. Here we come to the difficult problems of "bumping," seniority, relative power of various types of preference, and the like.

The idea of a national law enforcement APT career concept also needs "merchandising." Government agencies, civic groups interested in improved police personnel management, and perhaps even some foundations might well take up the idea so that it receives a fair hearing.

7. *Support of efforts to enlarge the supply of available talent.* Here we have a considerable heritage from World War II. The possibilities are almost endless and, since this will be covered next, there is no point in listing them all. But particular attention must be paid, especially in state and local departments, to executive development, in-service and other forms of education and training for the upgrading of personnel, the retraining of personnel whose occupations become obsolete, and the like. In-service training is a never-ending concept.

8. *Reinforcement of general police personnel management.* Finally, there are the myriads of actions which may be taken in general support of the police service and police personnel management. Here the guidelines laid down by the Municipal Manpower Commission in its report on *Governmental Manpower for Tomorrow's Cities* provide a most useful checklist. Nothing can transplant a combination of good management, in personnel administration and otherwise, coupled with a concept of end purposes deserving the attention and energies of men and women of great promise and energy.

IMPLEMENTATION

There are a great number and variations of methods to facilitate the L/E of experienced personnel into the mid-career levels of law enforcement. Some of the more popular, or at least often cited, are listed below without embellishment or arguments for or against each one. A progressive police personnel program with a positive outlook would use any or all, as the needs of the police community dictate.

1) Interchanges.
2) Short-term appointments.
3) Recruiting for career appointments.
4) Committee or advisory council assignments.
5) Job rotation.
6) Fellowships or post-doctoral assignments.
7) In-service training programs — cooperative agreements.
8) Merit system agreements involving rosters, central pool, or a clearinghouse of examination registers of various systems.
9) National career development action.
10) Direct L/E application to a specific department.

Local police departments can stimulate mobility by:

1) Assisting the local civil service to abolish restrictions based on the residence of prospective employees which close many doors for talents which are not locally available.

2) Establishing central rosters which inform potential career personnel of job opportunities throughout the country. Professional law enforcement associations can help, in collaboration with federal, state, and local law enforcement, by working out an effective system for creating manpower pools to promote interchange and mobility of APT personnel.

3) The development of nationwide recruitment program for local law enforcement employees so that the shackles of local retirement can be abolished. The pension factor is extremely important and will require extensive collaboration by all levels of government.

Action Program

There are many factors that will have a direct influence on any

Police Personnel Administration: Lateral Entry 153

action program. Before a law enforcement APT L/E program is implemented, thought should be given to the following:
1) Prestige of the department.
2) Integrity and quality of management.
3) Identification of needs of the department and applicants.
4) Recruiting program.
5) Allocation of adequate funds and people.
6) Conditions of employment including, (a) pay and fringe benefits; (b) opportunities for self-development, training and growth, and (c) adequate measures of job security.

There are many formidable problems; it is one thing to decide that L/E shall be an objective of effective police administration, another to develop the requisite programs to achieve that goal, and still another to secure the resources necessary to set those programs in motion. "It's easier said than done." In addition, a commitment to a program of police APT L/E needs some degree of informed and sympathetic understanding on the part of legislators and the public at large.

An interesting and noteworthy commentary appeared in *The Police Journal,* an English law enforcement journal, on the subject of L/E and is worthy of space here:

> *Promotion on Transfer.* It is becoming abundantly clear that the able and ambitious officer who wishes to enhance his career prospects can go far to do so if he is prepared to move in pursuit of higher responsibilities. A steadily increasing number of posts is being advertised, in ranks from inspector to chief superintendent. Forces benefit greatly from filling a proportion of their middle and senior ranks in this way, and the officers appointed, in addition to their step in rank, will gain much in the long term. Variety of experience is a high qualification, and service in two or more forces, together, perhaps, with secondment to the directing staff of the Police Colleges at Bramshill and Tulliallan, or to a regional detective squad, must notably improve an officer's chances of achieving a high appointment. The sense of belonging to the Service as well as to one's own force has become infinitely more pronounced in recent years, as the number of College-trained officers grows and Central Service provides so many national, regional and district posts.

There nevertheless remains a need for promising officers — and their wives — to be encouraged to look to forces other than their own for advancement. It is sometimes a great problem, with its factors of children's education, house-purchase and new environment. The domestic upheaval, though, sometimes turns out to be an adventure, rather than ordeal, for a family united in its feeling for the career on which all their futures really depend. The ladies, chief executives of removal operations, should be given every possible consideration by the senior officers who fix the timetable. In no public service does the officer's wife give more valuable and unselfish support.

One pleasing feature of recent advertisements is that applicants are rarely asked to forward testimonials or the names of referees. Chief constables have adequate facilities for providing one another with the necessary information and the officer concerned is saved the often embarrassing business of getting support. We entirely agree with a comment made by Mrs. R. S. B. Knowles, writing in *The Justice of the Peace,* not long ago, that "if one's selection process is sound, there is no need to rely upon another's assessment of a candidate's suitability in YOUR job." (72)

Demand for Police Employees

As the demand for police employees — federal, state, and local — is a major subject for another study, this discussion consists of highlights only. Essentially, two fundamental probabilities need to be held clearly in mind. First, during the next five to ten years relatively little increase is expected in the present 350,000 law enforcement personnel among our forty thousand law enforcement agencies at the federal, state, and local levels. As the U.S. Civil Service Commission stated in November, 1964:

> State and local employment growth continued to exceed Federal increases in the 1959-1963 period by margins of 6- or 7-to-1, for each year. . . . If this decade-long trend continues for five more years, state and local employment (which was only 4,340,000, or less than double the corresponding Federal total, as recently as 1953) will in 1968 outnumber Federal employment by more than 8,500,000, or almost 4-to-1.

---

72. "Commentary — Promotion on Transfer," *The Police Journal* (August, 1965), p. 352.

Between 1964 and 1968 the U.S. Civil Service Commission estimate that the federal service would grow by 2.7 percent, compared to a population increase of 6.1 percent, and a state-local employment increase of 20.5 percent. This will most certainly affect the police community.

As we have seen, it is among the police APT employees that scarcities have already been felt. But there is still another complicating factor of a demographic nature. This is the fact that due to prior birth rates little increase is expected during the next decade in that segment of the police labor force between the ages of twenty-five and forty-four years, the age group from which one would expect most APT employees to come. As there is some evidence that the upper administrative echelons of law enforcement, recruited heavily during the Depression era, are approaching retirement in rapidly increasing numbers, and this could further complicate meeting the prospective demand for quality executive and professional talent. The Municipal Manpower Commission has shown the same situation to prevail in many cities. Thus, given present personnel policies, the competition for APT personnel is expected to become acute not only as among various levels of the police community but between departments and private enterprise.

Thus, during 1970, for example, U.S. governments were expected to provide for 17 percent (11.5 million) of the total non-agricultural civilian employment, as compared to 15.7 percent (805 million) in 1960, the fulfillment of this potential demand will be anything but simple. For many governments — and law enforcement is an integral part — the experience may be traumatic indeed. At the very least the situation is such as to warrant experimentation and innovation in manpower, personnel, and general management policies over a wide front and on an intergovernmental and cooperative basis.

CONCLUSION

Certainly change, and the kaleidoscopic movement of individuals within our historic social structure, have characterized American life almost from the beginning. They are so a part of our inheritance of ideas that we take them for granted. We tend to forget that the kinds of almost perpetual motion to which most of us are so accustomed, and which we view so positively, are relatively novel in recorded history. (73)

Throughout most of history, migration, for example, has been seen as a cause of war and conflict, and technological change as a threat to, rather than bulwark of, the established order. It is only since the eighteenth century that social movement on a grand scale has been looked upon as a positive good and characterized as almost the essence of "progress." But this belated acceptance of societal motion and change has been almost as uncritical as feudal views of a neatly ordered society based on hierarchy and status were in their day. (74)

During the last century many experts and scholars have given a great deal of thought to the mobility of capital; this has provided a central theme for the economics of private enterprise. More recently, attention has been directed to try to understand the full direction and meaning of technology in relation to social change, especially as reflected in the ultimate form of automation. And now we find ourselves attempting to reflect in depth upon a major result of social motion, the great metropolitan or megalopolis (and conurbation) complex.

But, in comparison, the purposive allocation of money and brainpower to the systematic study of the mobility of people, either as individuals or in groups, and of the effects of mobility upon human personality and human organization, has thus far been minimal. To be sure, the term "personnel administration" has for a half century comprehended some of the factors involved, and the more recent rubric of "manpower management" has opened our eyes to a more comprehensive view of human resources. Persistent unemployment, scarcities of APT personnel, and the problems of women and minority groups among our workforce should sharpen our interest in "people." (75)

Nevertheless what we know about the reciprocal effects of "people in motion" is still surprisingly little. It is not the purpose here to fill this gap. This etude has, it is hoped, presented many of

---

73. Paul P. VanRiper, *Mobility in the Public Service as a Policy Problem* (Ithaca, Cornell University, 1966), an unpublished paper.
74. *Ibid.*
75. *Ibid.*

the aspects of L/E, such as (1) the major aspects of mobility and some of their direction and meaning in terms of the current law enforcement APT market; (2) some special factors affecting mobility in relation to the American police service; (3) certain pros and cons of L/E and mobility; (4) some lessons from abroad, and (5) a summary of the major policy considerations.

The following areas must receive much further study in order to develop a national action program:

1) How on a continuing basis can a merit system better identify and articulate L/E needs to which the police community can respond?
2) Can law enforcement organizations distinguish between needs of the service that can better be met from within and from without?
3) What are the inhibitions, real or imagined, that discourage progress in L/E?
4) Are merit systems exploiting the availability of potential sources of L/E recruits?
5) What similarities and differences exist between the jobs of police and private executives and middle managers? What is the transferability of executives among these organizations?
6) Can criteria be established to determine effective L/E?
7) What are the major innovations or reforms needed in the police service in order to implement a program of L/E?
8) Are we in favor of mobility for mobility's sake, or for improving law enforcement?
9) What steps are needed to fight the inertia of tradition that inhibits a program of mobility?
10) Are we clear about what we mean by a "merit system" when it comes to filling positions at all levels?

In sum, then, the "state of the art," insofar as it affects law enforcement L/E and mobility, is at a rather primitive and basic stage. We need data first, then thought, followed by action. It certainly appears the interest is present, and there is a strong hunch that the time is here.

Some philosopher, whose name is unknown, well described the task before the police community when he said: "The difficulty of the job is that there are no paths. The beauty of it is, there are no fences." (76)

---

76. Conklin, *op. cit.*, p. 11.

Professional public administrators must fully endorse the L/E concept and recommend its immediate implementation by the *entire* American police community.

There are inherent obstacles which must be surmounted. However, these barriers can, and must, be overcome. The concerted effort of all concerned with the administration of justice will see this concept through.

Law enforcement is no better than the moral precepts which bind its leaders and no stronger than the competence and loyalty of its staff officers and APT personnel. Law enforcement exists for the purpose of providing essential services to the community. It is not an abstract identity to which the people have no affinity. In a myriad of ways, the health, safety, lives and welfare of the people are entrusted to the officials and employees who serve the law enforcement community. The need, therefore, of competent, skilled, and loyal police officials is not a matter of convenience or accident; *it is a social imperative.*

CHAPTER 7

ISSUES IN
JOB PERFORMANCE EVALUATION

David D. Robinson

NOT more than a few generations ago most of our communities were small enough that nearly everyone was acquainted with everyone else, at least by reputation. Everyone knew the town constable, or the sheriff and his deputies, if he had any, and there was no doubt in anyone's mind as to the effectiveness of law enforcement or of individual officers. Those days are gone. Today in many locations, individual law enforcement officers are strangers to most citizens, and are not well known personally or professionally to department officials except to their immediate supervisors. Because of this fact, special efforts must be made to properly evaluate individual police performance.

WHY EVALUATE PERFORMANCE?

A systematic, timely, effective performance evaluation program benefits both the individual and the organization. A properly conceived and executed performance evaluation program should:

1) focus primarily upon results;
2) help the officer grow professionally;
3) bear upon motivation and job security;
4) provide sound bases for decisions regarding salary adjustments, promotions, job assignments, and other administrative matters.

Measuring Results

Three aspects of a man's work performance can be evaluated: Input variables, activity variables, and results.

NOTE: Reprinted from *Police* (January-February, 1971).

Input variables are what a man carries into an activity, such as the caliber and condition of his service revolver, the kind of a golf club he uses, or the dollar appropriation for running a department. Input variables should rarely be of concern in evaluating performance with the exception of safety related items, such as the condition of the service revolver or a patrol vehicle. Results are what count. For example, if a golfer uses a seven iron to hit the ball off the tee, and the ball goes 300 yards right down the middle and rolls up to the green, the fact that he used the wrong club (input variable) is much less important than the fact the ball went right where it was supposed to (the result).

Activity variables are concerned with the manner in which results are achieved. Managers who evaluate performance on the basis of activity variables are those who say, "I don't care if the ball did roll up to the green, you didn't keep your head down." Or, "Despite the fact that you fire a perfect score everytime, you shouldn't pull the trigger with your middle finger." Managers of activities tend to be overly concerned with form rather than results. They tend to confuse priorities in that regard. Some activities must be evaluated because a particular result may not be justified by the means used to achieve it. Matters of arrest, search and seizure, and interrogation fall into this category. (1) A confession is a desirable result of interrogation, but the ultimate utility of the confession depends upon whether or not it was obtained legally. In this case, the activity is at least as important as the result.

In most cases, however, the *result* is the most important variable, and with the exceptions noted, performance evaluation should focus upon results rather than upon input or activity variables. A full discussion of this topic is beyond the scope of this paper, but much has been written about the subject, (2) and in industry and in some government circles, it is considered to be a very hot topic.

---

1. G. Odiorne, *Managing by Objectives* (New York, Pitman, 1965). To some extent I disagree with Odiorne, who maintains that only results should be evaluated, but the issue is one of degree rather than of substance.
2. *Ibid.*

Professional Growth

Feedback in the form of performance evaluation is essential if learning is to take place. We must know the degree to which our behavior is appropriate to the task at hand so that we can repeat and improve upon appropriate behavior and discard inappropriate behavior. The shorter the interval between behavior and feedback, the faster and better we learn. Programmed instruction owes much of its success to the fact that it provides immediate feedback. With programmed materials the student responds to a question or a direction, and he knows immediately whether or not his response is correct. Without feedback we have no way to judge the degree to which our job performance is successful, and as often as not, our judgments of success or failure are incorrect. If we perform a given action incorrectly a number of times without feedback, "bad habits" are certain to develop and correct performance may never be attained. Feedback in the form of performance evaluation helps to "shape" behavior, and is absolutely essential to learning and professional development.

Motivation and Job Security

Most people want to do a good job. Psychologists have found that achievement itself is a strong motivator. (3, 4) "Common sense" says just the opposite — that a person has to be motivated to achieve — but in this case, common sense is wrong. Some of the necessary conditions for establishing or increasing motivation are: Good raw material in the form of people who have not been crippled by overexposure to bureaucratic red tape and other organizational hang-ups; responsibility with commensurate authority, and opportunity for performance feedback.

Knowledge of results and of how the boss views those results has a strong bearing upon our sense of security and well-being. Strange as it may seem, if we know that we are performing poorly, and how poorly, we are often more comfortable than if we have no

---

3. For example, F. Herzerg, "One More Time, How Do You Motivate Employees?" *Harvard Business Review*, 46:53-62 (1968).
4. A Maslow, *Motivation and Personality* (New York, Harper & Row. 1954).

information. Most of us feel that if we know what we are doing wrong and what to do to correct it, we still have an opportunity to redeem ourselves. Of course, it is extremely important to our sense of security and accomplishment for the boss to tell us that we have done well or that someone has complimented *him* on our performance.

A complaint heard in many organizations is "Around here no one ever knows how he's doing. That's why morale is low and turnover is high." Or, "You never know how you're doing until it's too late. It's better to beat them to the punch and quit." We can't estimate how many well-qualified people leave hard-to-fill jobs every year because of tension or resentment generated by a lack of feedback, but the figure must be astronomical. Absence of feedback can also be interpreted to mean that the department doesn't care about the officer. Few conditions can be more injurious to morale than the perception that management doesn't care.

A Sound Basis for Decisions

Administrative decisions relative to pay, promotions, work assignments and other factors must be made in every organization. Proper decisions can be made only if the officer's level of performance is well known to the decision makers. If not, important decisions are likely to be based on insufficient information or irrelevant criteria such as seniority, personal friendliness, athletic ability, or visibility to management. If promotion decisions are based on such considerations, unqualified or underqualified people will be promoted, and this has the ultimate effect of decreasing organizational effectiveness, reducing departmental morale, and increasing turnover among the better qualified people. An adequate performance evaluation system which is tied into the personnel, administrative decision-making system is necessary to maximize return on the huge investment represented by departmental manpower and equipment.

TIMING

Many organizations provide reviews annually. In effect, a year's critical comments are stored up and presented in a lump sum in which form they are likely to be ill-prepared and indigestible. Ill-prepared because in the usual system, the boss realizes in November that he must evaluate his subordinates in December, so he begins actually to eyeball performance for a month or so, and then relies upon memory for all that happened in the previous eleven months. What he tends to remember are the outstandingly good and poor aspects of the man's performance, but not his typical level of performance. Officers should be rated upon what they do consistently over the entire rating period, not upon the occasional high points or low points of performance.

The appraisee expects to hear the good things first — most bosses have learned to start with the compliments — but he is braced and waiting for the negatives. If a year has gone by since his last appraisal, the boss should have several negative points to discuss if the subordinate is as imperfect as most of us are and if the boss is at all perceptive. The appraisee will accept the first topic of criticism and will listen intently to the second one. After the third, he will probably tend to tune out all further criticism, constructive as it might be. We can absorb only so much criticism at any one time. More will be accomplished if criticism is focused on just one or two important areas than if all faults are catalogued. The same is true in a marital situation. Think of how you feel when your wife says, "You didn't clean the garage when you said you would; you're late to dinner; I need more money; you should spend more time with the children; and you don't spend enough time with me." Perhaps, all of these complaints are justified, and you know it, but by the time the third complaint is presented, you have tuned her out. Too many critical comments, especially a year's worth at once, tend to be indigestible.

A better approach is to evaluate performance as the need is apparent throughout the year. Performance evaluation really is a continuous process. In order to assist his men to develop professionally, the supervisor must adopt a full-time coaching attitude. He must spend time with them analyzing problems, reviewing plans, and carrying out "post mortems" on mistakes. An effective supervisor-coach does not necessarily give his subordinates answers to problems, and should admit that he doesn't know all the answers. He should serve as a sounding board for ideas, as a friendly critic of these ideas, as a resource person, and as a backstop when necessary. Most importantly, he must be committed to helping officers under his supervision to grow and develop.

A growing body of evidence indicates that if a subordinate is called upon to rate himself, the evaluation is accepted better and is less anxiety-provoking than the usual method of the boss telling the subordinate what his faults are. (5) In the self-review model, the situation is similar to a counsellor-counsellee situation whereas the traditional model resembles a courtroom scene with a judge and a defendant. A subordinate in the role of a counsellee is likely to derive much more benefit from the appraisal than if he feels like a defendant.

On an administrative level, certain decisions must be made which may require regular evaluations yielding quantitative data — numerical scores of some kind. These evaluations tend to be geared toward satisfying organizational needs rather than individual needs. As a matter of fact, rating scales and performance inventories rarely need to be shown to the individual because they give the impression of permanence and absolute constancy of behavior. Performance measurement techniques which yield scores are a very poor substitute for close contact and continuous feedback between supervisors and subordinates. Most quantitative scales are for administrative convenience, and are not designed for use in individual development. We will discuss quantitative methods in greater detail later in this paper.

VALIDITY CONSIDERATIONS

Several considerations affect the validity of performance

---

5. G. A. Bassett and H. H. Meyer, "Performance Appraisal Based on Self-Review," *Personnel Psychology*, 21:421-430 (1968).

evaluation. Although management has the right to evaluate performance however, whenever, and by whomever it desires, it has the obligation to do so as validly as possible. Surprisingly often, principles of validity are overlooked. Care should be exercised so that:

    1) The evaluator has opportunity to observe an adequate, timely sample of behavior.
    2) The appraisee is evaluated on the basis of *observable behavior*.
    3) The appraisee is given adequate opportunity to perform.
    4) Biases of memory, perception, and social pressure are avoided.

Observing an Adequate Sample of Behavior

A policeman's job performance depends upon three major factors: the actual performance, environmental effects, and chance variation. He may issue traffic citations in a middle class neighborhood in essentially the same way day after day. His performance is likely to change, though, if he is called upon to do the same job in a different environment, say a black ghetto. His behavior is likely to change as a result of such chance variations as a marital squabble, a nagging headache, or because the day before a fellow officer was feloniously assaulted in the course of a traffic arrest. The task facing the evaluator is to observe a large enough sample of the officer's behavior so that these environmental effects and chance variations cancel each other out — so that only "actual performance" or "true performance" is left.

The evaluator must be in a position to observe a timely sample of behavior, otherwise, his evaluation will be invalid. This consideration may best be illustrated by a military example. A young second lieutenant had even more difficulty adjusting to the military during his first year than most do. But suddenly he began to catch on, and during the next six months became so effective that he outshone his peers. His battalion commander was unaware of the improvement, however, and declined to promote him at the expected time. The lieutenant requested reconsideration and the battalion commander wisely gathered more data. These reports were so favorable that the lieutenant was promoted after all. Even though the battalion commander had the prerogative to evaluate the lieutenant, he should not have done so because he wasn't sufficiently acquainted with his performance to make an adequate judgment. Fortunately, the battalion commander was flexible enough to change his mind in the light of new information. Thus, he made a correct decision to promote the lieutenant and the lieutenant developed greater loyalty and respect for the commander because of his flexibility.

Evaluating on the Basis of Observable Behavior

The key words are *observable* and *behavior*. If an individual is to be evaluated at all, he should be evaluated on the basis of what can be *observed* rather than upon that which is inferred. For example, it is unfair to evaluate an individual on the basis of "poor attitude." His attitude may actually be favorable; his *behavior* should be challenged. For example, domestic problems may preoccupy an officer whose attitude is good, but his dress becomes sloppy, he becomes chronically late, and behaves in a surly manner. It would be legitimate to rate him on dress, punctuality, and surliness because these are observable, but not "poor attitude." Furthermore, in discussing these shortcomings with him, specific suggestions or demands for improvement can be made. It is not worthwhile to criticize on the basis of attitude because no clear path to improvement, that is, behavior change, is indicated. Besides, it is extremely frustrating to the individual not to have a clear indication of what he must do to obtain a more positive evaluation. Never criticize on the basis of unobservables or upon generalities if you can avoid it. Always try to give the individual a substitute for his unacceptable behavior in the form of positive things to do.

Opportunity to Perform

Obviously an individual must be given an opportunity to perform if his performance is to be evaluated, but surprisingly enough, men are rated up or down on the basis of what the boss assumes *would* happen or fail to happen under a given set of circumstances, rather than what *has* happened and can therefore be evaluated. For example, a young engineer was thought to be incapable of directing a project, was rated low, and was not given the opportunity to assume project responsibility until an emergency arose and no one else was available to carry the ball. Reluctantly, the chief engineer assigned him the job. His high level of performance amazed everyone, and management concluded that the individual miraculously had grown under pressure. The young engineer was not impressed with this conclusion, and despite the glory, soon left the organization because his prior lack of opportunity had soured his morale. In this case, the individual wasted career time, and the company lost a good man. Management assumed that the engineer was incapable of performing and had rated him low; no one gave him an opportunity to perform until it was too late.

Biases of Memory, Perception and Social Pressures

If performance evaluation is carried out continuously, memory and perceptual bias are likely to have less of an effect than if evaluations are performed annually or semiannually. We have examined memory bias in our discussion of timing the appraisal, and have pointed out that raters tend to remember examples of especially high performance, low performance, and recent performance. Thus, memory bias serves to highlight only selected aspects of performance. Consider perceptual bias: some raters see only the things that are done well; others tend to focus upon things that are done poorly. Some individuals misinterpret what they see. Ethnic or religious qualities can generate perceptual bias also. These biases operate unconsciously, and we are rarely aware that they are operating. The rater's voluntary behavior often affects the validity of performance evaluation, too. For example, social pressure may prevent a supervisor from giving a valid rating. He may be reluctant to give the chief's nephew an unsatisfactory rating. He may also be reluctant to render an unsatisfactory rating on an officer who pitches no-hitters in the

Police Association softball team.

Ways in which the effects of memory, perception, and social pressure can be minimized are to rate often, to keep performance records, to teach raters what to look for, and to have officers evaluated by more than one rater. These methods are so simple that they are overlooked because of time pressures or some other reason, but they pay off in terms of more valid evaluations.

QUANTITATIVE RATING METHODS

We have examined some of the conditions under which increased benefits can be derived from a sound program of performance evaluation. Throughout, we've said that continuous personal contact between supervisor (or coach) and subordinate is essential. Keep this in mind as we explore quantitative rating methods.

Within the last twenty years or so industrial psychologists have developed performance rating scales which yield numerical scores. These instruments have been received enthusiastically by administrators in many fields, since they are economical in terms of time and effort, and they permit individuals to be ordered along a scale of merit. However, like psychological tests, merit rating instruments must be used carefully and with discretion.

Quantitative scales are *never* to be substituted for close personal contact between supervisor and subordinate. They are of scant value to the subordinate in terms of improving his performance and probably need not be shown to him if supervisor and subordinate maintain close contact. Their value lies primarily in providing departmental administrators with quantitative data to be used *along with other data* in making decisions regarding salary adjustments, promotions, work assignment, and so on.

Decision makers should also consider such information as experience, training needs, the individual's present assignment, whether or not he manifests the qualities necessary for success in a job into which he may be promoted, and so on. The latter consideration is especially important. For example, sales executives have found time and time again that the best salesmen often fail as sales managers. Good teachers are not necessarily good administrators, and vice versa. In other words, the characteristics required for success in one job may be significantly different from those required for success in the next higher job.

Decision-makers can be lulled into a sense of dependence upon numerical scores. We have become conditioned to the fact that $50 is twice as much as $25, for example, or that six inches is precisely one inch less than seven inches. But measurement techniques in the behavioral sciences are not sufficiently precise to permit such interpretations. For example, the only conclusion that can be drawn from two IQ scores of 100 and 104 is that the individuals who attained them are of average and approximately equal intelligence. We have to know how large the error factors are in our measurement tools and techniques. Many factors contribute to the size of the error: biases of memory, perception, and social pressure, ambiguous wording in the rating scale, the length of the instrument, the size of the group upon which the instrument was standardized, the number of raters, their training and experience in rating, and a host of other factors.

One of the most important considerations in using a quantitative merit rating instrument is validity. Validity is heavily influenced by the factors we have just mentioned. A merit rating instrument must be validated for the group on which it is to be used. A systematic and consistent relationship between the score received on the instrument and some measure of performance must be demonstrated. If such a relationship can be demonstrated, the scale is valid. If not, it is not valid and must not be used.

How is validation carried out? First, a satisfactory criterion of job performance must be developed. Supervisors' rating of complaints versus compliments have been used to measure police performance. (6) Others are percentage of cases cleared, or ratio of arrests to convictions, or a combination of all of these. Criterion development is a highly technical subject about which much has been written. (7, 8)

---

6. D. D. Robinson, "Predicting Police Effectiveness from Self-Reports of Relative Time Spent in Task Performance," *Personnel Psychology*, Vol. 23 (1970).
7. B. F. Nagle, "Criterion Development," *Personnel Psychology*, 6:271-289 (1953).
8. E. E. Ghiselli and C. W. Brown, *Personnel and Industrial Psychology* (New York, McGraw-Hill).

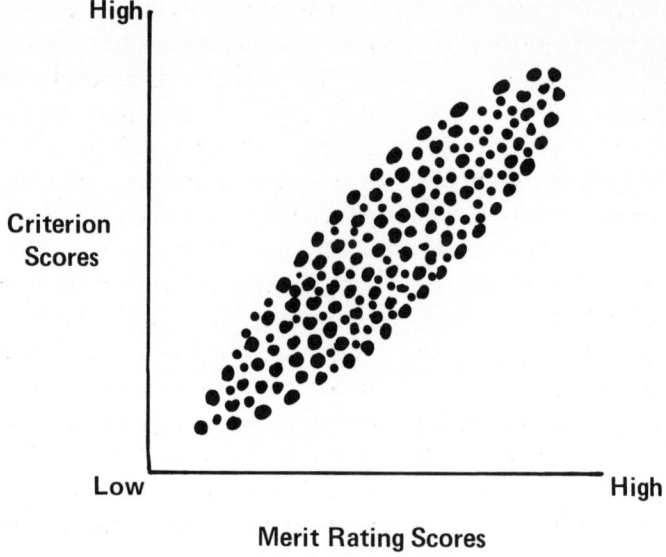

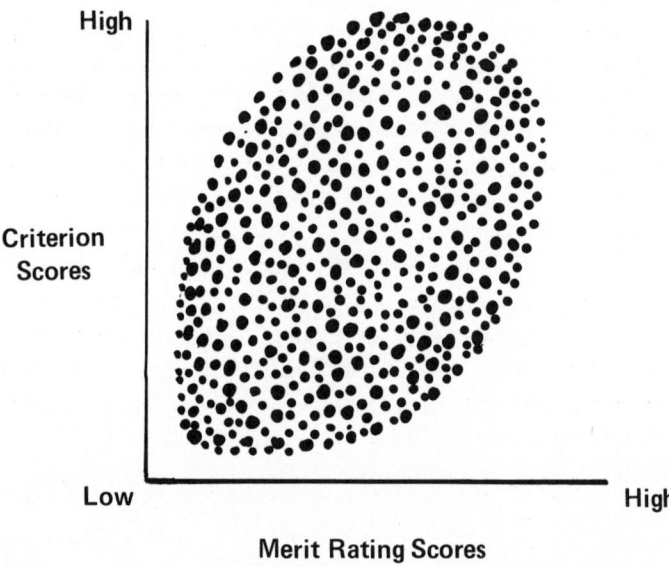

Figure 7-1. Scatterplots indicating relationship between criterion scores and merit rating scores (top) and an invalid relationship (bottom).

Once a satisfactory criterion has been developed, criterion scores for each individual are plotted against merit rating scores as shown in Figure 7-1. If the scale is valid, the points at which the criterion scores and the merit rating scores intersect will take on a cigar-shaped configuration. If not, the pattern will be irregular or even circular in shape.

The process of validation, especially criterion development and specification, requires technical guidance, and outside assistance probably should be secured. We have discussed quantitative methods of performance evaluation at some length, but have not specifically described or prescribed any.

SUMMARY

A sound program of performance evaluation should be focused upon results primarily. Such a program enables the individual officer to grow professionally, and bears upon his motivation and job security. It also provides a sound basis for personnel decisions. Performance evaluation should be carried out by direct supervisors on a continuous basis, and supervisors should adopt a coaching attitude.

In order for performance evaluation to be valid, the evaluator must observe an adequate sample of the subordinate's performance over a period of time, and he must evaluate *observable behavior* rather than inferred traits such as attitude, loyalty, or other factors. The appraisee must be given an opportunity to perform, otherwise, the evaluation will not be valid. Performance evaluation can be biased by the effects of memory, perceptual distortion and social pressure.

Quantitative rating methods are useful to departmental administrators as an aid to personnel decision making, but should never be substituted for close contact between supervisor and subordinate. Administrators should beware of over-dependence upon numerical scores, and should use performance evaluation (or test scores of any kind) in conjunction with other data. Merit rating instruments, like psychological tests, must never be used unless a consistent and systematic relationship can be demonstrated between measures of job performance and the scores yielded by the instrument. Like tests, merit rating scores must be validated.

CHAPTER 8

POLICE REVIEW BOARDS: AN HISTORICAL AND CRITICAL ANALYSIS

Lee P. Brown

POLICE review boards are not bonafide civil service commissions, nor are they boards established within a police department to handle internal investigations. Rather, a police review board is a committee established on a municipal level for the sole purpose of hearing complaints, charges, or grievances from citizens against police officers. The alleged complaints charging misconduct on the part of an officer may involve anything from verbal abuse, racial or religious discrimination, harassment, police brutality, to the violation of one's civil rights.

Such boards have the authority to set up their own rules governing their operational procedure. In this respect, the general rules of evidence exercised in the legitimate courts need not be followed. Evidence such as hearsay, second-hand and prejudicial opinion can be taken into consideration by the board during the course of its investigation.

It is not even necessary that the complaint be brought before the board by the aggrieved individual; rather, any group or organization may induce the board to conduct an investigation.

Police review boards are often referred to as being "kangaroo courts." This descriptive term has been used because such boards deprive the police officer of his basic constitutionally guaranteed rights, e.g. to face his accuser, representation by counsel, and protection against double jeopardy.

The most detrimental aspect of such boards is that they result in the demoralization of the police by exposing them to pressures over and beyond the proper ones available through departmental regulations, the law and the courts.

NOTE: Reprinted from *Police* (July-August, 1966).

In essence, a police review board is a quasi-judicial body established on a municipal level by a city government, having its members appointed by the mayor. Their existence tends to result in the impairment of law enforcement by conducting investigations, hearings, and administering judgments inconsistent with the existing safeguards abundantly present under our due process of law.

HISTORY OF POLICE REVIEW BOARDS

The concept of police review boards is by no means new. To fully understand the development of police review boards, it is necessary for us to go back to the early 1920's. Available information indicates that this movement had its beginning in 1922. It was during that year the American Civil Liberties Union (ACLU), through their affiliate in Maryland, protested the establishment of a state police force in that state. This protest was initiated in the form of a resolution. The ACLU based their opposition on the belief that such a force would be a "menace to civil liberties."

The most organized move to establish police review boards was initiated in the 1930's by the Communist Party. There is evidence to indicate that ever since the International Communist Party was founded, they have held as their goal the destruction of the local police agencies. According to Doctor Bella Dodd, who was a member of the National Committee, Communist Party U.S.A. (she left the Party voluntarily), the Communist Party launched its campaign to institute police review boards in the 1930's. She said that this program was part of a "continuous campaign against police which, to the Communist Party, represent the defenders of the bourgeoisie." (1)

The September 30, 1948 edition of the *New York Times* reported that members of the Civil Rights Congress had made demands for an investigation of police brutality exercised against Negroes and Communists in New York City. This request was rejected. However, the issue was re-opened on April 29, 1949,

---

1. E. John Keller, "Friend or Foe?" *Law and Order*, Vol. 13, No. 10 (October, 1965), p. 85.

when the National Association for the Advancement of Colored People (NAACP) complained to Governor Dewey about the brutality of the New York Police Department. Governor Dewey referred the complaint to the Committee on Unity, which had Franklin D. Roosevelt, Jr. as its chairman. Because of continuous pressure from the NAACP, in August of 1949, Mayor O'Dwyer appointed a three-man Negro committee to make a study of cases involving police brutality. This committee is believed to have been the forerunner of the Civilian Complaint Board which is presently in existence within the New York Police Department. This board is composed of only policemen and underwent a reorganization in May of 1955.

The February 8, 1949 edition of *The People's World,* which was cited by the House Un-American Activities Committee's Annual Report of 1958 as being a "West Coast Communist newspaper," supported the antipolice brutality resolution that had been adopted by the American Unitarian Fellowship for Social Justice. At that time, there were individuals attempting to make amendments to the Los Angeles City Charter which would set up an independent police trial board for the purpose of trying and disciplining police officers charged with brutality and other acts of misconduct.

During the first half of the 1950's the police review board concept was dormant. Then, in 1957, there was a move by the ACLU for the establishment of a police review board in Philadelphia, Pennsylvania. Their bid was rejectd by the Philadelphia City Council. To the surprise of the police department and many other citizens of Philadelphia, Mayor Richardson Dilworth, under the powers given to him by the Home Rule Charter, on October 1, 1958 appointed a five-man police review board affiliated with his office. This board was composed of: Doctor Thorsten Sellin, Chairman, Head of the Department of Sociology at the University of Pennsylvania; Clarence Pickett, Vice-Chairman, Executive Secretary Emeritus, American Friends Service Committee and holder of the Nobel Peace Prize; William T. Colemen, Jr., Esquire, Secretary, attorney; Rt. Rev. Monsignor Edward M. Reilly, Superintendent of Catholic Schools of the Archdiocese of Philadelphia; and

William Ross, labor leader.

It is interesting to note that Clarence Pickett (now deceased), one time Chairman of the Board, was for a long time closely associated with Communist organizations. (2) Mr. Pickett was at one time a national officer of the Communist front which had as its goal the abolishment of the House Un-American Activities Committee. (3) He spent considerable time traveling around the nation giving speeches as to why review boards should be established.

The most interesting point concerning the establishment of the police review board in Philadelphia is that Mayor Dilworth created it after the city council had voted down the ordinance which had been proposed to create it.

After being in operation only a short period of time, the Fraternal Order of Police (FOP), Philadelphia Lodge No. 5, received numerous complaints from its members about the way they were treated by the board. As a result, the FOP filed a suit and was given a temporary injunction preventing the board from conducting further hearings. The suit charged that the board was unconstitutional and violated the civil rights of policemen. It pointed out that there were cases where the courts of law had exonerated an officer, the police department cleared him of misconduct, and yet the police review board would hear the case for the third time and find the officer guilty.

This injunction was rendered by the Common Pleas Court against the City of Philadelphia in December of 1959. The City appealed the decision to the Supreme Court. While briefs were being prepared, the Fraternal Order of Police and the members of the board got together and reached an agreement. They made a compromise and the FOP withdrew its Complaint in Equity and the City of Philadelphia withdrew its appeal.

It was stated by Phladelphia Lodge No. 5 that the changes that had been initiated rendered the board "practically useless." However, it was stated by Martin Barol, Executive Secretary of the board, that "with the exception of a few minor points, i.e., changing the name from Police Review Board to Police Advisory Board, nothing was done in any way to interfere or curtail

---

2. *Ibid.*, p. 86.
3. *Ibid.*

activities of the Board."

In 1959, York, Pennsylvania created a police review board. This board existed, to the dismay of the city, for three years. During this three-year period, the York crime rate rose to its highest peak. There was an ultimate low in the morale of the police officers to make arrests because they feared reprisals from citizen groups. In 1962, Mayor John L. Snyder disbanded the board and announced that he would handle all charges of police misconduct himself. In 1963, the morale of the York policemen went up and the crime rate went down.

In 1960, Mayor P. K. Peterson appointed a police review board for the city of Minneapolis. At the first meeting of the board, Josiah Brill, Board Chairman, raised the question as to whether or not the members of the board would be liable for charges of slander or libel if their findings were made public, as necessarily would be the case. Mayor Peterson called upon a prominent law firm in that city to give an opinion on the problem. That opinion read as follows:

> I can find no statutory or charter authority for such a body as yours and therefore I am of the opinion that as now constituted each and every member of your committee would be assuming very considerable hazards in conducting any hearing at which any person other than one witness and yourselves might be present, and that each of you would run very definite hazards should you report orally or in writing to the mayor or verbatim statements or summaries of statements derogatory to the reputation of any member of the police force.

This opinion indicated that it would probably require an act of legislature to give such a board authority to conduct their investigations and that even then the protection against libel and slander would not be complete.

On the basis of this opinion, the board was shortly disbanded, with the approval of the mayor, before it carried on any activities.

In March of 1960, the Los Angeles Branch of the ACLU attempted to get an ordinance passed in that city which would by statute create a police practice review board, consisting of five members appointed by the mayor. This board would have the power to:

Receive, investigate, hear, and determine complaints by any person or organization of alleged misconduct to private citizens by personnel of the Los Angeles Police Department. The term 'misconduct' shall include, but not be limited to, mistreatment, abusive language, false arrest, unreasonable or unwarranted interference with private property or business, unreasonable or unwarranted use of force, unreasonable search and seizure, unreasonable or unwarranted interference with lawful associations and assemblies, and denial of civil rights or discrimination because of race, religion, or national origin.

The proposed ordinance would have granted the board unlimited power in that the board would be allowed to "adopt and promulgate such rules and regulations and utilize such procedures, methods and techniques as the Board finds necessary or desirable to accomplish its function."

In addition, the proposed ordinance would have placed a bounty on Los Angeles police officers by offering monetary consideration to a person lodging a complaint and the officer found guilty of misconduct. This was covered in the proposed ordinance which read as follows:

In the event of finding of misconduct by an employee of the Los Angeles Police Department, the Board may award the person injured by such misconduct compensation therefor not to exceed the sum of Five Hundred Dollars ($500.00), provided, however, that no such sum shall be paid or disbursed unless such claimant shall execute and file with the City Controller, within thirty (30) days following the date of such award, a written covenant not to sue the City of Los Angeles, the Los Angeles Police Department, or any employees thereof, for or on account of any acts giving rise to said claim.

At the same time, the proposed ordinance offered immunity to anyone lodging false complaints against the police. The ordinance stated:

No complaining party or witness therefor shall be prosecuted or punished for or on account of the filing of a claim with the Board, nor shall any complaining party or witness therefor be prosecuted or punished under the provisions of Section 52.50 of the Los Angeles Municipal Code, for or on account of the filing of a claim with the Board.

The Los Angeles Fire and Police Protective League, prominent Los Angeles citizens, and Police Chief William H. Parker launched an all-out attack against the proposal. Result: The Los Angeles City Council unanimously defeated the proposed ordinance.

Also in 1960, the ACLU attempted to create a police review board in Detroit, Michigan. They justified their demands by saying that a police review board would:

> . . . give the public a fairer means of appraising allegations of wrongful police conduct, promote greater citizen-police cooperation, promote greater respect for law and law enforcement, help reduce group and racial tension, protection of constitutional rights, secure a degree of assistance for citizens that makes police work less difficult and more effective.

The ACLU gained support in their bid from the NAACP who joined them in their demands for a police review board.

Opposition to the creation of such a board in the city of Detroit was voiced by three Detroit newspapers — the *Times,* the *Free Press,* and the *News.* In addition, the Detroit Police Officers Association and many influential Detroit citizens opposed the board. As a result, the police review board concept was defeated in Detroit.

During the year 1960, the ACLU also proposed the creation of a police review board in Cincinnati, Ohio. A pamphlet was distributed throughout that city entitled *The Case For a Public Review Board in Cincinnati.* This pamphlet said in part:

> When police authority is abused, to whom can a citizen complain — the police? Do we ask the police department to impartially investigate its own conduct? To ask the question is to answer it. An investigation of the police by the police is not an investigation. The citizenry must have an impartial body to whom it may turn when it has grievance against the police.

The ACLU contacted the Civil Rights Committee of the Cincinnati Bar Association soliciting support for the creation of a police review board. Resulting from this, a motion was put before this committee in an effort to obtain its support for the police review board move. This did not materialize, because shortly afterwards Colonel Stanley R. Schrotel, Cincinnati Chief of

Police received a letter from a ranking officer of the Cincinnati Bar Association which read as follows:

> I am pleased to advise you that at a special meeting of the Executive Committee of the Bar Association yesterday, held at my request, we voted unanimously to abolish the Bill of Rights Committee.

This did not stop the ACLU. They had Martin Barol, Executive Secretary of the Philadelphia Review Board, come to Cincinnati and speak in favor of the board.

In spite of this move, the review board proposal was defeated by the Cincinnati City Council, led by its five Republican members. Opposition was also supplied by local citizens, radio and television stations, the FOP associates, the American Legion, and the Hamilton County Police Association.

There was also an unsuccessful attempt to establish a police review board in San Francisco, California in 1960. It was publicly stated by the director of the Northern California Branch of the ACLU that they had been attempting to create such a board in that city for the past year.

In August of 1961, there was a move to establish a police review board in Providence, Rhode Island. This board was proposed by the NAACP to hear charges of brutality stemming from police suppression of a riot in the South Providence area. The mayor referred the matter to the Police Commission and, after hearing their report, refused to create a review board. He stated, "Existing and completely adequate and readily available means of redress have not been exhausted."

The next major city to establish a police review board was Rochester, New York. It was in March of 1963, resulting from a growing unrest among the Negro population who were charging police brutality, that Rochester created its review board. This board consists of nine members. These members are all appointed by the city manager and include representation of the Catholic, Jewish, and Protestant faiths, a professor from the University of Rochester, two business men, a union leader, an accountant, and a doctor.

According to an article that appeared in the July 31, 1964 edition of the *New York Times,* the Rochester board does its work in executive session and its power is limited to hearing complaints charging excessive physical force. The *Times* article said that the board is not considered to be an "all-purpose" solution for racial tensions.

The campaign for the establishment of the Rochester review board was spearheaded by the NAACP, with support from the ACLU. This issue became a political football, with incumbent Democrats in favor of it and the Republicans unanimously opposed to it. There was a threat from the AFL-CIO Council of Rochester to oppose the re-election of all the Democratic city council members unless they established a police review board. This undoubtedly influenced the Democrats in their support of the movement.

Not all the labor unions supported the police review board movement. The Communication Workers of America and the United Steel Workers were among those who opposed the board.

Neither were all Democrats in favor of the board. Mr. Goodman A. Sarachan, Chairman of the New York State Investigations Commission and a leading Democratic figure in the state, gave a denunciation of this plot to undermine the efficiency of the local police department by creating an unnecessary police review board.

Additionally, there were a great number of Rochester citizens opposed to this police review board movement. This was evident by the fact that 40,000 such citizens had signed a petition which was circulated by the police opposing the board.

On March 19th, a public hearing was held to discuss the creation of the police review board. Support for the establishment of the board was given by the Inter-Faith Clergy group, the AFL-CIO, various Negro groups, and the two local newspapers.

On March 26th, with the six Democrats supporting the board and the three Republicans opposing it, an ordinance was adopted by the City Council establishing a police review board in the city of Rochester.

On this subject, Chief W. M. Lombard, Rochester's Chief of Police had the following to say:

> This is different than the Philadelphia Board, which also reviews cases of police harassment, abuse of police authority,

searches and seizures, etc. Again I add that this community has a Human Relations Commission that does receive complaints from citizens involving police officers for other than use of force only.

. . . Council members were very much influenced by the Executive Director of the Philadelphia Board, who was invited to Rochester and did meet with them. Statements from him, such as the crime rate in the City of Philadelphia being reduced since the initiation of their board, had a definite effect in the thinking of many people. At the public hearing, figures were presented to refute such statements, but did not seem to penetrate.

According to the Rochester *Democrat and Chronicle* of December 31, 1965, the Rochester Police Review Board was stripped of virtually all its powers the previous day by a decision of the State Supreme Court. Justice Jacob Ark, in a ten-page decision, ruled that the board's authority to investigate and make recommendations on complaints of police brutality was illegal. He said that the board's only right was to listen to such complaints and pass them on, without comment, to the Chief of Police.

This decision was the result of a suit filed in April by the Police Locust Club and several of the officers being investigated by the board. The Locust Club received support from the Citizen's for the Abolition of the Police Advisory Board, a private group. The city asked for a ruling on this suit which challenged the legality of the board. The Genesee Valley Chapter of the American Civil Liberties Union supported the board.

Originally, an order restraining all board operations was issued. That order was later modified to limit the ban on board action to three of the seven policemen who were plaintiffs in the suit.

In the court decision, Justice Ark wrote that:

> The responsibility of making the preliminary investigation (should) be given to the commissioner (of Public Safety) who is experienced in police matters.
>
> He is in a better position to make a judgment as to what force was necessary under a given set of circumstances and whether the police officer was faced with a situation that gave no time for

calm reflection but acted reasonably under the exigency that confronted him.

The board overlooks the fact that although its membership consists of nine highly respected members of the community, when it makes a public statement it does not speak for them as individuals, but with the authority of an official body of the City of Rochester.

Its public criticism of a police officer bears the imprimatur of the City of Rochester . . . The board, in that respect, seeks to do that which can be done only by the commissioner, after a hearing and a finding of guilt against a police officer.

Justice Ark went on to say that the functions of the board had become "intertwined" with the operation of the police bureau in a way that violates "the rights of a police officer against whom a complaint was filed." He added that his duty was not to "pass upon the philosophy of a police advisory board . . ., but only upon its legality."

Rosario J. Guglieimina, the agency's executive director and legal counsel, commented on the board by saying, "If this decision is permitted to stand, it means the death of the board. Who would want to be associated with an agency that can serve no useful purpose? Not me certainly!"

An Associated Press dispatch from Philadelphia, dated July 28, 1964, noted that five members of the New York City Council were studying the operation of the Philadelphia Police Advisory Board searching for ways to ease relations between police and private citizens in New York City. It is interesting to note that the New York policemen made a public display of their opposition to the establishment of a police review board in that city by staging a protest march, participated in by thousands of the members of the New York Police force. As of this writing, a police review board has not been established in New York City.

However, on February 16, 1966, newly elected Mayor John V. Lindsay announced that he was replacing New York City Police Commissioner Vincent L. Broderick. Broderick, who would not accept the idea of establishing a police review board in that city, was replaced by Howard R. Leary, who at the time was police commissioner in Philadelphia.

Leary said that he would prefer not to have a civilian review board, but he would "absolutely" cooperate within one.

It appears as if Mayor Lindsay was determined to create the board, despite the protests from the New York policemen.

There have been major pushes for the creation of police review boards in Pittsburg, Pennsylvania; Balitmore, Maryland; Washington, D. C.; San Diego, Oakland, and San Jose, California, and other cities.

In California, the proponents of the police review board concept received minor support from the California Democratic Council, who in 1960, went on record in a policy platform urging all cities and counties throughout the state to establish police review boards.

In October of 1964, Peter J. Pitchess, Sheriff of Los Angeles County and President of the Peace Officers' Association of the State of California, requested that a survey be conducted to determine the attitude of candidates for state office toward the establishment of police review boards. District Attorney J. F. Coakley, Alameda County and Chairman of the Association's Law-Legislative Committee, addressed a questionnaire to all candidates. Of those responding to the questionnaire, ninety-four expressed opposition to police review boards. Only five expressed support for such boards and thirteen abstained from expressing an opinion. No legislation proposing establishment of police review boards was introduced at the 1965 session of the California legislature.

As of this writing, Philadelphia, Pennsylvania and Rochester, New York are the only two major cities in the United States in which police review boards exist, and pending further court action, Rochester's board is now defunct.

WHAT GROUPS ADVOCATE POLICE REVIEW BOARDS?

Ohio Congressman Gordon H. Scherer, a member of the House Un-American Activities Committee, was asked to comment on the police review board movement in Cincinnati. He stated that "in a Police review board like this, it is always helpful and sometimes quite significant if one considers the persons and organizations who are agitating for such an innovation."

The September 26, 1960 edition of *U.S. News and World Report* carried an article in which Stanley R. Schrotel, Chief of Police of Cincinnati, Ohio, was interviewed. Parts of this interview went as follows:

Q. Who are the pressure groups?
A. From my point of view, they are organizations such as the national Association for the Advancement of Colored People and the American Civil Liberties Union.
Q. What are they doing?
A. Right now, for instance, the Civil Liberties Union is militantly urging the formation of "Police Review Boards" in urban centers throughout the country. These would be boards of private citizens formed for the exclusive purpose of passing upon complaints made against police officers. This, in my opinion, is a poor idea.
Q. What's wrong with it?
A. I thing that this idea plagues the policeman who is trying to do his job. If he knows his actions will be second-guessed by someone not acquainted with the problems that attend police work, and if he knows that his job may depend on this outside judgement, one of two things will occur; he will either leave the police force because he knows it is no longer a career service, or he will become a neutral. He will not take aggressive action.

Throughout the national campaign for the establishment of police review boards, one group always seem to be an active and vocal supporter — The American Civil Liberties Union. The ACLU claims to have in excess of forty thousand members, with chapters in the major cities in the United States.

The development of the ACLU in the United States has a very interesting background. It goes back to 1915, after the start of World War I, when the American Union Against Militarism was formed to prevent United States involvement in the war. Lillian D. Wald was the chairman and Crystal Eastman and Charles T. Hallinan were his executives. In 1917, Roger N. Baldwin joined the staff and a Civil Liberties Bureau was created to handle the many Bill of Rights violations brought before the American Union Against Militarism.

Shortly afterwards, the Civil Liberties Bureau became an

independent body under the name of the National Civil Liberties Bureau and had the following board members: L. Hollingsworth Wood, Chairman; Norman Thomas, Vice-Chairman; Helen Phelps Tokes, Treasurer; Walter Nelles, Counsel; Crystal Eastman, John Lovejoy Elliott, John Haynes Holmes, Agres Leach, Owen Lovejoy, Rabbi Judah L. Magnes, and John Nevin Sayre. This organization handled many cases involving freedom of speech, press, association, and particularly cases involving conscientious objectors.

In September of 1918, the Justice Department, under the belief that the National Civil Liberties Bureau was encouraging resistance to the draft, raided its offices and seized their files. The files were examined and then returned after no evidence for prosecution was found.

In January of 1920, the National Civil Liberties Bureau was reorganized under the name of the American Civil Liberties Union, with Albert DeSilver, a New York attorney, as its director. The ACLU devoted its first year of operation to defending the members of the Industrial Workers of the World, which was considered a controversial organization.

Since that time, the ACLU has been closely associated with numerous controversial organizations and, in the last two decades, has provoked a continuous attack against law enforcement.

At the National Congress level, there is a House Report 22900, 71st Congress, 3rd Session, January 17, 1931, pursuant to H. Res. 220, which states:

> The American Civil Liberties Union is clearly affiliated with the Communist movement in the United States, and fully 90 percent of its efforts are on behalf of Communists who come into difficulty with the law. It claims to stand for free speech, free press and free assembly, but it is quite apparent that the main function of the ACLU is to attempt to protect the Communists in their adovocacy of force and violence to overthrow the Government, replacing the American flag by a Red flag . . .

The California Senate Fact Finding Committee on Un-American Activities in its 1943 report said:

> The American Civil Liberties Union may be definitely classed as a Communist front of 'Transmission Belt' organization. At least 90 percent of its efforts are expended on behalf of Communists who come into conflict with the law . . .

The Commonwealth of Massachusetts, in a special commission to investigate Communist activities stated:

> The ACLU, with its front of respectability and with its large membership of sincere, worthy citizens, has provided important legal talent and a camouflage of decency behind which Communist forces have agitated and promoted their campaigns.

A speech given by Sergeant William H. Petersen, which appeared in the Policemen's Benevolent and Protective Association of Illinois magazine in 1961, gave a stern warning against the ACLU when he said that the ACLU was "waging an all-out war against law-enforcement agencies in America." Sergeant Petersen said:

> Among the Communist fronts that honeycomb the U.S. today, the American Civil Liberties Union is the most active in plaguing the nation with oblique attacks on American institutions and constitutional safeguards.
>
> Paradoxically, the ACLU operates under a pretext of protecting those very constitutional rights. But whose rights? Oddly, and it is enough to arrest the suspicion of every policeman as to the policy of the ACLU, it runs to the aid of suspected criminals and is rarely concerned about the rights of the law-abiding citizens.
>
> Behind the facade of a misleading title, this organization is waging an all-out war against law enforcement agencies in America. It is seeking to establish so-called Police Review Boards in every city. Existence of such boards provide the means for harassing and intimidating police officers who are overworked in their efforts to protect lives, liberty, and property against the deadly assaults of crime, both organized and otherwise.

The ACLU is indeed a very controversial organization. It has often been alleged that many of its members are or were Communists. On the other hand, the organization has listed as members some very respectable American citizens, e.g. Francis Biddle, Attorney General of the United States, 1941-1945; Msgr.

John A Ryan, Catholic University, Washington D.C., Robert M. Hutchins, Director of the Center for the Study of Democratic Institutions, Santa Barbara, California; Arthur Schlesinger, Felix Frankfurter, Frances Perkins, and others.

> The Fact-Finding Committee on Un-American Activities of the State Senate has corrected an old injustice, and enhanced its own reputation, by setting its records straight about the loyalty of the American Civil Liberties Union . . . it was said in complete honesty that the committee declares itself 'convinced that (the ACLU) is not a Communist-dominated organization of a subversive front in any sense.' This is a complete reversal of position . . .

On August 18, 1960, President Eisenhower sent a letter to the ACLU which read as follows:

> In this fortieth anniversary year of the American Civil Liberties Union, it is a special pleasure to send greetings to those attending your biennial conference . . . There is work to be done, and while I remain in office — and for as long as God gives me to live — I will continue to combat every threat to our sacred principles of freedom, liberty, and equal justice under law. It is good to be reminded that the members of the American Civil Liberties Union and the overwhelming majority of my fellow citizens are working together in this field with steadfast vigor and understanding.

The controversy surrounding the ACLU still exists, and so does the ACLU. Yet, the fact cannot be denied that many members of this organization have been pointed out as being affiliated with the Communist movement. For example, Roger Baldwin, founder and leader of the ACLU for over thirty years, was cited in the Congressional Record of May 26, 1952, as being affiliated with Communist-front organizations. Doctor Harry Ward, once chairman of the ACLU, was also one-time chairman of The American League for Peace and Democracy. On June 1, 1948, that organization was placed on the Attorney General of the United States list of subversive organizations. Doctor Ward is also the author of two books — *Soviet Democracy* and *Soviet Spirit*. A. L. Wirin, who according to the *Los Angeles Daily Journal*, January 13, 1954, was a candidate for the executive board of the National Lawyer's Guild, which was cited by the House Committee on Un-

American Activities on September 21, 1950, as being a Communist front organization.

Additionally, the ACLU has received grants from the Garland Foundation. The Garland Foundation was cited by the United States House Special Committee on Un-American Activities as follows: "The Garland Fund was a major source for the financing of Communist Party Enterprises . . ." (H., Rept. 1311, March 9, 1944).

Although the ACLU has never been placed on the United States Attorney General's list of subversive organizations, it is very easy for one to take a position regarding this group and support it with valid references. However, to be completely objective, one must form his conclusion about this organization after viewing all of the facts. Otherwise, a valid appraisal of the ACLU cannot be obtained. Whether or not the ACLU is a Communist front organization remains a matter of conjecture — some say it is, and others say it is not.

On the other hand, there is no controversy over the Communist Party's relationship to law enforcement. They see law enforcement as an enemy of the Communist movement in America.

The Communist Party, USA was first started in 1919. Since its inception, it has waged a continuous war against law enforcement. They have picked law enforcement as their target on the basis of logical reasoning. The Communists are striving to overthrow the United States Government by force and violence. They know that the concept of law and order is in direct opposition to the concept of force and violence. In America, the law enforcement agencies are the ones charged with the responsibility of maintaining law and order. Therefore, the Communists reached the conclusion that the policemen and law enforcement agencies must be discredited so that the citizens will eventually lose respect for law and order. This plot was outlined by Fulton Lewis III, of Washington, D. C., a former research analyst of the House Committee on Un-American Activities and an expert on Communism, in a speech he delivered at the annual convention of the Policeman's Benevolent and Protective Association of Illinois, in Peoria, on October 17, 1961.

Mr. Lewis included in his speech a statement made by M. J. Olgin. Mr. Olgin was at one time a member of the Communist Party, USA. He made the following statement in a pamphlet published by the Communist Party in 1935, entitled, *Why Communist?* Mr. Olgin said:

> The Communist Party is active directly as an organization and indirectly through its members within other organizations. The Communist Party leads political as well as economic struggles, and the right against governmental terror. These fights are conducted through literature, through mass meetings, through demonstrations and when occasion demands, through open mass combat with the police in the streets.

To illustrate what implications the Communist movement has for law enforcement, it is only necessary to go back a few years for a clarification. On June 13, 1961, there was testimony given before the Senate Internal Security Subcommittee that showed the Communists are engineering a well-planned program aimed at the destruction of police action. At this hearing, Lyman B. Kirkpatrick, Inspector General of the Central Intelligence Agency, produced the official Communist training manual which is used by the Red action units. This manual contains diagrams which illustrate how a few agitators can induce a crowd to surround the police, pinning them in human pockets and immobilizing them. Other Communist manuals tell how to weaken a police department by spying on the individual officers. This plan calls for the agitators to "first, make investigations and report on the activities of the police and security services. Secondly, investigate and repress those security organizations which support goverment. Third, find ways to infiltrate into police and security organizations to steal documents (particularly those reporting their knowledge of Communism) and destroy everything of value."

Herbert Romerstein, a former member of the Communist Party, USA, gave a clear picture as to what would happen should this country accept the police review board idea:

> You'll be facing fire from two sides. One is a question of establishment of the Police Review Board which can become a

permanent instrument of attacking the police: that is, as each case comes up the leftists and their friends can make complaints before the Police Review Board and keep the police department tied up in constant agitation and litigation . . . The fire on the other front is the picking out of individual cases and attacking them and embarrassing the police department in regard to these. It is necessary to organize a counter campaign.

Mr. Kirkpatrick, in his testimony before the Senate's Subcommittee, also stated:

Our police are among the foremost guardians of freedom and thus a major target of the Communist. The better the force, the greater its efficiency, the higher its competence in preserving peace, the more vital it is for the Communist to destroy it. They strive to degrade the police in the eyes of the people, and engage in smear campaigns to discredit the leaders among the rank and file policemen. Police brutality has become a commonplace expression, and accusations against arresting officers are growing most frequent. Furthermore, the courts have not distinguished themselves by sustaining the police in the legitimate exercise of their duties, but too often find reasons to justify the culprit under the fallacious guise of 'rights and legal technicalities'!

The Communist handbook which was seized by the CIA had the following to say in respect to the police:

. . . police are the enemies of Communism, if we are to succeed we must do anything to weaken their work, to incapacitate them or to make them a subject of ridicule.

It is clear, without a doubt, that the Communist Party is waging an all-out war to discredit the police. One of the weapons used in this war is the police review board. For that reason, when the cry for the establishment of a police review board arises, it would be well to check and see who is making the bid. It may not be readily obvious that there are Communist overtones, but more times than not they are present. This is evidenced by a work entitled *Advice to the Lenin School of Political Warfare,* by George Dimitrov and quoted in the report of the American Bar Association Committee on Communist Tactics, Strategy and Objectives — Congressional Record, August 22, 1958, page 17719:

As Soviet power grows, there will be greater aversion

to Communist Parties everywhere. So we must practice the techniques of withdrawal. Never appear in the foreground; let our friends do the work. We must remember that one sympathizer is generally worth more than a dozen militant Communists. A university professor, who, without being a party member, lends himself to the interests of the Soviet Union, is worth more than a hundred men with party cards. A writer or reputation or a retired general are worth more than 500 poor devils who don't know better than to get themselves beaten up by the police. Every man has his value, his merit.

It is not the intention of this paper to go into detail about the Communist Party beyond the scope to which it applies to police review boards; however, if there is an additional interest in such, the writer recommends:

1) *Masters of Deceit,* by J. Edgar Hoover.
2) *The Witness,* by Whitaker Chambers.
3) *The Naked Communist,* by Skousen.
4) *The Techniques of Communism,* by Budenz.
5) *Problem of Communist* and other publications issued by the House Committee on Un-American Activities and available through the U.S. printing office in Washington, D.C.

Law enforcement people do not have any quarrels with the various civil rights groups, e.g. the National Association for the Advancement of Colored People, the Congress of Racial Equality, the Southern Regional Council and others. However, in any discussion of police review boards, these organizations can not be overlooked, for they are very active in their demands for the establishment of such boards. It is, however, important to point out at the onset that it certainly is not the intention of this writer to categorize the civil rights groups with the previously discussed advocates of police review boards.

The minority groups' demands for the creation of police review boards stem from their charges of excessive police brutality against minority group members. It is their contention that the establishment of police review boards would be one way of obtaining equal treatment from the enforcers of the law.

The Negro people are very sincere in their claim that there is unequal administration of justice and that the police are guilty of brutality against the Negro.

There is a great number of Negroes who dislike and distrust the police. They see the police as representing the authority of the white power structure. They do not feel a part of the community and, consequently, they view the action of the police as being discriminatory.

This aspect of the problem was outlined by Joseph Lohman, Dean of the School of Criminology of the University of California, in his appearance before the California Advisory Committee to the United States Commission on Civil Rights in August of 1963, when he said,

> The police today in the North and West often find themselves caught between pressures from the Negro and white communities. Negroes are fighting for a change. Whites often are resisting and call on police to aid them in their effort.

Professor Lohman stressed that the police are a symbol of white authority and the legacy of suspicion and distrust brought to the North by Southern Negroes.

For those reasons, the NAACP and other civil rights groups advocate the establishment of police review boards. Their intent is honest, and as stated earlier, the police are not opposed to what the civil rights groups stand for. People in law enforcement are aware that the NAACP has done a commendable job in the area of civil rights. However, the police do take issue with their shotgun charges of police brutality and their demands for the establishment of police review boards.

POLICE BRUTALITY

The major reason voiced for the creation of police review boards is the repeated complaint of police brutality. One would indeed be naive to postulate the idea that police brutality is nonexistent — it has existed in the past and it does exist today. However, a distinction should be made between police brutality and brutality of the police.

When we speak of police brutality, we are making a very broad generalization and the term then becomes a generic term, void of real meaning. This term is used by the minority groups to mean more than physical violence on the part of the police. It is used to mean both physical violence and police harassment. Police harassment usually in the form of being stopped and interrogated by the police. The minority group member feels that the reason he is being stopped and questioned is because he is a member of a minority group and thus, being accorded an inferior status by the police. They feel that the police, representing the authority of the white man, are placing them in this inferior position just because they happen to be Negro. They feel that the police are enforcing the discriminatory practices of the white power structure. These feelings are also given the title of police brutality.

Brutality of the police, on the other hand, eliminates the generalization that law enforcement is universal in nature and kind, and refers to a specific policeman or group of policemen. This term is more useful than the former in that it permits one to be specific in his charge of misconduct on the part of the police and therefore adds meaning to the subject. One can no more say that all police are alike, there is police brutality; therefore all policemen are brutal, than we can say that brutality does not exist at all.

J. Edgar Hoover, in the September 27, 1965 edition of *U.S. News and World Report,* had the following to say about police brutality:

> Our investigations indicate that a large number of police brutality allegations have no basis in fact. Police brutality and police misuse of authority are rapidly becoming issues of the past. Responsible law enforcement officials are dealing with these transgressions quickly and emphatically.
>
> The great specter of police brutality is being exploited by some selfish-minded, irresponsible men who apparently are concerned only with what they can gain today and who are totally oblivious to the great disservice they are doing their country.

The allegation of police brutality does, however, serve a function. This function is related to the demands for the establishment of police review boards. The logic is — if the police are brutal and nothing is done about it, then there is good reason to establish police review boards to correct this misconduct on the part of the police. Subsequently, the cry of police brutality is alleged indiscriminately, based on the philosophy that if a lie is told often enough, it will be believed.

As stated earlier, brutality on the part of the police has existed in the past and it does exist today — this we cannot deny. However, it certainly is not as prevalent today as in the past. The police themselves are concerned with the few policemen who engage in misconduct of any sort. Those men are being weeded out of police work — for there is no place for them in the profession of law enforcement. It is important that we judge each police department on its own merit. Law enforcement should not be categorized as being literally universal. To be completely objective, we must not be oblivious of the fact that law enforcement is continuously attempting to improve itself.

> We have seen the caliber of man entering the field of law enforcement undergo a drastic change. Because of improved working conditions and improved pay, law enforcement is now attracting many men with a college background. . . . We find that the days when a policeman was hired because he fitted the 'tough cop' stereotype by being big and aggressive have disappeared. Today's policemen are hired because of their physical and mental capabilities, with greater emphasis being placed on the latter. (4)

If an officer is guilty of police brutality, he should be punished. Otherwise, methods should be developed to prosecute those who allege police brutality merely for the purpose of discrediting the police or to cover up their own activities. It must be remembered that policemen are also entitled to protection under the law.

SHOULD THERE BE POLICE REVIEW BOARDS?

A complete and objective evaluation of the police review board concept leads this writer to be totally convinced that such boards are an unnecessary hindrance to effective law enforcement.

Consideration of one factor alone — morale of the policemen

---

4. Lee P. Brown, "An Unforeseen Problem Resulting from College-Educated Policemen," *Police,* Vol. 10, No. 3 (January-February, 1966), p. 73.

— is sufficient to reach this conclusion. The fact that virtually 100 percent of the nation's policemen are opposed to the establishment of police review boards is ample evidence that the creation of such boards would contribute a damaging blow to the morale of the policemen.

One might ask the question, what is the importance of police morale? Webster defines morale as "moral or mental condition with respect to . . . enthusiasm." By defining the term, it gives us a clearer understanding as to what we are talking about.

Obviously, a police department is composed of human individuals, and these individuals deal in "people work," meaning that they work with people rather than inanimate objects. Leading men in the field of police administration have often stated that a policeman spends about 90 percent of his time dealing with people. Therefore, it is easy to see that the values and attitudes of these individual policemen play an important role in determining the quality of service rendered to the community. (By values, we mean that which has meaning for a member of a group, and by attitudes we refer to that which determines activity).

A high degree of morale, e.g. desirable working conditions, adequate pay, community backing and confidence, etc., is conducive to molding the policemen's values. These values in turn will determine the policemen's attitudes. These attitudes will dermine the manner in which the officer performs his duty.

So we see that morale plays a very important role in establishing the caliber of law enforcement service rendered by a police department.

Experience has shown that in the cities where police review boards have been established, the morale of the officers has correspondingly dropped to an all-time low. This has had a direct effect upon the crime rate in those cities. For that reason, police review boards do more harm than good to a community.

Additionally, it is quite conceivable that police review boards would tend to generate the very things which they are established to eliminate. One manifest function of a police review board is to "shape up" the police department and thereby accord all citizens of the community equal protection under the law. Another manifest function is to eliminate police brutality and to have the police accord all citizens equal respect, regardless of their racial or religious background. This will, in the minds of the police review board advocates, create a more favorable climate between the police and the minority group members. Supposedly, this will be accomplished by creating a board to receive, investigate, and punish cases of misconduct on the part of police officers.

These verbalized manifest functions attributed to police review boards are indeed very noble ideas; however, as stated earlier, such a board would tend to generate the very things which it is established to eliminate. As an example, the latent function of such a board would make it impossible to improve the community's law enforcement service.

One latent function of a police review board would be that many of the men presently engaged in police work would leave the profession to engage in less sensitive work. Additionally, the existence of a police review board would create a very serious recruitment problem for the police departments.

Thomas J. Gibbons, former Police Commissioner of Philadelphia, in an article in the *Saturday Evening Post*, July 9, 1960, entitled "Watch Out For The Bullies With The Badge", had the following to say in respect to recruitment:

> In 1953, we had examinations for police recruits, we beat the bushes in local colleges, pestered veteran's organizations and citizens' groups to send us good men. We attracted about two thousand applicants to draw from; we hired almost a thousand. I would say this was one of the greatest crops of recruits in our department's history. But, in 1960 things have changed, the simple truth is that hardly anybody wants to be a policeman in my city. Instead of giving one exam for four or five thousand men each year, we give the test a couple times a week for just a handful of men.

This is the city which initiated the first police review board!

Philadelphia police officers were interviewed concerning their opinions of the police review board in that city. A commissioned officer said, "It stinks." A patrolman on the beat said, "If I made an arrest in the minority groups, I know I'd be hauled before the board to explain why and it doesn't matter what the circumstances of the arrest were." A veteran officer said, "I've got seventeen years on and can retire in twenty. I'm going to coast the rest of the way." A detective said, "I'll only make an arrest in that section of town if there's no way out of it."

So we see that the latent functions of a police review board are such that they make the manifest functions unachievable. Instead of improving the police service, it destroys it. The policemen will refuse to do their job because of the fear of repercussions from the board. Qualified men will refuse to enter the police service because they want no part of such an unstable occupation. Trained policemen already working the the service will start looking for jobs because they know that police work will no longer be a career profession and they prefer not to work under such pressures.

Would these conditions improve the police service? They certainly would not. What we see is the police review board creating exactly what it is established to correct.

Another reason for opposing the creation of police review boards, centers around who is going to control the police department. As stated by Inspector Edward M. Davis of the Los Angeles Police Department in an address before the Peace Officers' Association of the State of California,

> The right to discipline carries with it the power to control the conduct, actions, and attitudes of the employees of an organization. When the right to discipline is vested with management, management has the essential tools with which to attain the desired behavior from employees. If, however, the ability to discipline employees is taken away from management, or if management must share this responsibility with some outside person or organization, management is then stripped of the most essential powers in the operation of any organization. When employees are subjected to disciplinary actions from outside the organization, a fundamental rule of organization has been breached and the employee becomes confused, diffident, and inefficient.

If a police review board is established, the possibility of people wishing to serve selfish motives by obtaining appointment to the board is very great. This would be one step toward taking the control of the police department out of the hands of the police chief and other elected city officials and placing it into the hands of an outside agency which knows nothing about running a police department. This brings politics into police work, and every informed person knows that there is no place for politics in law enforcement.

The proponents of police review boards continually bring up the subject of individual rights. Are they going to deny the fact that policemen also have civil rights? This writer maintains that they do. Among the rights of the police officer, as a citizen, which would be infringed upon by the actions of a police review board are the following:

1) The right to have his conduct judged according to due process of law in a civil or criminal tribunal created for that purpose.

2) The right to answer but once for the civil or criminal consequences of his act.

3) The right to have his reputation protected against public attack by a governmental body.

4) The right to a trial by jury and the right of appeal in accord with the requirements of law.

5) The right to be protected in his occupation and reputation against the actions of public authority not based upon established principles of law.

6) The right to equal protection of the law.

If an officer is deprived of his fundamental rights, how can we expect him to respect the system of criminal justice which he is hired to enforce.

CONCLUSION

Charles Reith, in his book entitled, *The Blind Eye of History*, traced law enforcement through past centuries. He reached a very interesting, and I think appropriate, conclusion when he said that every nation which has failed to support its laws has perished. Are we, the leading nation in the world today, going to ignore this important lesson of history and follow the path of downfall experienced by previously great nations? Are we going to let self-serving groups destroy our local law enforcement agencies — our first line of defense — by creating unnecessary police review boards? If we condone the establishment of such boards, that is exactly what we would be doing. We would be placing a bounty on the head of every police officer, subjecting him to false complaints from a carefully planned plot to undermine the efficiency of our law enforcement agencies.

The outward appearance of police review boards is such that an uninformed person would not readily see the inherent dangers. For that reason, it is the responsibility of all policemen to become familiar with the complete police review board concept and take the initiative in informing the public. Keep in mind that case law has stated "municipalities have no constitutional right to vest judicial power." (*The State, ex rel. Charrington, Prs. Atty. vs. Davis et al County Commissioners*, 119 O.S., 596 Cincinnati, Ohio).

As law enforcement officers, we must realize that we cannot fight this battle alone. We need the assistance of the general public. When the public has been adequately informed about police review boards, they will join us in the battle — for in supporting our cause, they are insuring themselves of well-being. In the words of Plato:

> Do not allow distrust of law to gain a foothold and to propagate itself in your city. Distrust for law is the poison that causes the dissolution of the state: Distrust for law brings anarchy.

CHAPTER 9

POLICE AND MINORITY GROUPS: TOWARD A THEORY OF NEGATIVE CONTACTS

Jack L. Kuykendall

INTRODUCTION

THE police in the United States are a focal point of conflict during periods of social change. As the state's instrument of legitimatized force they are representatives of the existing social system. Yes, in a democratic society which emphasizes the "rule of law" the police must act as a governing mechanism for the processes of social change: "To maintain a balance between conflict and consensus necessary to a democratic society, the police hold to the old value system and, simultaneously, protect legitimate social change resulting from society's structural strain." (1)

A major source of "structural strain" in society results from the aspirations of minority groups as they press for equity in the distribution of social, economic and political rewards. Challenges to the "system" and strategies utilized to effectuate change continually place police and some minority groups in confrontation. The pervasive hostility and danger inherent in these conflicts has caused a proliferation of anxiety, distrust, and hatred. The police and some minority groups often view each other as enemies — each group representing an obstacle to what the other is trying to achieve. The National Advisory Commission on Civil Disorders says that ". . . abrasive relationships between police and Negroes and other minority groups have been a major source of grievance, tension and, ultimately, disorder." (2)

These "abrasive relationships" are viewed as an immediate

---

1. Vernon Fox, "Sociological and Political Aspects of Police Administration," *Sociol Soc Res*, (October, 1966) (Reprint).
2. National Advisory Commission on Civil Disorders, *Report* (Washington, D.C., U.S. Government Printing Office, 1956.

consequence of a continuing series of negative contacts between police officers and members perceive they have been treated inequitably by police. Such contacts have the possible implicit dimension of initiating or reinforcing negative stereotyping of one group by the other. The purpose of this paper is to move toward development of a theory of the negative contact situations.

In analyzing police behavior five factors will be considered: selective recruitment; socialization process of the organization; dual responsiveness of the police system to a "legal" and "order" orientation; the institutionalization of the police as a power group, and the conflicting and discretionary aspects of the police role.

The minority groups, that is, Indian-Americans, Oriental-Americans, Spanish-speaking Americans, and Black Americans, are evaluated in terms of factors which will bring them into contact with police. These include their spatial location, the cultural norms which conflict with implicit and explicit values of the police, the degree to which a minority is pressing for change in status and the strategies utilized to effectuate such change, police perception of the minority as a "problem," and specific complaints of inequitable police treatment.

After a discussion of the police and each minority group, a section on the dynamics of the negative contact situations is presented. The final section suggests propositions that may be useful in theory building.

THE POLICE

Selective Recruitment

There has long been a concern about the possibility of "undesirables" being attracted to the police profession. (3) Supposedly, the role provides the opportunity for individuals with personality, emotional, or character disorders to act out aggressive or inappropriate behavior in a societally sanctioned capacity. Such behavior could include dominance drive,

---

3. Richard Blum, "Psychological Testing," In Richard Blum (ed.), *Police Selection* (Springfield, Thomas, 1964), pp. 85-139.

sandomasochism, a desire to control one's anti-social tendencies or to legitimatize criminal impulses, compensatory reactions for inferiority feelings, displaced aggression, authoritarianism, immorality, and dishonesty. (4, 5) Under the guise of legitimate justification, individuals can indulge in behavioral excesses without explicit condemnation. The number of such "types" actually recruited into law enforcement is not known; however, there is important information available concerning the individuals who do become police officers.

Lohman and Misner (6) have assumed that a great majority of police officers are recruited from the lower socioeconomic or "working" classes. Studies by Niederhoffer (7) and Bayley and Mendelsohn (8) confirm the predominance of police recruits with "working class" backgrounds. Vander Zanden (9) points to several studies which indicate that prejudice is more likely in lower class whites than in members of higher socioeconomic groups because of the threat blacks (and other minority groups) pose in social and economic competition.

The individual from the "working class" also brings to the police role a "preoccupation with maintaining self-respect, proving one's masculinity, 'not taking any crap,' and not being 'taken in'." (10) The emphasis upon masculinity among police has been substantiated in the studies of Matarazzo, *et al.,"* (11)

---

4. Jacob Chwast, "Value Conflicts in Law Enforcement," *Crime and Delinquency*, 11:151-161 (April, 1965).
5. O. W. Wilson, "Problems in Police Personnel Administration," *J Crim Law, Criminology and Police Sci*, 43:840-847 (March-April, 1953).
6. Joseph Lohman and Gordon Misner, *The Police and the Community: The Dynamics of Their Relationship in a Changing Society: Field Survey IV*. Report for the President's Commission on Law Enforcement and Administration of Justice (Washington, D.C., U.S. Government Printing Office, 1966).
7. Arthur Niederhoffer, *Behind the Shield: The Police on the Urban Frontier* (Garden City, Doubleday, 1967).
8. David H. Bayler and Harold Mendelsohn, *Minorities and the Police: Confrontation in America* (New York, Free Press, 1969), pp. 4-6.
9. James W. Vander Zanden, *American Minority Relations: The Soliology of Race and Ethnic Groups*, 2nd ed. (New York, Ronald, 1966), p. 105.
10. James Q. Wilson, *Varieties of Police Behavior* (Cambridge, Harvard University Press, 1968), p. 34.
11. Joseph D. Matarazzo, et al., "Characteristics of Successful Policemen and Firemen Applicants," *J Applied Psychol*, 48:123-133 (1964).

and Dillman. (12) The results of the Edwards Personal Preference Schedule given to eighty-one sucessful police applicants by Matarazzo indicate that '. . . [they] describe themselves as having strong needs to excell or achieve, be the center of attention, understand and dominate others, stick to a job until it is done, and to be 'one of the boys' among men." Similar findings were derived from Minnesota Multiphasic Personality Inventories completed by thirty-five applicants: ". . . [The aspiring police officers were found to be] typical of the enlisted man one often encounters in the military service: blustery, sociable, exhibitionistic, active, manipulating others to gain their own ends, opportunistic, unable to delay gratification, impulsive, and showing some tendencies toward overindulgence in sex and drinking. In a word, fitting the lower socioeconomic groups' stereotype of the 'man's man.' " (13*) Dillman also analyzed police recruit responses to the Michigan Sentence Completion Test and concluded that among other factors there was an "idealized and highly masculine" relationship with the male parent.

There are indications that some police departments intentionally recruit from the "working class" strata of society because of the type of skills developed during socialization. These individuals have stood the test of a "street-corner" or "gang" society, and have the ability to better understand and cope with the element of the community the police most frequently contact. (14, 15)

The prevalence of explicit recruitment from the "working classes" is not known. The social and economic characteristics of law enforcement may attract a predominance of such individuals to police ranks. Regardless of the causes, individuals with

---

12. Everett G. Dillman, "Analyzing Police Recruitment and Retention Problems," *Police*, 8:22-26 (May-June, 1964).
13. Matarazzo, et al., *op. cit.*
* Examinations administered to 243 successful police (116) and fireman applicants in Portland, Oregon, were the Wechsler Adult Intelligence Scale, Rorschach Inkblot Test, Miale-Holsopole Sentence Completion Test, Taylor Manifest Anxiety Scale, Saslow Psychomatic Inventory, Cornell Medical Indes, California and Adorno Authoritarian F Scales, and the Edwards Personal Preference Schedule or Minnesota Personality Inventory. This study also found that most of the applicants were from lower socioeconomic backgrounds. The general result was that of intelligent, emotionally stable young men.
14. Niederhoffer, *op. cit.*, pp. 37-39.
15. Thomas M. Frost, "Selection methods for Police Recruits," *J Crim Law, Criminology and Police Sci.*, 46:135-145 (May-June, 1955).

"working class" backgrounds bring to their jobs attitudes and experiences which have important implications for the police system.

The Police Organization†

The police organization is an agency of social control whose function is to minimize criminal activity and maintain order through the enforcement of laws. Criminal law is both substantive and procedural — substantive laws define the elements of a crime, and procedural laws, in part, determine behavioral guidelines for police tactics. Within the existing legal framework the maintenance of order does not always follow the enforcement of laws. Consequently, the organizational response becomes a function of not only a legalistic perspective, but also police perceptions of minimal acceptable levels of order and the degree to which an organization is responsive to public demands to suppress disruptive elements in society.

The police organization is a dual structure — manifest and latent — fluctuating between the "legalistic" and the "order" orientation. Each structure has its own goals, normative standards, customs, and socialization process. Although these are intricately intermixed, they are discernible and provide support and a rationale for behavior as either a "legal actor" or as an "agent of order," or both.

The manifest, or legal function, is the idealized organizational role. Collectively, the police function in this capacity during periods of social stability. Individually, they may invoke the latent, or order structure, for support during situational crises. It is possible to have collective observance of the legalistic perspective, and individual and subgroup observance of the order perspective.

During periods of social stress it is possible for the police, collectively, to assume a posture which emphasizes order.

---

†Numerous writings have provided substantially to this section's evaluation. See Fox (1966), Chwast (1965), Lohman and Misner (1966), Niederhoffer (1967), Bayley and Mendelsohn (1969), Wilson (1968), Skolnick (1967) and 1969), Black and Reiss (1966), Reiss and Boruda (1967), Stoddard (1968), Lundstedt (1965), Levy (1968), and Goldstein (1968).

However, the "rule of law" (legalistic perspective) is sufficiently internalized among the police, and in some segments of society, to preclude the police from acting indiscriminately. Therefore, they revert to a traditional means of exercising influence — politics. They assert a philosophy of order which posits restrictive conformity to accepted standards, and suppression of deviations from those standards. The instrument for order becomes a viable political force, competing as a strategy to determine the extent and direction of social change rather than as an overseer to its legitimate processes.

The police can become institutionalized as a power group in society, responsive neither to law nor the public, but instead, to their own philosophy which has evolved from role requirements, perceptions of how behavior is controlled (punishment), and a capitalistically cultivated ideal to compete successfully.

This latter factor has resulted in a formal internal reward structure in police departments which encourages managerial efficiency and a "production" orientation. Success is measured quantitatively in terms of arrests, contacts, crime rate, etc. The reward system is identical for both latent and manifest structures. Both determine success in terms of "counting." However, each structure has separate "means" — order or legal. In a given situation the officer can shift from one structure to the other depending upon which means provides the greater support for behavior; and as noted previously, there can be collective reliance upon the order structure during periods of social stress.

The police system also provides the officer with values which emphasize conforming patterns of behavior that are akin to those of the middle-class. The officer develops a "control" orientation in behavior from the socialization processes — for example, training and customs — in the department. He becomes conditioned to seek out "disruptive" or non-conforming clues as indicators of criminal activity. This results in the development of stereotypes of "trigger cues" that activate action.*

In summary, the organization provides the police officer with personal values emphasizing conformity, reinforces his desire to compete quantitatively for success, provides reference group

---

* For a discussion of the concept of "law and order" see Skolnick (1967, pp. 6-22).

support for legalistic or order-oriented behavior, or both, and socializes the officer to be sensitized to stereotyped "cues" which portend of disruptive or criminal activity. When the policeman goes into the streets to perform the police role his perceptions are shaped by his experiences in the organization and the characteristics of his personal background.

The Police Role

Police work requires that the officer have both the willingness and capacity to use force. Westley (16) says that violence is an occupational prerogative of the police. Danger necessitates the use of force (violence) and the role demands assertion of authority in many situations. However, the danger/authority trait of the police role results in conflicting demands on behavior. Skolnick (17) has commented most aptly in this regard:

> The combination of danger and authority found in the task of the policeman unavoidably combine to frustrate procedural regularity. If it were possible to structure social roles with specific qualities, it would be wise to propose that these two should never, for the sake of the rule of law, be permitted to coexist. Danger typically yields self-defensive conduct, conduct that must strain to be impulsive because danger arouses fear and anxiety so easily. Authority under such conditions becomes a resource to reduce perceived threats rather than a series of reflective judgments arrived at calmly.

Danger can result in potentially disruptive social situations which the officer must attempt to structure in a manner acceptable to the authority dimension of his role. The reactive nature of the police response limits the officer's ability to predetermine a choice of tactics which can be successfully employed. Since all situations cannot be precisely defined, guidelines for behavior are often vague or sufficiently abstract to be subject to a variety of interpretations.

Consequently, the officer must develop an interpersonal role style in "handling" the various contacts that are made. This

---

16. William A. Westley, "Violence and the Police," *Amer J Sociol*, 59:34-41 (July, 1953).
17. Jerome H. Skolnick, *Justice Without Trial: Law Enforcement in a Democratic Society* (New York, Wiley, 1967), p. 67.

results in a wide range of approaches to situational problems. (18, 19, 20) As a result of this the police have traditionally had implicit discretionary powers. † This provides a latitude in responding to calls, but can also result in insufficient control over the response employed by the officer. In many situations the role gives the officer the opportunity to do exactly what his personal values dictate: He becomes the sole arbiter of guilt or innocence — he becomes the "law."

MINORITY GROUPS‡

Indian-Americans

During westward expansion in the United States Indians were dominated through treaty, or by violence, and finally placed on reservations under control of the federal government. The Indians have remained a depressed minority and many of them still reside on reservations where they have their own tribal laws, police and judicial system. (21, 22)

In growing numbers, Indians are now leaving the reservation and settling in urban areas. Often they have become "ghettoized" as the result of discrimination (23) and tribal kinship and cultural traits. Kuttner and Lorinez (24) in their study of Omaha,

---

18. John H. McNamara, "Uncertainties in Police Work: The Relevance of Police Recruits Background and Training," In David J. Bordua (ed.), *The Police: Six Sociological Essays* (New York, Wiley, 1967), pp. 163-252.
19. Albert J. Reiss and David J. Bordua, "Environment and Organization: A Perspective on the Police," in David J. Bordua (ed.), *The Police: Six Sociological Essays* (New York, Wiley, 1967), pp. 25-55.
20. James Q. Wilson, *op. cit.*, pp. 57-83.

† Failure to provide guidelines for the discretion of the officer can also result from managerial inadequacies in the police department. (President's Commission on Law Enforcement and Administration of Justice, 1967, pp. 13-41).

‡ Robin M. Williams, Jr., (1964, p. 304) defines minority groups as " ... any culturally or physically distinctive and self-conscious social aggregates, with hereditary membership and a high degree of endogamy, which are subject to political, or economic, or social discrimination by a dominant segment of an environing political society."

21. Peter I. Rose, *They and We: Racial and Ethnic Relations in the United States* (New York, Random, 1964), pp. 20-24.
22. U.S. Commission on Civil Rights, *Justice* (Washington, D.C., U.S. Government Printing Office, 1961), pp. 144-148.
23. Rose, *op. cit.*
24. Robert Kuttner and Albert B. Lorinez, "Alcoholism and Addiction in Urbanized Sioux Indians," *Ment Hyg*, 51:530-542 (October, 1967).

Nebraska, found that Indians had been assimilated, but into the "skid row" community. This was the result of patterns of alcohol consumption — the Indians failed to adapt to the more demanding social roles. Perhaps this is the consequence of the indirect effects of historic discrimination.

One study (25) indicates that police perceptions of Indians as a "problem" involve drinking and sex crimes; however, this study does not apply to urban areas. Kuttner and Lorinez (26) found high crime and delinquency rates among Indians in Omaha and there are indications that crime is one means employed to support alcohol and drug usage. If Indians reside primarily in "slums" or ghetto areas they are probably heavily policed, but there is no evidence that Indians are presently viewed as a crime problem.

Violation of treaty rights of Indians have lead to open confrontation with law enforcement officers in rural areas. During a "fish-in" to protest laws limiting fishing in Washington, Indians accused police of beating women and children without provocation. "Fish-ins" are an indication of the rapidly increasing organized efforts of Indians to effectuate a change in status. Reliance on "red power" and a swing toward harsh militancy is becoming apparent. (27, 28, 29, 30)

Indian complaints against police concern the lack of maintenance of "law and order" in Indian sections of towns and cities; a tendency of officials to "throw the book" more at Indian violators in comparison to whites; the ignoring of Indian violations against Indians, but a severe response when Indians become involved with whites; the use of excessive force in making arrests; and the "rolling" of intoxicated Indians. (31) The relationship between reservation police and Indians is not known. There are indications of a greater latitude in criminal

---

25. Norman S. Hayner, "Variability in the Criminal Behavior of American Indians," *Amer J Sociol*, 47:602-613 (January, 1942).
26. Kuttner and Lorinez, *op. cit.*
27. *New York Times* (October 12, 1969).
28. Hamilton Binus, "Indian Uprising for Civil Rights," *Ebony*, 22:64-72 (February, 1967).
29. Wilcomb E. Washburn, "Red Power," *American West*, 6:52-53 (January, 1969).
30. *Time* (July 4, 1969), pp. 16-21; (February 2, 1970), pp. 14-20.
31. U.S. Commission on Civil Rights, *Justice* (Washington, D.C., U.S. Government Printing Office, 1961), pp. 144-148.

proceedings, but any implication for police behavior is speculative. (32)

Oriental-Americans

Japanese and Chinese constitute almost the entire Oriental population in the United States. Although dispersed throughout the nation, they are primarily located in rural and urban areas in the western states and Hawaii. Initially "ghettoized" in Chinatown, succeeding generations of Chinese-Americans have become increasingly integrated into the white community. Japanese-Americans have been assertive in obtaining integration, and are even more assimilated than the Chinese. In large measure this is the result of the acquisition of economic skills and strong cultural and family institutions which have led to an enhanced socioeconomic status. As a group, the Oriental-Americans are not economically deprived, and there is presently no evidence of militant efforts to alter their status. (33, 34, 35, 36)

Historically, the Chinese have had "tong" wars (gang activity), and there have been perceptions of licentious, corrupt and exotic behavior in the "yellow ghetto," but in recent years this has apparently subsided. Generally, rates of criminal activity among Orientals have been low, but there are indications that among Chinese there is "hidden" crime and delinquency. Reasons given for the success of Orientals in maintaining effective social control and minimizing proliferation of marginal groups are the strength of community and family institutions. However, as the Orientals have become increasingly acculturated there is evidence of rising rates of delinquent activity. (37, 38, 39)

---

32. Warren H. Cohen and Philip J. Mause, "The Indian: The Forgotten American," *Harvard Law Review*, 81:1818-1858 (June, 1968).
33. Rose, *op. cit.*
34. Vander Zanden, *op. cit.*, pp. 255-262.
35. Harry H. L. Kitano, *Japanese Americans: The Evolution of A Subculture* (Englewood Cliffs, Prentice-Hall, 1969).
36. Rose Hum Lee, *The Chinese in the United States of America* (Hong Kong, University Press, 1960).
37. *Ibid.*
38. Kitano, *op. cit.*
39. U.S. Commission on Civil Rights, *Hearings in San Francisco: May 1-3* (Washington, D.C., U.S. Government Printing Office, 1967), p. 207.

One aspect of Oriental culture which has led to conflict with the police is the Chinese interest in gambling. This is the basis for the only complaint of Orientals against the police that could be found. Chinese believe that they are disproportionately arrested for a gambling game that is almost exclusive to their culture. Japanese-Americans have indicated that there is little, if any, discrimination against them. (40, 41)

Police do not perceive that Orientals present any "problem" other than a proclivity of the Chinese towards gambling, and believe the social control mechanisms of the Oriental family to be the reason for low crime rates. (42)

Spanish-Speaking Americans

The Spanish-speaking minorities consist of Puerto Rican, Hispano-, and Mexican-Americans. Puerto Ricans are scattered throughout the United States but are primarily concentrated in New York City. Hispanos are of Spanish-Indian ancestry and reside primarily in the urban and rural areas in Arizona, New Mexico, Texas, and California. Mexican-Americans are immigrants from Mexico and their descendants. Many of the Mexican-Americans are seasonal farm workers and are a transient population for part of each year. While the majority of Mexican-Americans reside in the southwest (including California) there are sizeable populations in some midwestern and western urban areas. (43, 44)

In New York City, Puerto Ricans are concentrated in a ghetto area called Spanish Harlem. The Hispanos are predominantly an agricultural people and reside in rural slums. They face less discrimination than blacks, but in urban areas they generally live in segregated areas. Mexican-Americans, when present in large numbers, are segregated into "Mexican Colonies" in

---

40. ———— *Hearings in San Francisco: January 27-28* (Washington, D.C., U.S. Government Printing Office, 1960), pp. 746-762.
41. ————, *Hearings in Los Angeles: January 25-26* (Washington, D.C., U.S. Government Printing Office, 1960), pp. 111-115.
42. ————, *Hearings in San Francisco: January 27-28, op. cit.*
43. Rose, *op. cit.*, pp. 43-3.
44. Vander Zanden, *op. cit.*, pp. 242-254.

southwestern urban areas. (45, 46) Although generally segregated, the Spanish-speaking minorities have made some progress in integrating white communities. Puerto Ricans with "fair" skin are able to leave Spanish Harlem. Hispanos- and Mexican-Americans in the higher socioeconomic strata of society are considered "Spanish" and therefore acceptable. In southern California where they are the single largest minority the Spanish-speaking Americans have gradually become more integrated since World War II. (47, 48)

An important aspect of this minority's culture is the language. Breakdowns in communication have led to complaints of police nonresponsiveness in protection and services. (49) A popular cultural pattern of the Puerto Ricans is "street corner" gathering for recreational and social activities. (50) Migrant Mexican-Americans often gather in cities and towns during non-working hours and generally concentrate in one area for recreational and social reasons. Undoubtedly, inadequate recreational facilities, housing, and perhaps unemployment, have resulted in ghetto minorities developing cultural patterns of activity which place them on the street more frequently than dominant groups.

Spanish-speaking minorities, to the extent that they live in identifiable ethnic communities, are viewed as a police problem. These segregated areas are typically disadvantaged; they present the most ambiguous law enforcement encounters and a greater perceived danger for the officer. (51) Police have a tendency to view high-crime-rate areas, which is a trait of most lower socioeconomic urban areas, as enemy territory. (52) The general police perception of the Spanish-speaking minorities as being "racially" criminal is not known. However, from the author's

---

45. Rose, *op. cit.*, pp. 42-44.
46. Vander Zanden, *op. cit.*
47. *Ibid.*
48. Fernando Penolosa, "The Changing Mexican-American in Southern California," *Sociol Soc Res*, 51:405-417 (July, 1967).
49. U.S. Commission on Civil Rights, *Hearings in Newark, New Jersey: September 11-12* (Washington, D.C., U.S. Government Printing Office, 1962), pp. 455-461.
50. *Ibid.*
51. Bayley and Mendelsohn, *op. cit.*, pp. 81-108.
52. Harold Black and Marvin J. Labes, "An Analogy to Police-Criminal Interaction," *Amer J Orthopsychiat*, 37:123-129 (July, 1967).

experiences and observations. Mexican-Americans in the southwest are seen by some police as "sneaky, dishonest, and immoral," with a proclivity towards use of drugs and intoxicants. When migrant farm workers are present in these communities the police often show a marked concern about the possibility of increased crime and personal danger.

The depressed socioeconomic status of the Spanish-speaking minorities is resulting in rapidly increasing and militantly organized efforts to effectuate change. In Spanish Harlem indications are that Puerto Ricans believe legalistic strategies have failed. They are beginning to adopt aggressive action which has already led to a confrontation with the police. (53, 54) "Brown power" is becoming an outcry for Mexican-Americans and Hispanos in the southwest. This is illustrated by the recent marches, strikes and violent confrontations in New Mexico, Texas, and California. (55, 56)

Complaints against the police are the emphases placed on property rights to the exclusion of individual rights and liberties; verbal harassment, that is, use of derogatory words such as "pancho," "muchacho," and "amigo"; excessive patrolling of minority neighborhoods: use of excessive force; unnecessary interrogations and searches, and in general, violation of constitutional rights. Two recent landmark Supreme Court cases — *Escobedo v. Illinois* and *Miranda v. Arizona* — which limit police interrogation of suspects, involved Spanish-speaking minorities.

Mexican-Americans are particularly fearful of the Immigration Service and Border Patrol, whom they view as the "Gestapo." A major problem of these agencies is the use of Mexican bracero (legal entrants) and "wetback" (illegal entrants) as seasonal farm workers. Officers are authorized to question and search within one hundred miles of the border, without warrant, anyone suspected of being an alien. With the influx of "wetbacks" this

---

53. Armando Rendon, "El Puertorriqueno: No More, No Less," *Civil Rights Digest*, 1:27-35 (Fall, 1968).
54. Richard Hammer, "Report from a Spanish Harlem 'Fortress,' " in Bernard E. Segal (ed.), *Racial and Ethnic Relations* (New York, Crowell, 1966), pp. 324-330.
55. *Time, op. cit.*
56. *Newsweek*, (March 25, 1968), p. 37.

Police and Minority Groups 213

undoubtedly leads to harassment of many lawful Mexican-Americans. (57, 58, 59, 60, 61)

Black Americans

Evolving from a heritage of slavery, black Americans in this century, and particularly in the last three decades, have steadily mced fr n rural to urban areas — and from the south to the north and west. Approximately 70 percent of the black population now resides in metropolitan areas. In all parts of the United States blacks are racially segregated and have suffered extensive discrimination. (62)

The black culture is often characterized by personal and social disorganization. Black ghettoes typically have high crime rates that are disproportionate to white, lower socioeconomic areas. Unemployment, lack of adequate recreational facilities, inadequate housing, and masculine gang activities frequently place blacks on the streets. There exists among black Americans a subculture that has high aspirations but limited available opportunities, sees the "power structure" as remote and impersonal, and that sanctions violence. (63, 64) These factors create potentially challenging and disruptive situations for the police.

Blacks are militantly, even violently, organized to Christian Leadership Council, to the aggressively violent tactics of the Black Panthers, blacks are demanding a change in the distribution of power. They want to determine their own future — they want "Black Power." (65, 66, 67, 68)

57. U.S. Commission on Civil Rights, *The Mexicans* (Washington, D.C., U.S. Government Printing Office, 1968), pp. 15-21.
58. _____, *Hearings in San Francisco: May 1-3, op. cit.*, pp. 25-252.
59. _____, *Hearings in Los Angeles: January 25-26, op. cit.*, pp. 300-301.
60. Hammer, *op. cit.*
61. Rendon, *op. cit.*
62. National Advisory Commission on Civil Disorders: *Report* (Washington, D.C., U.S. Government Printing Office, 1968), pp. 203-247.
63. *Ibid.*, pp. 224-236.
64. Kurt Lang and Gladys Engel Lang, "Racial Disturbances as Collective Behavior," *Amer Behavioral Sci*, 4:11-13 (March-April, 1968).
65. Vander Zanden, *op. cit.*, pp. 220-228; 356-757.
66. National Advisory Commission on Civil Disorders, *op. cit.*, pp. 299-322.
67. Eldridge Cleaver, *Soul on Ice* (New York, Delta Books, 1968).
68. Skolnick, *op. cit.*, pp. 125-176.

Police, collectively and individually, believe that blacks represent a serious law enforcement problem. Black ghettoes are the most dangerous areas to work in, and civil disturbances have, at times, led to open "warfare." (Bayley and Mendelsohn, 1969, pp. 46-108; National Advisory Commission on Civil Disorders, 1968, pp. 299-339; Skolnick, 1969, pp. 241-292; Lohman and Misner, 1966). Police resources are usually assigned on the basis of criminal incidents and potentially disorderly areas. From the police perspective, these traits characterize black communities.

Black complaints against police include the following: police are viewed as representatives of an inequitable "system," and as an army of occupation; police do not respond to complaints and have inadequate grievance mechanisms; they are either oppressive or fail to provide sufficient protection; exclusively black incidents are underenforced while black/white incidents are overenforced; police are either too impersonal or too personal, that is, paternalistic or condescending; verbal and physical harassment and abuse is believed a common practice; police patrolling tactics are seen as suppressive; constitutional rights are consistently violated, and blacks in white neighborhoods are harassed, as are black men in the company of white women (69, 70, 71, 72, 73, 74, 75) Lohman and Misner, 1966, pp. 53-103; Michigan State University, 1967, pp. 13-18; Bayley and Mendelsohn, 1969, pp. 137-138; Fogelson, 1968; Skolnick, 1969, pp. 211-288; Edwards, 1968, pp. 28-31).

---

69. National Advisory Commission on Civil Disorders, *op. cit.*
70. Lohman and Misner, *op. cit.*, pp. 53-103.
71. Michigan State University, *A National Survey of Police and Community Relations: Field Survey V*. Report for the President's Commission on Law Enforcement and Administration of Justice (Washington, D.C., U.S. Government Printing Office, 1967), pp. 13-18.
72. Bayley and Mendelsohn, *op. cit.*, pp. 137-138.
73. Robert M. Fogelson, "From Resentment to Confrontation: The Police, the Negroes, and the Outbreak of the 1960's Riots," *Poli Sci Quart*, 83:217-247 (June, 1968).
74. Skolnick, *The Politics of Protest*. Report to the National Commission on the Causes and Prevention of Violence (New York, Ballantine, 1969), pp. 211-288.
75. George Edwards, *The Police on the Urban Frontier* (New York, American Jewish Committee, 1968).

DYNAMICS OF NEGATIVE CONTACT SITUATIONS
*Macro Level Analysis**

Police/minority-group negative contact situations can be analyzed from the "power maintenance" function of police and the overt threats posed by a minority group in power challenges. Minority-group segregation is a consequence of dominant group rejection and ingroup solidarity of minorities, and represents distinct boundaries of separation. Dominant groups also possess the power — economic, social, and political resources — often sought by the minority group.

Denial of equitable distribution of power is based on the threat minorities pose in being permitted access and control of resources. In one sense a minority can be viewed as a resource by which certain power is maintained. For example, provide cheap labor; they are an acceptable outgroup for scapegoating; enhance the status of lower strata dominants by providing an inferior hierarchial group, and minorities can often be manipulated to alter the success of competing political dominants.

Minorities are dominated through an intricate network of overt and covert, informal and formal techniques. The extent to which they continue to accept dominance is a function of their own resources — possessed upon coming into contact with the dominant group, or that are subsequently acquired. Minority resources for consideration here are their adaptive capacity, visible concentration and organized pressure tactics for status change.

Oriental-Americans have demonstrated a high adaptive capacity with strong community and family institutions, and the acquisition of economic skills which have led to enhanced acceptance by the dominant group. Initially, the possession of economic skills and concentrated visibility posed a serious threat, but the availability of adequate resources and the general rapid acculturation of essential skills has led to increasing assimilation.

Indian-Americans, to date, have not manifested any

---

* Concepts used in this analysis are taken from authorities previously cited, Blalock (1967), and Cloward and Ohlin (1960). In addition, the author's own ideas are incorporated.

meaningful adaptive capacity in assimilation. Not only have they faced *de facto* segregation, they have been visibly segregated (isolated). With increased movement to cities and a recent "red" awareness, Indians may rapidly become more visible. Use of militant tactics for status changes, plus visible ghettoization, may lead to conflict with police. There are recent indications of this in Minneapolis where an "Indian Patrol" has been developed to prevent "harrassment by police." (76)

Spanish-speaking Americans have manifested a limited adaptive capacity. In part, this is due to some higher socioeconomic positions which can be related to a "Spanish" heritage and varying degrees of visibility of physical identification. In the main, however, they represent a concentrated and visible minority which is increasingly employing militant tactics to obtain equity in distribution of resources. They are a perceived threat to power and therefore a police problem.

Blacks are more threatening than the Spanish-speaking minorities because they are intensely visible and concentrated, and they are the principal power-challenge group in society. Their use of pressure tactics has resulted in rewards being administered by the dominant group. Blacks have institutionalized militancy through white recognition, and other minorities are emulating black successes. However, the blacks' adaptive capacity is limited and has not correspondingly increased with the success of pressure tactics. Therefore blacks become even a greater threat because power is redistributed only on the basis of institutionalized aggression.

An important aspect of a minority's adaptive capacity is cultural strengths and weaknesses. Discrimination can influence cultural characteristics of minority groups. Important considerations here are cultural influences on behavior of minority members and the implications for relationships with police — as a law enforcing institution of the dominant group.

Law represents a formal mechanism by which power contests

---

76. *Time, op. cit.*

and individual behavior are regulated. As lasw can represent the dominant group interests, they can also be equitable in evaluating individual deviance reprehensible to both dominant and minority groups. However, dominant influenced power laws coupled with informal and interpersonal acts of discrimination often lead to extensive personal and social disorganization in minority-group cultures. With denial or resources legitimate opportunities are limited, and a deviant or illegitimate opportunity structure develops. This often leads to extensive violation of equitable substantive laws governing personal conduct which, in turn, provides perceptions of a collective minority deviancy. Negative stereotyping ensues and reinforces the dominant groups rationale for continued discrimination and resource denial.

Police, as a "power-maintenance" agency, are involved in enforcing both dominant influenced and equitable laws. Cast in this role they have an institutionalized self-conception as a moral and just power group. The police and some minority groups are traditionally in conflict by virtue of extensive and visible minority deviancy and perceptions of minorities as distorted by on-going experiences, and when trying to maintain the power distribution desired by the dominant group they are, in effect, fighting a "holy war."

Police have a vested interest in their own power, the existing distribution of power, and are in large measure responsible for its maintenance. If the minority becomes collectively disruptive and highly visible anxiety prevades the dominant group, and police responsiveness leads to an invoking of the order posture. The police, to the degree they have the resources, will be required to suppress civil disturbances. If minority activity does not become collectively violent some officers indulge in situational suppression, supported by the latent order structure of the organization. The police role is personalized and institutionalized; the police are arbiters of dominant values and not objective and responsive regulators of human conduct. Not only are they a symbol of an inequitable society, they are, in fact, frequently and perhaps unavoidably inequitable.

Micro Level Analysis*

In negative contact situations the minority-group member perceives he has been treated inequitably by police. The police officer brings to these situations an ethnocentric background, a need to maintain his masculinity, values which emphasize conforming patterns of behavior, a sensitivity to disruptive or criminal activity as identified by stereotyped cues, wide discretionary powers in enforcement encounters, reference group support, and emphasis upon "order" oriented or "tough" responses. If he is bigoted as well he is very close to inappropriate responses whenever he enters the minority-group culture. Moreover, the challenges to the various dimensions of his role are unusually high in the environment. In fact, they are so numerous that it is not only the individual minority-group member, but the collective, visible, and segregated minority that becomes a threat. Collective minority violence is met with collective police violence; individual minority violence is met with individual police violence; the anticipation of either is met by police suppression.

The police and minorities are sensitized to each other — the police officer as an individual and a representative of the "system" controls the life of minority citizens; members of the minority are a threat to the police, both to the individual policeman doing his job and to the organization as a whole. As the police anticipation of situational and organizational threats fluctuate, so will their response. When the officer enters a threatening situation he is likely to employ some form of abuse, especially if the actor(s) is a minority-group member. The power maintenance role of police, and the extensive and social disorganization in the minority culture create numerous stressful situations. When a policeman enters this kind of situation, and it is not quickly structured to minimize personal danger, he will employ the strategies needed to control the situation. These strategies may be in accord with the officer's personal values and not those of the law. Often his response is perceived as inequitable, and frequently that perception is justified

---

*Concepts used in this analysis are taken from sources previously cited and those developed from the author's experiences and observations.

If the police organization lacks sufficient control mechanisms, the officer's response will often be indiscriminate without regard to precipitous situations.*

The police represent a readily available target for outlets to minority dissatisfactions. The minority individual often expresses his frustration in challenging those he thinks are suppressing him — he gets the "pigs."

The police-minority contact situation often becomes a vicious circle perpetuating negative reinforcement of each group by the other. The police by their power position *are* oppressive, and when minorities begin to exert pressure for redistribution of power, conflict results. This conflict becomes personalized in the interaction of the minority-group member and police officer. When either can be "read" as manifesting what the other already believes, the situation becomes negative and enhances the possibility of negativism in future contacts. Repeated situations may preclude positive contacts of any nature between police and minorities.

TOWARD A THEORY OF NEGATIVE CONTACTS

1. The police "power maintenance" function in society establishes dual organizational structures in police departments that are responsive to "legalistic" and "order" perspectives.
   a. Legalistic behavior is emphasized during periods of social stability in society.
   b. Order, or suppressive behavior, is emphasized in periods of social stress and acceptable during situational stress for the individual officer.
2. Police negative perceptions of minority groups are a function of
   a. concentrated visibility,
   b. extent of personal and social disorganization of the minority culture which is determined by the police on the basis of the
      (1) prevalence of perceived minority criminal deviance, and

---

* See Kuykendall (1969) for an analysis of a response hierarchy of police power strategies used in controlling various types of situations which police officers encounter.

(2) prevalence of perceived threatening and challenging situations.
   c. pressure strategies utilized for effectuating changes in status.
3. Police negative perceptions of minority groups are perpetuated by
   a. selective recruitment from working classes of dominants,
   b. inadequate control mechanisms in the organization,
   c. reward (quantitative evaluations) structure of the organization,
   d. implicit and explicit socialization in the use of stereotyping as a skill requisite.
   e. danger-authority conflict of the police role,
   f. dominant group support and encouragement for the use of suppressive tactics, and
   g. latent order structure which tolerates and reinforces situational order-oriented behavior by police officers.
4. Minority-group negative perceptions of police are a function of
   a. the "power maintenance" function of police,
   b. non-responsiveness of police to minority needs and grievances, and
   c. the perceived, and actual, verbal and physical abuse and harassment resulting from factors in hypotheses 2 and 3, and which create negative contact situations.
5. Minority Group negative perceptions of police are perpetuated by negative contact situations which reinforce factor c in proposition 4.
6. Police negative perceptions of minority groups are also perpetuated by negative contacts which reinforce factor b in proposition 2, and factors c and d in proposition 3.
7. Repetitive and frequent negative contact situations lead to individual and collective polarization of police and minority groups, and individual and collective confrontation and violence.

CHAPTER 10

THE ROLE OF THE COURTS IN A STATE-WIDE CRIMINAL JUSTICE INFORMATION SYSTEM

Robert R. J. Gallati

STATE-WIDE criminal justice information systems are being developed in several states and they may be expected to exist in one form or another in every state within the next few years. There are a number of reasons for this trend, including the following:

1) It has become almost universally accepted that there is an urgent need to make more systemic the present processes of criminal justice, and that a criminal justice information system is the essential foundation upon which a more coherent system of criminal justice may be structured.

2) It is generally accepted that such a system is most properly a state function, for data files containing people information have greater scope and are more meaningful (and in some cases more secure) at the state level than at the local level; likewise, comprehensive data banks at the federal level pose more sensitive civil liberties issues than similar record keeping at state level.

3) From a practical standpoint, the planned expansion of the FBI's National Crime Information Center (NCIC) Computerized Criminal History Program is based upon the development in each state of a central data bank of criminal offender record information from all functional branches of criminal justice administration. The role of the FBI/NCIC is to be limited to that of an index or directory and the various state data centers are conceived to be the actual information sharing mechanisms for the exchange of records between and among the nation's criminal justice agencies.

There is on-going at this very moment a frantic attempt on the part of a great many states to develop compatible state-wide criminal justice information systems as rapidly as possible. Most of these states are utilizing the New York State Identification and Intelligence System (NYSIIS) as a model, supplemented, of course, by indigenous modifications. We may very well, therefore, examine NYSIIS and understand not merely the concept of a state-wide criminal justice information system, but also observe how such a system has been created, developed, maintained and placed in operation.

NYSIIS was created as an agency in 1965. The concept of NYSIIS, as expressed in its enabling legislation, rests upon the following basic principles affirming the unitary nature of criminal justice: all criminal justice agencies need to participate in and share a joint data bank; the submission of information thereto should be primarily voluntary; NYSIIS is to be a service agency only, with no powers, duties or facilities to arrest, prosecute, confine or supervise; security and privacy considerations must permeate the system and involve central and remote NYSIIS operations; new dimensions of science and computer technology can be applied to provide greater effectiveness in filing methodology and the utility of processed data; and that criminological research will be supported by a vast resource of computerized empirical data available for variable searching to test theses, hypotheses, theories and pilot projects, thereby enabling criminal justice administration to evaluate its own procedures, practices and operations.

It was very evident from the start that if NYSIIS was to function effectively as a criminal justice information system serving all functional areas of criminal justice, there were some conditions that had to be met.

1) NYSIIS had to be created and maintained as an independent agency so that it could serve all functions without fear or favor;
2) NYSIIS had to have a vast computer capability and engage in massive historical and on-going data conversion of the millions of records contained in its and contributing agencies' manual files;
3) NYSIIS had to advance the state-of-the-art of computer-related technology;

4) NYSIIS had to provide computer-related communications systems for remote access to the system data bank and for computer interface with interstate information exchange systems;
5) NYSIIS had to embrace a sophisticated security and privacy program and adopt a Code of Ethics in order to counter the possible threat that computerized data banks containing derogatory data about individuals posed to civil liberty;
6) NYSIIS had to encourage the utilization of its incredibly vast computerized empirical data base by social scientists as well as criminal justice professionals for purposes of research, evaluation and monitoring of criminal justice administration in all of its manifestations.

NYSIIS has achieved a vast computer capability and has converted several million records for automatic data processing. Since criminal offender record information provides the background and status of persons of interest to all elements of the criminal justice process, the computerization of individual criminal histories and related identification files was given top priority. At this point in time the identification function is almost totally automated; however, the manual system must still be maintained and gradually phased out as more and more records are converted for computer processing. To this end the following have been accomplished:

1) 375,000 criminal case histories have been converted and an additional 10,000 are being added each month;
2) 2.5 million fingerprint classifications are "up" on the computer;
3) name and wanted search at NYSIIS is now computerized for rapid determination of individual status in the criminal justice process;
4) both wanted persons and summary case histories are computer-interfaced with NCIC providing a nation-wide record in many instances.

NYSIIS has also developed a number of computerized analytical capabilities, such as criminalistic data analysis, organized crime intelligence, latent fingerprint search, etc. All of these analytical modules are theoretically viable for investigative purposes by all branches of the criminal justice process. However, as a practical matter, they are most often in the police domain, and I would prefer to focus upon the identification function which is more relevant to the role of the courts.

One of the prime benefits, but by no means the sole benefit, to be derived from the computerization of identification records is the speed with which state-wide records can be made available at the time and place they are needed. Procedures for release on own recognizance, forthwith sentencing, rapid arraignment and felony bail require swift and complete criminal history record responses. Obviously, however, speedy processing alone will not deliver the needed data within the required time frame; it is essential concomitantly to develop a computer compatible communication system. NYSIIS now has a state-wide facsimile transmission network, as well as computer-to-computer interface, and various other telecommunication devices. Our facsimile system enables us to receive copies of fingerprints from remote locations throughout the state in fourteen minutes, and, upon the completion of the identification process, to transmit a response at the rate of six minutes per page of offender record. Our average elapsed time for inhouse processing of submitted prints and production of the individual's criminal record is less than 2½ hours. Thus, a state-wide criminal offender record based upon fingerprint identification is available to the courts of New York State in an average of approximately three hours. This is a 12,000 percent improvement over the former ten to fourteen day response cycle for state-wide criminal history records before NYSIIS.

Another significant benefit to be derived from computerization is the capability of storing vast amounts of data and retrieving discrete portions thereof, as required for particular purposes. Thus, for arraignment purposes a summary of the arrestee's criminal history may suffice, whereas, for police or probation purposes, a much more comprehensive case history is required. Likewise, the offender's criminal status anywhere in the nation is readily obtained by NYSIIS through computer interface. However, the most significant benefit to criminal justice in the long run is the capability of obtaining feedback and evaluation of the entire process from arrest to parole and analyses of the contributions of each functional branch to the objectives of the system. Certainly, complete, rapidly available and relevant data concerning persons involved in the criminal act will make offender files more meaningful for each agency involved. Statewide criminal justice information systems thus support areas of criminal justice administration by correlating data resources and pointing the way to more coherent and coordinated criminal justice administration, thereby demonstrating the ultimate potential of a true criminal justice system.

What is the role of the courts? I submit that the courts have several parts to play in their participation as an integral part of state-wide criminal justice information systems.

1) Generator and contributor of criminal offender data for the benefit of all branches of criminal justice. A most critical example of this is the reporting of disposition data.
2) Consumer of criminal offender record information for purposes of arraignment, release on own recognizance, bail, sentencing, referral, etc.
3) User of empirical data and computer analyses to evaluate the effectiveness of judicial decisions and the court system itself as it may be constituted at any particular time, including the application of operations research, criminological research, etc.
4) Guardian and protector of the rights and liberties of offenders whose records comprise so very critical a portion of state-wide criminal justice information systems.

Of course, there is another aspect of computerization of court data which should be mentioned, although it is beyond the scope of my presentation; that is, an internal information system for case files, dockets, caseloads, etc. Some portions of what we have to say about the court's role in a state-wide system would have applicability to such a system, even though it is designed primarily as an operational aid for a particular court or group of courts.

THE COURTS AS CONTRIBUTORS OF DATA TO A STATE-WIDE CRIMINAL JUSTICE INFORMATION SYSTEM

The courts generate and are in a position to contribute vital data to a state-wide criminal justice information system. The most essential of all these data are court dispositions. The need for effective court disposition reporting procedures has been recognized for some time. The basic statutory requirement for disposition reporting was contained in the old Code of Criminal Procedure and has been in effect since 1928. Unfortunately, not all dispositions were reported because reporting procedures were a separate matter for each court to establish. In 1963, the Judicial Conference was authorized to develop a state-wide reporting system. Considerable study and restudy have been undertaken by the Judicial Conference which has not developed an automated system for reporting dispositions to NYSIIS. Likewise, their computer will have significant data concerning the progress of cases through the courts. We provide the Judicial Conference with computer data concerning arrests and later receive computer tapes with dispositions of such cases.

Unfortunately, while the Judicial Conference Statistical System was being developed, a serious backlog of unreported dispositions accumulated. The result is that many of the criminal offender records in NYSIIS do not presently include required disposition data. However, much of this backlog is currently being overcome and the Judicial Conference System is expanding to counties throughout the state. It is anticipated that computerized criminal offender disposition reporting for the entire state will be operational during 1972. This is a matter of highest priority because incomplete records hobble the courts in their efforts to deal intelligently, fairly and accurately with current cases involving former offenders. Likewise, police, district attorneys, probation and parole officers, and correction officials are handicapped by incomplete records. Perhaps the most important consideration of all is that the lack of disposition data prejudices the arrestee who may have been acquitted of the charge or a defendant who was convicted of a lesser crime than that for which he was arraigned.

So serious, indeed, is this gap in an otherwise effective statewide criminal justice information system, and the national system that is derived from it, that it compelled J. Edgar Hoover, Director of the FBI, to address a letter to all fingerprint contributors as follows:

> We ask your special attention to the urgent need to report a final disposition for each charge.... We have made this request previously, but never under conditions of such urgency as those which now prevail.... A number of civil suits have been filed, all undecided as yet, demanding that the FBI cease dissemination of any part of a record that is incomplete, for lack of disposition shown and/or totally expunge from the record any notation of arrest or charge unsupported by a disposition. ...If the FBI . . . should be required to expunge all arrest notations for which dispositions are available but not reported, every element of the criminal justice system will be handicapped, deprived of information pertinent to the protection of society.

Another area in which the courts could contribute very significant data to the state-wide system is in the matter of bail reliability. At the present time NYSIIS does not receive any information from the courts relative to arrestees on bail or recognizance, except as it may be obtained in a limited number of cases where a warrant is issued. In these days when preventive detention is being considered, a viable alternative might be for the court of arraignment to have information concerning the defendant's conduct in previous cases where he had been released on bail or on his own recognizance. I am confident a host of other data will eventually be contributed by the courts as they rely more and more upon the benefits of state-wide criminal justice information systems.

THE COURTS AS CONSUMERS OF STATE-WIDE CRIMINAL OFFENDER RECORD INFORMATION

In order to carry out their responsibilities within the judicial process, the district attorney and the court have definite needs for records of the accused person. Prior criminal history is needed at arraignment to establish the court's jurisdiction to admit the accused person to bail; it is also needed to determine the correct charge for crimes in which a second offense calls for a higher level of crime and penalty. After the trial has been completed and if the accused person has been convicted, the criminal history is needed once again to justify, in certain cases, a higher sentence for a second offense. Importantly, as well, non-criminal data will be useful when sentence is to be passed as it may determine whether the convicted person can be released on probation.

If there is a lapse of time between arraignment and trial during which the accused has been free on bail, the court may want to know whether any additional criminal history information is available that would be pertinent to the case. During the trial itself, circumstances may arise which require further information about the defendant or witnesses. Once the trial has been completed and if a guilty verdict has been reached, the court must determine the sentence to be imposed. In exercising its discretion, the court needs all relevant data, including both criminal and non-criminal information about the arrestee that will be pertinent to the sentence determination.

Therefore, the significance to court proceedings of full and accurate state-wide criminal offender record information is undeniable. A question that is being raised at the present time is the need to meet extremely demanding New York City Court arraignment response time requirements for state-wide "rap sheets." As I mentioned previously, we are responding to fingerprint submissions in an average total elapsed time of approximately three hours. At this time no other state can do nearly as well; however, we hope to improve on even this remarkably rapid service. NYSIIS is keenly aware of the desire of the New York City Criminal Courts to expedite arraignment and sentencing, and we are exploring every possible means to meet these stringent demands. Further automation of the identification function — in particular, an automatic fingerprint classification capability — would make the hope of additional reductions in response times more realistic.

The understandable desire to obtain state-wide "rap sheets" in the least possible time for arraignment should not obscure the importance of these documents in aiding court decision making at various other stages of court procedure. Probation investigations are assisted by NYSIIS summary case histories. These histories quickly provide information upon which recommendations for ROR, bail, and sentencing may be made to the court. Likewise, if the court places the offender on probation and he is arrested again while on probation, NYSIIS will automatically make the necessary notifications. As more and more pertinent data are added to the computerized state-wide record, probation officers and the courts they serve will be able to rapidly retrieve required data and thereby expedite sentencing.

The courts will also be indirect generators and/or consumers of criminal offender record information. As the courts issue criminal warrants for individuals, these are recorded by the police as *wants* in the offender file at NYSIIS, and, when certain criteria are met, in the FBI/NCIC Wanted System, as well. Obviously, the status of a defendant in terms of outstanding warrants against him is of critical importance at arraignment. Similarly, when our system is expanded to include the offender's record while on bail or recognizance, this status will be of prime interest to the courts, regardless of what agency may have entered the data into the system. Thus, as we continue to expand the scope of criminal offender record information to include, for example, post-adjudicatory data, the courts will have rapid access to a wealth of state-wide information not presently available except after lengthy and exhaustive investigation.

THE COURTS AS USERS OF EMPIRICAL DATA AND COMPUTER ANALYSES FOR RESEARCH AND EVALUATION

State-wide criminal justice information systems offer the courts unprecedented opportunities to critique their own operations. Of course, the Judicial Conference Statistical System specifically offers the courts an opportunity to develop statistical profiles of their operations in terms of how types of cases are handled, elapsed time involved in court proceeding, percentages of convictions, pleas, acquittals, etc., in particular courts or in discrete groups of courts. However, in a much broader sense, a state-wide criminal justice information system, which includes relevant data from the Judicial Conference Statistical System, as well as additional data from all functional branches of criminal justice administration, offers opportunities for research and evaluation never before available.

One of the principal purposes of NYSIIS has been to develop a total information system that supports the total decision-making processes of criminal justice administration. Of course, the decisions of our courts, both in reference to the disposition of particular individuals and in reference to the interpretation of statutory law, are of overriding importance for the entire structure of the administration of justice in our society. Use of the term "total information system" does not imply the development of a massive central file that will capture and keep all records generated by the criminal justice process. Some records — such as prisoner confinement records — are only of incidental significance. Other records — such as certain pieces of evidence — must be maintained at the place of trial. Other records — such as Grand Jury minutes — are regarded as confidential documents and are filed locally. Therefore, some agency information has been specifically left out of NYSIIS because of legal restrictions, the context of data in local operations, the sensitive nature of certain files, and exclusion policies of NYSIIS itself. Some of the specific decisions relating to exclusion include the following: witness sheets, indictments, evidence, full text of probation and parole reports; confidential medical and psychiatric narrative; general categories of abnormal sex behavior; IQ and personality test results; notation of illegitimate birth; paternity warrants, and comments on extent of religious participation or activity.

In developing its information system NYSIIS has concentrated on the facts on which decisions are made and from which documents are produced. The sum of these data at this time represents the world's largest empirical data base of computerized criminal justice information.

I would not presume to attempt to advise the court system as to how they could best use this fantastic resource. However, I would suggest that, as in all other branches of criminal justice, there is an on-going need to ascertain the effectiveness of policy decisions from an operational standpoint. This suggest that the enormous potential of sophisticated operations research could be considered to update and improve the structure of our court system, or at the very least to flash early warnings of impending crises and indicate the need for aggressive preventive maintenance. You will recall the statements of Chief Justice Warren Burger relative to deferred maintenance of the American system of criminal justice in every phase — including the courts. He stated in part:

> ...those who are apprehended, arrested and charged are not tried promptly because we allow unconscionable delays that pervert both the right of the defendant and the public to a speedy trial of every criminal charge; and...convicted persons are not punished promptly after conviction because of delay in the appellate process. Finally, even after the end of litigation, those who are sentenced to confinement are not corrected or rehabilitated, and the majority of them return to commit new crimes.

While the blundering of the constable or the failure of the prisons cannot be charged to the courts, there is still very much that the courts need to know in terms of criminological research as to the effects of their decisions upon the court system itself and upon the effectiveness of all other functional branches of the criminal justice process. By what objective criteria do we exercise our court sentencing powers? Do our courts fully comprehend the systemic consequences of their procedural, sentencing, and statutory interpretation decisions? I would suggest that only a minimum of empirical research has been done in the past to assist the courts in their olympian tasks. It appears that the new technology should be utilized to improve, not only the true administration of criminal justice, but also the wisdom with which it is administered. The enormous resources of state-wide criminal justice information systems are at your service.

THE COURTS AS GUARDIANS AND PROTECTORS OF OFFENDER RIGHTS AND LIBERTIES

The noble purposes of our courts as the ultimate guardians of individual human rights are placed into sharp focus when we consider the incredible advantages of computerized criminal justice information systems and balance these benefits against the possible compromise of civil liberties and individual freedom. I will not be so presumptuous as to address these problems in a general way — there are panelists here today far more qualified than I to speak on these burning issues. However, I would like briefly to present some insights on these crucial issues from one who must deal with the operational aspects of security and privacy in a state-wide criminal justice information system and the possible impact upon such operations of court discretion.

As the director of an operational state-wide criminal justice information system, I am directly involved in the task of providing dynamic security and privacy to balance the sometimes contrary but equally valid tenets of the right of the people to know versus the right of the individual to his privacy. This is something we have to pretty much play by ear, for very little legislation to date has been provided which defines or limits the legitimate interests and rightful functions of government in the area of record-keeping and personal dossiers. Two obvious, though often overlooked, exceptions to this rule are those provisions of the Criminal Procedure Law which constrain release of information on Youthful Offenders, and those provisions of the Civil Rights Law of New York State which require criminal justice agencies, on demand, to return the fingerprints of those who are acquitted or whose cases are dismissed prior to or during prosecution, provided they have no prior conviction.

I freely admit that the creation of centralized computer banks does increase the risks to civil liberties, through coordination of material from diverse sources, as well as through encouragement of a wider spread of data collection activities due to the lower per item cost of data stored and the speed and ease of access. I nevertheless feel strongly that in the centralization process, with computerization of records, there is a much greater degree of control that a central, detached agency such as NYSIIS can exert for the protection of the right to privacy. There exist various sophisticated technologies, computer programs and peripheral protective or encoding devices which can be marshalled to protect the integrity of a large computer system. Likewise, the very existence of a state-wide system has great potential for raising and enforcing standards that would not be possible for widely dispersed manual files.

NYSIIS and its users have subscribed to a very advanced Code of Ethics and use and dissemination agreements have been

required to assure conformity with privacy criteria. Some additional measures that have been provided and are available to protect the privacy of individuals whose records are contained in the system include:
1) Users of the system are limited and specified by statute;
2) Classes of information included in the system are specified by statute;
3) Unauthorized disclosure by an employee is forbidden by statute;
4) An individual is permitted access and review of his identification files and has the right to have corrections made where substantiated;
5) Employees and system participants are closely disciplined;
6) The concept of redemption or the "forgiveness principle" has been adopted.

The very existence of state-wide information systems, the addition of computers and related technology to the identification function, coupled with the judicial interpretation of privacy as a constitutionally protected right — all have contributed their share to a renaissance of interest and support for the adoption of measures to strengthen the hands of administrators in the prevention of possible compromise of personal privacy and individual civil liberties. However, there is still a serious problem. The core of the problem is the lack of clear law and guidance in this area of privacy which has now been made more complicated by computer technology. There is no clear-cut judicial definition of personal information as a precious commodity as exists in the law of property. Likewise, there is an absence of institutionalized court procedures to protect against the improper collection of information, or storage of inadequate or false data.

Recent decisions of some courts give evidence of increasing judicial sensitivity to the rights of privacy in computerized criminal justice information systems. Far from resenting these exercises of judicial discretion, NYSIIS welcomes the guidelines judicial opinions afford. We applaud this concern on the part of the courts and look forward to its impact upon future legislation which must take cognizance of these decisions. As an operating agency, we are besieged with non-criminal justice agencies seeking to avail themselves of these state-wide records. Undoubtedly, more and more legislation will be introduced to seek to open up criminal offender files for other than law enforcement purposes. I believe the continued viability of computerized state-wide criminal justice information systems depends upon scrupulous concern for privacy, and perhaps the most significant way to impress both government and the general public with the crucial importance of security and privacy is for all to know beyond a doubt that the courts will strike down any unreasonable invasion of the right to privacy.

CONCLUSION

Automation in the courts is bound to be. The question is not whether it will occur, but how soon it will occur and in what configuration. I submit that the existence in New York State of a state-wide criminal justice information system provides a tremendous assist to the courts in their efforts to automate. As we have seen, many of the criminal justice information needs of the judiciary may very well be satisfied by participation in the state-wide system made available by NYSIIS. Undoubtedly, however, there is need for computerization of many facets of court administration, procedure and record-making and record-keeping beyond that which can properly be expected to be provided by NYSIIS.

I am delighted that the Judicial Conference Computerized Criminal Statistics System has been planned to follow the history of arrest for a fingerprintable crime from the moment of arraignment to the final disposition, and NYSIIS is proud to be able to interface with this important development. Likewise, I applaud State Administrator Thomas F. McCoy's statement at the N.Y.U. Second Annual Conference on Applications of E.D.P. Systems for State and Local Government:

> The contradictions I referred to... between the speed of computers and the 'deliberate speed' of the judicial system, between the sophistication of the computer and the still traditional and often primitive methods of the judicial system must be gradually eliminated. This is the task of the unified

court system in this state. It will not happen overnight, but it will happen.

I would like to add to Administrator McCoy's fine statement the observation that not only methods and procedures may be improved but in the criminal sphere also judicial understanding of the effects of court decisions upon victims, offenders, the criminal justice system and society at large.

I trust that NYSIIS will be able to continue to meet the needs of the courts and that the court system will continue to provide the inputs required for a viable state-wide criminal justice information system. I look forward to the increased utilization of both the operational and research, planning and development potentials of our state-wide system by the judiciary. Finally, let us all hope above all that our courts will vigorously uphold the right to privacy and thereby give the green light to administrators of computerized criminal justice information systems to stringently enforce reasonable regulations for the security and confidentiality of their files, as well as provide offenders with fundamental rights that will encourage redemption.

The role of the courts is crucial to the success of any state-wide system. State-wide criminal justice information systems can provide critically needed services for a more effective criminal court system. At this juncture in our nation's history, when law and order with justice is priority number one for everybody from the President on down, such a partnership is decidedly in the public interest.

CHAPTER 11

THE POLICE AND THEIR PROBLEMS

Marvin E. Wolfgang

THERE are several reasons which make me less than comfortable writing for this particular group on this particular topic: first, I am likely to say things which hit sensitive concerns and might be uncomplimentary to the very group that reads this paper. This is quite a different situation from being with my usual graduate seminar discussing theoretical and methodological problems in criminological research. Secondly, there is such a dearth of research on community attitudes toward the police that I must speak in sweeping generalities and speculative suggestions rather than rely much upon carefully designed research.

There have been some studies of the police, and there are many observations made in a somewhat clinical and anthropological way. I have been fairly close to the police department in Philadelphia for about fourteen years, having spent three intensive years working closely with the homicide squad. Our own research activities at the University of Pennsylvania's Center of Criminological Research are intimately linked with the Philadelphia police department, without whose cooperation we would not have been able to conduct some of our most meaningful work. Thus, at least in our own area, we enjoy that kind of peculiar position which permits us entree and rapport while granting us freedom to make suggestions — hopefully constructive — and criticism of the police organization and of the community's attitudes toward and relationships with the police.

To ask "Who are They?" poses more than one question because we can hardly speak of a collective consciousness, a community consensus in this regard. The police represent not only persons or a subgroup in a society, but also a symbol of social values, of authority, of formal and codified rules of conduct. The police are

---

Reprinted from *Police*. (March-April, 1966).

the guardians of a system of values that have historical continuity and contemporary coherency; they are the executors of middle-class values reflected in the criminal law and community norms of right and wrong conduct. They are the front-line reconnaisance troops of these values; their functional role is to discover, detect, and deter deviance from those values while protecting vulnerable victims from the offensiveness of others. In this sense, the community of individuals is primarily composed of persons who accept, internalize, and themselves teach and represent in their roles the very values the police are expected to uphold.

Most communities, however, are also made up of interest groups, at least two sexes, different ethnic groups, social classes, important age differences, occupational categories, wealth and poverty, a power elite, and an impotent minority. These are only broad and gross classifications we use to simplify analysis; there are obviously many more. These suffice, however, to show the range of variation in differential perspectives relative to the police and their functions. Moreover, there is a dichotomy we must never forget, e.g. that the community is composed of criminals and noncriminals, delinquents and nondelinquents. The attitudes of these groups towards the police serve both to divide the community response to police power and to cause a response in the policeman's psychology. Sometimes, as we shall see, the police tend to exaggerate this response and view the community of citizens and of criminals as only saints or sinners, as respectably good or irrefutably bad. Instead, the community comprises a continuum, a distribution like IQ ranging along an axis from good to bad, with most of us in the model sweep of the bell-shaped curve.

We must also keep in mind that the police themselves do not represent an entirely homogeneous group. Having a police badge does not make men alike. The uniform does not cause uniformity of ideas, hopes, aspirations, and achievement. While there may be more similarities among persons in a police organization than in the community at large, each officer comes to his profession with his own peculiar personality, abilities, and talents to handle ideas and people. If there are sadists in the police force, they must be extremely rare, and the idea is more of a myth than a reality.

However, there are some men more aggressive, more prone to

violence, more hostile, more prejudicial than others. To say that these same variations exist in all occupations is not a sanguine response, however, for the police are in a special kind of relationship to the community that most other occupational groups do not enjoy (or suffer).

Therefore, to speak of the police in general, as one is required to do in a short paper like this, is somewhat in violation of our recognition of the heterogeneity among the police. We shall nonetheless keep this fact in mind.

I have said that we don't know enough about the social organization of the police and of the community's attitudes. We have more than rumors, however, and are better off than in many other things where our notions are only rumors. My grandfather reminded me during the Second World War of a jingle popular during the First World War:

> My aunt's charwoman's sister's son
> Heard a policeman on his beat
> Say to a nursemaid down the street
> That he knew a man who had a friend
> And he could tell when the war would end.

We are better off than this, and before saying more about the specific relationship between the police and the community, let me pay my debts generally to some writers and researchers whose work influenced my thinking on these matters. I am referring, for example, to the unpublished material of Doctor Jerome Skolnick (1) at the Center for the Study of Law and Society at Berkeley, California; to the newly published work by Michael Banton in England, *The Policeman in the Community,* (2) to William Westley's "Violence and the Police" (3) and others. I do not always agree with all of these writings, but I do occasionally draw upon them.

THE ROLE OF THE POLICE IN RELATION TO THE COMMUNITY, AS THIS ROLE AFFECTS ATTITUDES IN BOTH DIRECTIONS

It is axiomatic that the police officer's role represents a conflict

---

1. Jerome Skolnick, *Justice Without Trial.* (Mimeographed, forthcoming publication).
2. Michael Banton, *The Policeman in the Community* (London, Ravistock, 1964).
3. William Westley, "Violence and the Police," *Amer J Sociol.* 59:34-41.

of values in many specific situations. Policemen participate in the same community as the people whose conduct they are supervising. William Foote Whyte noted in *Street Corner Society,* his account of the social structure in a Massachusetts Italian neighborhood, the contradiction between the policeman's formal obligations and the relationships he needs to build up in such a community if he is to keep the peace. Taking a strictly legalistic view of duties cuts him off from the personal relations necessary to enable him to serve as mediator of disputes in his area. Yet, the policeman who develops close ties with the local people is unable to act against them with the vigor prescribed by the law. (4) Accepting free coffee or meals, shirts or hams at Christmastime, may be innocuous behavior in one sense and at one time, but it creates ties of trouble between the generous citizen and the policeman. It is not merely that the police officer may be more lenient in permitting minor violations of his benefactors. Even if the gift-giving citizen never performs any law violation, the actual conflict is potentially present and therefore promotes a moral conflict harbored by the organization of the police, if not by the officer himself.

As an organization, the police force is expected to perform successfully. The police force, like any other group, wishes to be successful, to conceive of themselves as performing their roles with efficiency, for efficiency is one of the main virtues in the American ethos. Similarly, the community wants the police to function efficiently. The measures of success, however, of this organization are probably harder to obtain than for most organizations. The automobile industry and most businesses measure success by economic rewards, by net profits. A university is performing its role if it teaches, does research, grows in quantity or quality; a professor by his publications, research, and teaching and administrative skills. There are, of course, problems of weighing these ingredients, but they are consistent and form a logic of function. For the police organization, there are conflicting values expressed by the community itself. The police must meet many criteria and it is difficult to compare the value of

---

4. William Foote Whyte, *Street Corner Society* (Chicago, University of Chicago Press, 1943), p. 136.

success in one direction at the expense of shortcomings in another. A police force which solves more crimes but which treats suspects with undue severity is in one sense more efficient, but its practices would excite public protest. The police have a variety of objectives but they are simultaneously subjected to many restrictions about the ways in which they attain them, and the interplay between ends and means is much more complex than in most organizations. The efficiency of the police may be less important than their responsiveness to the community they are required to serve. (5)

Moreover, the structure of the police organization, the way information upon which to act is fed into the system, and the way supervision in the bureaucracy is performed help to promote ambiguities and sometimes conflicts. As the density of population increases and police work becomes more complex with greater division of labor and specialized skills, a bureaucratic system emerges. We are not using bureaucracy in a pejorative sense, but in a sociologically descriptive way. Bureaucracies create hierarchies of command and impersonalized regulations. Unlike most formal social organizations — industry, hospital staffs, business — where directives come from above, from the upper echelon, as the basis for dealing with people from the outside, most police activities are originated by members of the public — motorists, drunks, lost children, crowds, burglars. Information about these events, as Banton points out, reaches the organization through the men at the bottom. The patrolman first on the scene must make a judgment and this decision may affect the entire organization. His supervisors are in a real sense dependent on him. Yet, while these cases are fed into the system from the bottom, and the supervisors cannot be looking over the shoulders of the officers at all times, the men at the top must control their subordinates. Discretion at the bottom is permitted and this creates a break in the link of supervision.

This issue of discretion is an important one, both from a constitutional or legal perspective and from the viewpoint of community values. Police power is a mighty force for many

---

5. Banton, *op cit.*, pp. 105-106.

objectives. How that power is used is a function of how the community perceives the police and how the police perceive the community. If there is inadequate communication between these two groups — as I fear there is — then a condition that my friend, David Matza, calls "pluralistic ignorance" is maintained; that is, both groups are ignorant of or inadequately informed of one another's wishes and expectations. (6) As Michael Banton suggests, "The only long-term solution to the problem of police discretion is for the police and the public to share the same norms of propriety." (7)

Now the community often sees the police as employees of the state, not as public servants, and rarely, if ever, as the formal guardians of the community's sentiments. As I shall emphasize in a moment, the heterogeneity of our American communities with many different social groups and classes, has much to do with the fact that there is not *one* community but many which the police serve on one hand and contain on the other. While I referred earlier to the police functioning as guardians and executors of middle class values — at least from a sociologist's functional view of society — the community as a whole probably does not share this perspective. The police are invested, the community generally feels, with *legal power* only. Although it is true that the police officer does not enjoy many more rights, privileges, or power than the ordinary citizen, the police officer does perform a role that clusters certain rights, responsibilities, and power that the citizen has only in a diffuse and uncommitted sense. That is, the police officer, when he takes a salary and signs up for the job, is committed to performing certain limited activities that express this power, while the citizen is working in a factory, an office, or a classroom and does not use this same power. The investment of time, labor, and ego make the difference.

However, if the police officer had power, concentrated in his role, he also wants authority — that is, rightful or moral authority. It is this exact kind of authority the community often appears unwilling to grant. Power itself is not necessarily rightful.

---
6. David Matza, *Delinquency and Drift* (New York, Wieley, 1964).
7. *Ibid.*, p. 146.

As has been said elsewhere, legal power itself "gives one man the ability to force another to do his will. But if this power is seen as rightful, as authority, the second man will probably comply with the former's wishes because he feels morally obliged to do so." (8) In these terms, policemen could possess both authority and power. Many criminals and many lawbreakers (if I may assume the difference is being communicated) do not consciously recognize policemen as having moral authority over them. In most situations, the police expect that the persons with whom they deal will regard the police as being morally justified in dealing with them as they do. The police try to get offenders to recognize what the norm of proper conduct is and to agree to observe it in the future. If the "client" must be made a "captive," the police really prefer that the offender believe that he deserved it. This is one of the reasons that homicide squad officers generally have less trouble with the parties they arrest. Most homicide offenders who killed their spouses or loved ones or friends in a quarrel feel remorse, shame, or guilt, and in so expressing it, they accept the moral authority of the officer who is obliged to make the arrest. This is the same reason which accounts for the American police officer's general reluctance to make arrests as well as his explaining or arguing with the persons he arrests — to confirm his moral authority.

The police officer, we have said, is himself a member of the community whose norms he has to enforce. The community, however, does not make the police and the norms moral equivalents. This difference means that the policeman often does not receive the moral support of his community. I shall point out later that one of the reasons for the lack of moral support is the police emphasis on their own solidarity and the community's apathy and forced isolation. The police officer really wants the goodwill even of the offender and will sometimes treat him leniently in order to be thought a "human" and good-hearted person. When he must make an arrest, he is often in a conflict situation and is almost in one sense "betraying" the arrestee.

---

8. *Ibid.*, p. 147.

Banton (9) draws a parallel to the agents in society who are responsible for having persons committed to a mental hospital. This unattractive status requires restricting a man's freedom while simultaneously trying to suggest that it is for his own good and for the good of others.

The police are known to complain that the lower or higher courts often release offenders they (the police) felt firmly about as real criminals. Lack of evidence, legal technicalities, political corruption may separately or concomitantly be responsible for the releases or for light sentences. The conflict between protection of society and protection of private individual rights plays a part in these disparities between what the police believe and what the courts may do. The police are more interested in security; the courts, it seems, are more concerned with freedom. Whatever the reason for the disparate views — arrests too readily made without sufficient evidence, or release by the courts because of over-concern for technical freedom — there is no denying that the police view the arrested offender who's back on the street the next day as a negative judgment of the policeman's role and moral authority. Either the specific circumstances causing this judgment must be changed, or the police should re-evaluate their role so as not to perceive this kind of event as an indictment of their authority. Under present conditions, the police are forced to retreat into themselves and become less identified with the community that seems not to support them. As Durkheim, a French sociologist, said, one of the purposes of punishment is to reinforce the social norms of right and wrong conduct. (10) When the police are rebuffed, they can no longer be seen or see themselves as executors of that reinforcement process. When this happens, their moral authority is chipped away until only legal power, which is in itself ineffective, remains. The motorist who is stopped comes then to be intimidated by the legal power of the police to make an arrest but does not comply with requests out of a belief in the officer's rightful authority to require conformity. The more society is in this condition, the weaker are the police,

---

9. *Ibid.*, p. 150, n. 1.

the more alienated they become, and the less secure is the community.

Finally, within this context of the policeman's role and the community attitudes, let me suggest that there is much similarity in values regarding the degree of offensiveness of certain crimes. Being members of the community, we have said, policemen share the same values as many other members. In a study designed to measure people's attitudes regarding seriousness of delinquency, Thorsten Sellin and I studied police officers, juvenile courts judges, and many university students. (11) These are admittedly and generally representatives of middle-class values. In short, we found no significant differences among the three groups with respect to their ratings of seriousness. This finding reveals that the police do in fact share the same relative perspective on crimes as do these other groups. It further indicates, however, the rightful authority the police should have to perform their roles of enforcement.

THE SOCIAL ISOLATION, ALIENATION, AND SOLIDARITY OF THE POLICE—THEIR EFFECT ON THE POLICE AND THE COMMUNITY

The police are often attacked by the community for not being sufficiently aggressive in apprehending an offender. However, if the police are too aggressive and use too severe yet efficient means of solving a crime and making an arrest, the American Civil Liberties Union, the NAACP, the courts, and other agencies will attack them for undue process of law. When the police perform their duties with alacrity and comprehensiveness, often the paradoxical situation occurs that the crime rate seems to go up. The more they work, the more they discover. The more thorough the policeman is, the more he may offend some groups — like catching speeding motorists. If he is lenient, he does not discourage; if too harsh, he's criticized for discourtesy (although this is a reaction of particular segments of the class structure.) In short, he is vulnerable to abuse by his very role, not by his

---

11. Thorsten Sellin and Marvin E. Wolfgang. *The Measurement of Delinquency* (New York, Wiley, 1964).

personality; and this kind of community reaction generates alienation from the public. The cleavage is crowned by the need to stick together. In sociological terms and generalization, the more the outgroup attacks the ingroup, the more prominent become the differences between the outgroup and the ingroup, and the greater is the solidarity of the ingroup. The similarities rather than the differences between members of the ingroup are stressed. In our specific context, the police fraternity becomes a solidified front both as a protection against the outside and as a status-retaining force within. In England, we are told by one author: "British policemen have much less cause than American ones to feel that they must keep together in face of the public. Their organization can therefore tolerate more internal strains than could be the case across the Atlantic. There is a longer hierarchy of ranks in Britain; pay differentials are greater; the sense of opposition between the men and the bosses (and vice versa) seems stronger; discipline is stricter; constables show less solidarity with one another, and more competitiveness." (12)

There is another point to keep in mind: the police officer in certain neighborhoods is viewed as alien by definition. He is apart, and his separateness makes him lonely except for his own brotherhood of officers. James Baldwin describes some of this feeling of the soldier walking through enemy territory in *Nobody Knows My Name:*

> ...The only way to police a ghetto is to be oppressive. None of the Police Commissioner's men, even with the best will in the world, have any way of understanding the lives led by the people they swagger about in twos and threes controlling. Their very presence is an insult, and it would be, even if they spent their entire day feeding gumdrops to children. They represent the force of the white world, and that world's criminal profit and ease, to keep the black man corraled up here, in his place. The badge, the gun in the holster, and the swinging club make vivid what will happen should his rebellion become overt...
>
> It is hard, on the other hand, to blame the policeman, blank, good-natured, thoughtless, and insuperably innocent, for being such a perfect representative of the people he serves. He, too,

---

12. Banton, *op cit.*, pp. 118-119.

believes in good intentions and is astounded and offended when they are not taken for the deed. He has never, himself, done anything for which to be hated — which of us has? — and yet he is facing, daily and nightly, people who would gladly see him dead, and he knows it. There is no way for him not to know it: there are few things under heaven more unnerving than the silent, accumulating contempt and hatred of a people. He moves through Harlem, therefore, like an occupying soldier in a bitterly hostile country; which is precisely what, and where he is, and is the reason he walks in twos and threes. (13)

A policeman expressed his isolation to a researcher recently in terms of the following incident:

I try not to bring my work home with me, and that includes my social life. I like the men I work with but I think it's better that my family doesn't become a police family. I try to put my police work into the background, and try not to let people know I'm a policeman. Once you do, you can't have normal relations with them. (14)

DANGER AND VIOLENCE

The exposure to danger and potential violence is one of the most important ingredients separating the policeman from the "civilian." Policemen may be assaulted or insulted just because of their occupation; they are more likely to be assaulted or murdered in executing their duty than are others. Hence, policemen have sympathy for any of their own members who makes an error in judgment, as when an officer shoots an innocent person in a dark alley, believing him to be a dangerous suspect or escapee from prison, etc. The public is quick to condemn; the police have sympathy where there is public indignity. In the light of our previous remarks, it is understandable that the police rally around their own member to protect him and symbolically expect a similar display of sympathy should any of them perform the same kind of error.

In 1962, seventy-eight law-enforcement employees were killed

---

13. James Baldwin, *Nobody Knows My Name* (New York, Delta, 1962), pp. 65-67, cited by Skolnick, *op. cit.*
14. Skolnick, *op. cit.*

in the line of duty; forty-eight officers were victims of direct attack by criminals, most of them dying by gunfire. Over a three-year period, 26 percent of police officers killed by felons were responding to "disturbance" calls (family quarrels, man with gun, etc.); 12 percent were investigating burglaries in progress; 22 percent were pursuing robbers; 25 percent were attempting arrests or transporting prisoners; 11 percent were investigating suspicious persons; 4 percent were killed without warning by deranged persons. Of every 100 police officers, ten were assaulted at some time during the year. (15) Part of the reason for much of this is the ease with which guns are acquired, and the association between the gun and virility in regions of American culture. When people possess guns, there is a standing temptation to use them when circumstances do not justify their use, and this fact increases the policeman's burden.

It should be noted that because the policeman lives under a more constant threat — if not actual use — of violence, he tends to collect, like a clinician, certain clues of danger: the black leather jacket, a particular strut, the demeanor and language, particularly of juveniles, and the gesture toward a pocket that is quick and threatening. Living on the threshold of violence, whether or not he ever experiences it, creates suspicion. This cognitive awareness again sets him apart from civilians.

Dealing with criminals, as most nonpolice persons do not, tends to develop a defensive reaction, often in the form of violence by the police themselves. In one classic study in the Midwest, William Westley asked policemen under what circumstances they thought officers were justified in "roughing a man up." More frequently mentioned than any other reason was the reply that violence might be justified when a man showed disrespect for the police — twenty-seven out of seventy-three men (or 37 percent) felt this way. According to Westley, if a policeman uses violence to make a difficult offender show respect for the police, he is requiring that the man show respect for him as an individual; his action is not meant to exact respect for law and order and the policeman as its representative, but simply for him as an

---

15. Data cited by Banton, *op. cit.*, p. 111, from *Crime in the United States*, 1961, pp. 21-23, 110.

individual. (16)

The police tend to view flagrant disrespect as a personally ego-deflating experience, partly because of the lack of court and public support. In England, I doubt that this is the case. As one officer in Westley's study put it:

> There was the incident of a fellow I picked up. I was on the beat and I was taking him down to the station. There were people following us. He kept saying that I wasn't in the army. Well, he kept going on like that, and I finally had to bust him one. I had to do it. The people would have thought I was afraid otherwise. (17)

As one who handles violence, the policeman becomes associated, in the eyes of the community, with something dirty and nasty. Moreover, the citizen, realizing the necessity for such work, wants to be disengaged from it and those who do it. Keep in mind that one idea of power, status, and respectability of a group is its ability to tolerate having jokes made about it. Psychiatrists can afford to have jokes about their profession. The police have not been able to enjoy such a level of tolerance.

SOCIAL VARIABLES IN THE COMMUNITY: ATTITUDES TOWARD THE POLICE

In my conversations with middle-class women, asking them how they felt about the police, the answer was almost invariably that they had been treated with respect and dignity. They felt either warmly protected by the police ("I like to see patrolmen on my street") or had a sense of social distance, as if the police were impersonalized agents of the body politic. This protective feeling is probably much more commonly a female than a male response. A father or big brother image is fairly common.

There is, however, a difference by social class. When a police officer rings the bell of a home in a middle-class residential area, the respondent's expectations are centered around such items as the following: "Is he going to tell me that my little daughter is lost? That someone was seen prowling around the house? Or that

---

16. Westley, *op. cit.*, p. 38.
17. *Ibid.*, p. 39.

he has tickets to sell to the policemen's ball?" In a lower-class neighborhood, the respondent has more focal concerns around "trouble." "What did my kid do now? Did Bill (the husband) get drunk again last night?"

The lower class gets into trouble more often and comes to view the policeman as an unfriendly intruder in the neighborhood. In a sense, he is, as the excerpt from Baldwin graphically stated. The reaction of the police officer is affected by the social class of the offender, or by the suspect he must question and arrest.

Relative to the slum dweller, the police officer is socially superior. When the lower-class suspect tells the officer to go to hell, the officer can respond with swearing (thus giving the other party a kind of privileged familiarity) or he can remain aloof with an air of dignified middle-class morality, representing that morality in appropriate conduct. The interaction between officer and suspect should be reduced to physical force *only* by the suspect, else the inference of moral authority is lost by the officer and it is only the legal and physical power that remain as weapons of control. That the latter are necessary many times is not to be denied; but the ready resort to violence by the police is more denegrating to the police than to the offender.

Deference to middle or upper-class status in suspects is probably less common in the United States than in England, but it is there, nonetheless. Particularly in dealing with traffic violators does this kind of interaction occur. When the officer receives comments, such as — "Who do you think you are, anyway? You should be spending your time chasing criminals." — from the Cadillac owner, the policeman may either feel a sense of deference to superior social and economic status as he projects beyond the immediate situation; or he may enjoy the experience of exercising a moral authority over the offender by reminding him of his duty to obey the law. In either case, the upperclass offender's attitude is a personal rebuke that is best responded to by an impersonal stance represented in the law's requirement of obedience and the officer's being the representative guardian of social harmony and order.

In the lower-class area, the police are perceived more as the "long arm of the law" reaching into a subculture easily vulnerable to detection of deviance. In the middle and upper-class area, the police represent rules established by the group itself. Too often, however, the policeman is viewed as a hired hand, a servant, rather than a mirrored and visible reflection of the mores.

Juveniles comprise another group attitude toward the police. They generally reflect their parents' attitudes which vary by social class. Do the police represent authority figures to adolescents? In an interesting study in upstate Pennsylvania, Edward Rothstein questioned junior and senior high school students who were nondelinquent, and he did the same with delinquent boys. He found that the leading authority figures for all boys were, in rank order, mother, father, judges. The police, clergymen, and teachers were lowest for both delinquents and nondelinquents, but whereas nearly 70 percent of the nondelinquents rated the police as being important authority figures, only 31 percent of the delinquents did so. (18)

Once again, the right of the policeman to feel that he signifies society's moral authority is shown to be in conflict with that segment of the juvenile population which fails to see him in this role and which also is the group most likely to violate the law.

We do not have time to analyze special interest groups, juvenile gangs, minority populations, and so forth in further detail. Obviously, they each contain their own attitudes towards the police. The professional criminal who sees all life as a racket too often finds reinforcement for his view in the handout to the police. The informant for the police requires some moral compromises for the sake of expediency. The rioting strikers, the militant minorities, the drug pushers, and the friendly prostitutes form different subsocieties of response to the police. "If they're not with us, they're against us" may be a common and illogical perspective. They all contribute to the isolation and insularity which the police feel in relation to these clusters of clients.

CONCLUSION

In a society which permits as many alternatives and as much

---

18. Edward Rothstein, *An Analysis of Status Images as Perception Variables Between Delinquent and Nondelinquent Boys.* Ph.D. dissertation, New York University, 1961. See also, this same authors Attributes related to high social status: "A Comparison of the Perceptions of Delinquent and Nondelinquent boys," *J Social Problems*, 10:75-83.

personal freedom as does a democracy, deviance that takes the form of crime may be viewed as the price we pay for permitting these liberties. We should remember that there are many offenses committed by generally lawabiding citizens and that total efficiency in law enforcement would mean totalitarianism and would be unthinkable. The community of citizens cannot expect perfect security from wrongdoers. The role of the police should be viewed as an integral part of that effort to strengthen and sustain the chief values of our culture — freedom from attack on our persons and our property. They are part of our collectivity and need the confidence of the community in order to perform their roles. They should be freed from conflicts that occur in their tasks. They should be less required than they are to take solace in their own solidarity and should be made to feel more a part and reflection of the larger community of which they are in fact and in attitude. The police will always be a special agency of society, facing changes and having experiences most of us will never really know. They should be seen not apart from, but as part of, the community in which they work and live.

CHAPTER 12

TRADITIONAL POLICE ORGANIZATION: A PORTENT OF FAILURE?

Robert D. Pursley

TRADITIONAL para-military police organization has been with us for a long period of time. Myopically, police administrators tenaciously adhere to their deities of the scalar principle (chain of command), span of control and unity of command concepts with no provisions for new aspects of organizational research findings. This classical approach is almost entirely concerned with the organization's anatomy, its structure and the manner in which orders are transmitted through and results achieved.

Even the noted writers on police administration perpetuate this type of organizational construct with little or no innovative thought or adoption of the behavioral aspects of organizational theory. Under traditional police organization, it is the organization that molds the parameters of responsibility and action and the individual is required to fit, period! There exists absolutely no assessment of human resource potential available around which the organization is woven. Perhaps with the past caliber of personnel that was attracted to law enforcement the need for control and narrowly defined job description was the best arrangement; however, changes occurring today and in the near future will cause this type of organizational pattern to fail unless substantial, basic modifications are made.

Traditional police organization will fail in all but the smaller departments because of its inability to contend with two major factors; one of which is external to the organization and the other a burgeoning internal phenomenon. Both of these factors unless given careful consideration and prompt action will in the

---

NOTE: Reprinted from *Police* (Oct. 1971).

forseeable future cause increasing loss of public confidence and respect toward uniformed law enforcement and significant reduction in efficiency levels.

The operative external factor is society itself and its power to redefine aspects of the police role. Unquestionably, in some way law enforcement's role is being redefined somewhere while you read this article. The police are caught up in a vortex of changing attitudes which have a direct bearing on the police mission itself. Society is forcing law enforcement to reemphasize and modify its traditional role in light of newly generated standards and by closer scrutiny over police action through newly defined areas of accountability.

The operative internal factor is a rising level of expectation and self-concept among some police officers themselves. At this time these officers usually are the younger and more highly educated men who for the first time are starting to trickle into some uniformed law enforcement agencies. These young men are often over-achievers as attested by their educational attainments and they possess different motivational levels, needs, career aspirations, and role concepts than similar police applicants just a few years ago. It is with these men that the hopes for a new emergent police service of the future is founded.

When a man enters law enforcement with a high level of formal education it is to be expected that his perspectives will differ because he has been exposed to different frames of reference and experiences. This type of individual seeks out a career in police work not because it offers security, or because of personal lethargy or because he views the occupation of a policeman on a higher status than he could achieve elsewhere in another occupation due to his limited education and personal characteristics. They come because they, like many of the young college people today, feel a strong sense of committment to social activism and help. They often sense a different role concept of themselves as policeman with a closer identification with the idea of social involvement and help and less emphasis on what policemen traditionally have described their role namely as that of a law enforcer with all the connotations of punitive action so ascribed.

Here then, we have three forces operating. A tradition system of organization which is inflexible and unresponsive with its overpowering mechanistic system; societal pressure for redefinitions and reemphasis and the appearance of a new type of police officer. Together these act as our agents for a necessary catalysis of change.

What must law enforcement do in order to fulfill their future responsibilities? The immediate need is for a major reorganization of the traditional police department in a way that higher levels of efficiency, responsiveness and integration are met.

This can be done by recognizing a system approach while like any system must take cognizance of its particular elements. The immediate task is to redefine the role of the patrolman by increasing his parameters of responsibility and thus, his opportunities to become more involved in higher levels of police work. This approach is not feasible for all patrolmen, but for the new class of highly educated and motivated officer this is a necessity. To relegate this type of an individual to mundane tasks for a significant portion of his career will frustrate his need to achieve and self-actuate. Failure to recognize this need and adamant refusal by police administrators to realize that not all of their men are alike and to continue to insist that they all serve a lengthy apprenticeship regardless of education, former training etc. (which has long ago been given up by private industry) is the primary reason so many of these highly qualified individuals cannot be retained, and why it is so difficult to interest them in potential careers to begin with.

A few inroads are being made in this area. One which holds great promise for the future and which is a significant departure from traditional departmental organization is the new concept of the police agent.

Equally promising and even more innovative is the creation of agencies structured around crime control teams made up of highly educated and trained individuals who serve the dual function of behavioral specialists and law enforcement officers. The department is integrated around these teams who are assigned to work very closely with the residents of a particular geographic area within the agency's jurisdiction.

Agencies of the future must deemphasize the military standards and trappings and reorganize around a social service modulus of total integration within the department. This will mean a closer identification with a social work role which is anathema to the role concept possesed by most policemen today. Notwithstanding present aversion to this role, the police will be drawn in this direction, and to fulfill this responsibility they must be able to recruit and retain significantly higher standards of personnel. To make the nature of police work more meaningful and attractive police agencies must divest themselves of such tasks as licensing, parking control, etc. These tasks must be given to municipal agencies whose caliber of personnel and standards are lower, thereby freeing the police officer (or whatever he might be called in the future) to function at the more significant levels of crime prevention, behavioral modification, social service, apprehension, etc.

There are chiefs of police who will read this article and scoff; others will see the significance and realize that the day is approaching when far-reaching changes are going to be made in police organization to fulfill the increasingly complex role which our modern society thrusts upon them: A role which demands that law enforcement at the local and state levels be able to compete in attracting and retaining the best talent possible — but how long can we afford to wait?

CHAPTER 13

POLICE PLANNING: A STIMULUS FOR NEEDED ORGANIZATIONAL CHANGE

George T. Felkenes

THE concept of planning continues to increase in popularity. In fact, there appears to be a growing tendency to accept the notion that many of the problems of police agencies can be solved through use of management techniques which have proved successful in other organizations. As one who accepts the values of planning, I am specifically disturbed by such trends when they are not based upon a healthy skepticism and a reasoned commitment to a particular planning effort. I shall, therefore, examine some negative points before discussing various benefits derivable from a planning effort. Finally, we will look at the planning process itself.

SOME NEGATIVE ASPECTS OF PLANNING

In many ways, police agencies are very different from other organizations. For example, colleges and universities tend to hold that the institution exists to increase the contents of the sets of knowledge, aspirations, values, and mental skills associated with *each* individual involved in the academic process. Thus, we have students undergoing experiences intended to expand their knowledge and we have faculty engaged in research and scholarship to enlarge their own understandings. Even when academic activities are intended to contribute to goals more general than individual growth, these goals tend to be extrainstitutional. So we have a physicist working to add to knowledge in his discipline and we have an agronomist seeking methods of overcoming starvation, but such motivations also tend to be highly individualized. These are some of the realities in

---

Reprinted from *Police* (June, 1972).

a number of other professions, but they are not to be found to the same extent in most other public service organizations. Consider industry, for example; the preservation of the integrity and continuity of a company's own purposes are paramount. Individuals may relate to the organization to achieve personal fulfillment, but only in ways which contribute to organizational goals. Exceptions, when discovered, are usually not tolerated for very long.

I am definitely committed to the police and want to make every effort to increase the workability of their organization. This commitment is well worth the income lost by avoiding more lucrative pursuits. Now, suppose that under the struggle for institutional survival we decide to introduce planning and other management techniques. What we must recognize is that planning brings the tendency to focus attention upon institutional goals. It also introduces many concepts, activities, and uses for data which are strange to the police environment. By what it carries with it, planning is capable of transforming a police department into a completely new organizational configuration from that which previously existed. Planning is based partly on the new and innovative, often some of which has not been adequately tested and analyzed for workability. By precipitously adopting new ideas as part of the planning processes, the wise administration will always keep in mind that traditional operating methods will change. He must likewise weigh carefully the freedom given by perpetuation of traditionally adequate operations with some uncertainty and temporary restrictions found by adopting the new.

Another way of looking at it is that one purpose of planning itself has side-effects which may create unwanted change. All that can be done is to urge any planner to be constantly critical of what he is doing. In fact, one of the personal frustrations of the planner — namely, an inevitable agency resistance and skepticism — is actually an excellent means of protecting this critical attitude. What may appear to be recalcitrance is often a natural tendency to conserve that which is valued, and the planner should be sensitive enough to ferret out the meaning of such "conservatism."

Another important negative aspect of planning is the tendency to generate a *plan*. This plan is considered a blueprint of the future. It is the *way* the organization will go. Such plans are normally quickly forgotten, except perhaps when resurrected occasionally to demonstrate to outsiders (legislators, civic leaders, and budgetry analysts for example) that the institution *knows* its own purposes and methods of achieving them. While planning should be somewhat predictive, it should be so by revealing future possibilities and by getting people to use their imaginations. It would encourage people to think in terms of alternatives. The plans, rather than being a static blueprint, should be a "roadmap" which reveals numerous paths into the future. Planning should be open and dynamic and it should never tend to preclude the spontaneous creativity which is so important to institutional vitality.

Another danger inherent in some planning systems, such as those built upon computer-based information systems, is that a set of relationships is built into the system, often at great expense. When many thousands of dollars are spent in developing such a system, it is not easy to let go of it. Consequently, there can be a tendency to try to maintain the invariance of the relationships. To illustrate what I mean, take the fictitious overly-simplified example of the formula: "Patrol vehicle = the number of street miles X number of serious crimes in the particular area." In this simple formula you are free to insert a number of street miles and the number of serious crimes in order to determine the required vehicle density. My contention is that street miles may have some vague statistical meaning for traditional policing, but I would not be able to assign any meaningful value under a drastically modified and highly diverse urban setting. Now, imagine that the preceding formula has been highly elaborated. It is still based upon many traditional experiences and assumptions concerning the forms of relationships in a police agency. It has been very expensive to develop. Along comes some innovative thinking, creating new theories which do not fit this elaborate formula. What goes, the formula or the innovation? Ultimately, the formula will go, but probably not without some undesirable resistance.

The final point is that planning is hard work and that it creates new demands for both information and effort. Expansion of personnel and resources to accomplish successful planning may not be possible for many smaller departments, but there is always a price to be paid. The question to the answer is: "Will the benefits of planning offset the price?"

SOME BENEFITS OF PLANNING

Only you can answer the preceding question. I can, however, describe some of the possible benefits of planning one police agency is trying to realize.

In these days of conflict, job pressures, and competition for personnel among various police agencies, it is very easy to lose the silent people. In losing them, we lose their ideas and energy and the opportunity to give them relevance. A planning system can be designed to involve these people and to give agency relevance to their thinking and actions. When you look, you find these people among the students, practitioners, other departments' personnel, and with your own agency. At the same time, the planning effort can channel the energies and enthusiasms of the more aggressive people and groups within the department.

In focusing attention upon change and potential actions (i.e. because of its future-orientation) planning tends to intellectualize conflict. It gets people together to argue and discuss differences before they occur. This, it seems, is far superior to having an evolutionary process create unexpected conflict conditions; and it is also consistent with the traditional organizational commitment to rational processes.

Closely coupled to the aforestated benefit is what might be called the integrative function of planning. By this, I mean the bringing together of individuals, groups, efforts, and goals. Planning should tend to counteract the isolation of groups so common among bureaus, divisions and sections in a police department. The detective division, for example, does not communicate with the patrol division. The command, field, and administration personnel view themselves in separate ways. Distinctions are made between operational goals and administrative goals. Such distinctions may be valuable for some purposes, but they should not prevent people from interacting in meaningful ways. I believe that planning can be designed to remove these barriers.

Another important integrative benefit of planning is related to what we might call the community-relations function. An integrative planning system can contribute to increased understanding of both the organization functions and its external environment. Personnel officers, for example, can be encouraged to remain alert to social changes which may affect the operations of the community relation function as well as remaining aware of innovations in normal work techniques in the particular field of expertise. This process of organizational awareness might also be called a process of "searching the field" for new ideas, techniques and innovations. In an integrated planning program, organizational awareness can easily be made one of the steps in the planning activity. For example, given the opportunity to interact in new ways with command and field persons, the personnel officer can become acquainted with some of the realities of agency needs. Patrol leadership decisions also can lead to a greater appreciation of the personnel selection methods. Thus, operations personnel can be given the chance to develop insight into the fundamental administrative goal of preserving the organizational equilibrium by careful utilization of personnel resources.

One of the principal reasons for planning is to introduce conscious intelligence into the change process. This puts the department in the position of being able to pursue change rather than being pursued by it. Anticipating change means that the agency need not merely react to every chance event, but rather that it can establish a creative balance between intelligent choice and evolution.

Once the alternative departmental plans are developed, they can be used to design various support programs; such as community relations, capital construction, public relations, and personnel development and recruitment. They can also be used for monitoring program activities, for allocating space and for budgeting. In other words, planning can serve the purposes of "effective management;" but "effective management" may be secondary to the opportunities for leadership which can be created by planning.

Police Planning

In conclusion, some of the goals of planning as I see them from the perspective of an educator viewing a police department are:

1) To bring people together in performance of significant actions and, in general, to develop an integrative force within the agency.
2) To provide a basis for monitoring programs, allocating resources and using information.
3) To provide for experiences and exchange of information which serve to create mutual understanding in the various groups within the organization.
4) To associate decisions with people having the information and expertise to best make them.
5) To seek out and solicit the thinking of people from all groups within the department.
6) To create a method for using mathematical and computer techniques in ways which support, not supplant, the full range of human intelligence and aspirations.
7) To provide guidance for future action without destroying the possibility of rapid departmental evolution.
8) To encourage investigation of the behavioral aspects of administration to assist in satisfying human needs, goals, and desires.

THE PLANNING PROCESS — AN OVERVIEW

There are many steps in the planning process as used in most police departments. Details are often described in departmental manuals. However, no attempt is made here to cover the details, but rather to set forth a broad general overview of the planning process.

The first general step is to prepare some of the background information needed for the planning. In most cases, budget projections should be developed, personnel figures for the various divisions projected in detail, and space needs projected. I call these numbers "planning parameters" or "optimal desires." It must be emphasized, however, that many agencies will not have the data base, manpower, or computer capability support to make projections as reliable as those generated in the large police departments. In the system, as envisioned by me, the "shaky" data is not critical, as the developing of alternatives is an answer to incomplete or inaccurate assumptions.

The next step is that of orienting the department to the new concepts, language and processes involved in planning. Most people will have difficulty in appreciating the purpose of planning or the importance of making much effort to understand it. One approach would be to conduct a two- or three-day workshop for all the command staff and chief administrative personnel. This workshop would include several talks and some simulation of the planning process. Although a fair degree of enthusiasm can be generated during such a workshop, one cannot expect to have communicated full and lasting understanding. If an expectation that something is about to happen is created, and the notion that what is about to happen is not undesirable, label the workshop a success.

The third general step is to organize the personnel into working groups. A central planning committee consisting of key departmental personnel should be formed. This committee sets the parameters, reviews plans and makes recommendations to the Chief. A very important innovation in the planning process is to create a number of subplanning committees consisting of interest groups within the department, patrol officers, and perhaps unions. These committees conceivably do the actual program planning. A planning office must also be formed to do the staff work involved in coordinating the planning effort and in making calculations and analyses of plans.

The fourth step is to set up a provocative situation for each of the planning committees and to record the reactions in a uniform way. The provocation (or system perturbation) is amply provided by the parameters given to the committees. Each committee is told that they must design a program which does not generate more departmental resources and use more money or space than the central planning committee says they will have in five years. They may also be given other constraints which are non-quantifiable and are issued as statements, such as: "You cannot plan a public relations program," or "You must develop three general training courses to show the relationship of your division to other divisions in the department." Sometimes I suspect that inadequate data will be an advantage in that it often created a strong enough reaction for attention to be captured. One important purpose of the planning, however, is to get the committees thinking the terms of *alternatives*. Consequently, they also should be told that they are free to generate as many alternative programs as they wish. This instruction serves both as a means of getting alternatives and also as a safety valve.

The fifth stage is to analyze the plans to put them together in a comprehensible form. During this state the central planning committee reviews all plans and seeks trustee approval.

the sixth stage, following the approval of the Chief, is to design implementation programs — including the seeking of funds and creation of time schedules.

The final stage is to use the plans as part of the budgeting process and to provide for their annual review and modification.

In the final analysis planning involves a major effort. Since the program budget is becoming more popular as a method of management decision making, it must be remembered that police program planning assimilates into it the budgetary processes. Consequently, by implementing a program planning approach, the former line-item budget is cast into a different mold to permit a more rational decision at the various organizational levels. Basically, the purposes of the program approach (i.e. creating thought stimulation, utilization of intelligence, involvement of outside groups, increased communication, and creation of an orientation toward the future), creates a system oriented toward people as an integral part of planning. As most executives in police work realize, planning is done in an environment of probabilities, possibilities, and uncertainties. Precise information is often non-existent and definite answers are unavailable. To overcome those hindrances, there must be a willingness to intelligently guess and explore alternatives. Program planning permits this and reemphasizes that there is no such thing as *The Plan*.

CHAPTER 14

POLICE UNIONISM: IMPROVING POLICE AGENCY AND EMPLOYEE PERFORMANCE THROUGH COLLECTIVE BARGAINING

John H. Burpo

IN January, 1973, the Police Foundation funded a project for the IACP Public Safety Labor Relations Center. One of the programs in the project is to develop management responses to police unions that would foster harmonious labor-management relationships within police agencies. This project calls for the development of responses to such labor-management problems as divisiveness between line and command personnel, lack of participation by employees in the decision-making process, and communication gaps between labor and management.

One of the major areas of concern in the IACP project is the improvement of public administrators' collective bargaining techniques. The Labor Relations Center is developing management strategies that can be applied in collective bargaining negotiations to enhance the public employer's bargaining position, and contract clauses that can be used as guidelines to attain a bargaining contract with optimum benefits for employees, yet one that retains management's power to operate the police agency.

One collective bargaining strategy the Public Safety Labor Relations Center is examining closely is public employers negotiating over policies and programs that will improve the overall performance of police agencies and the performance standards of individual police officers. The specific objective of this part of the project is to develop the collective bargaining process for use in raising agency and employee performance

NOTE: Reproduced from *The Police Chief* magazine, February and April issues, with permission of the International Association of Chiefs of Police.

standards. This article will focus on collective bargaining as a mechanism for achieving this objective.

HISTORICAL PERSPECTIVE

The term "collective bargaining" is used to describe a process whereby an employer and employees represented through a recognized union negotiate a formal written agreement over wages, hours, and terms and conditions of employment. (1) Collective bargaining has been a long established practice in the private sector, where the Wagner Act and the Taft-Hartley Act, passed in 1935 and 1947 respectively, created mandatory guidelines for private industry employers and labor unions to follow in the pursuit of improved employee benefits. (2)

Police departments and other public agencies have not had the collective bargaining experience which exists in the private sector. For many years, resistance existed in state legislatures against the extension of collective bargaining rights to public employees. The rationale for this resistance was that collective bargaining would infringe upon the sovereignty of governmental bodies charged with the establishment of wages, hours, and terms and conditions of employment. This article was reinforced by a number of state court decisions denying collective bargaining rights to public employees. (3)

The sovereignty argument lost its persuasive effect in the sixties, however, and several states enacted collective bargaining legislation for public employees. Among the leaders in extending this right to employees were New York State, (4) Wisconsin, (5) and the federal government. (6) Since this initial legislation, other state, county, and municipal governments have recognized the advantage to stabilizing labor-management relationships in the public sector through collective bargaining. There are now

---

1. See "A Dictionary of Arbitration," American Arbitration Association, 1970, pp. 49-50.
2. See 29, U.S.C.A., 141 *et. seq.*
3. See, for example, *Weakley County Municipal Electric System v. Vick*, 309, S.W. 2d 792 (1958).
4. Conden-Waldin Act, sec. 108. Civil Service Law. This legislation was amended in 1967 as the Tayler Law.
5. Subchapter IV, Chap. 2, Wisconsin Statutes, Sec. 111.70, enacted 1959.
6. Executive Order 10988, issued by President Kennedy in 1962.

thirty-five states that permit collective bargaining for some or all public employees by virtue of statute, court decision, or attorney-general opinion. (7) Twenty-seven of these states offer this right to police employees. (8) In the absence of state legislation, a number of county and city governments have extended their employees collective bargaining rights through legislative enactment.

COLLECTIVE BARGAINING DISTINCTIONS

There are several distinctions between collective bargaining in the public and private sectors that become immediately apparent. Several labor commentators have noted that private industry labor relations operates in an *economic* environment, where labor disputes are resolved on the basis of a decision by the employer and union as to whether the costs of agreement or disagreement are more economically feasible, e.g., the employer might decide the losses incurred from shutting the plant down due to a strike would be less in the long run than granting employees a fifty cents per hour pay raise. (9) On the other hand, public sector labor relations operates in a *political* environment, where the costs to the employer and unions are more closely tied to the presence or absence of support by the public, which is expressed at the ballot box.

Another manifest distinction is the centralized legal structure of private sector labor relations versus a more decentralized situation in the public sector. Private industry is regulated by one law — the Taft-Hartley Act. In public employment, however, there is a proliferation of collective bargaining legislation, with each state establishing different criteria for regulating the relationship between public employers and employees.

Another important distinction between the two sectors is the nature of the entity called the "employer." In private industry, the union deals with a person, or group of persons, who represent one

---

7. See "Summary of State Policy Regulations for Public Sector Labor Relations," U.S. Department of Labor, Labor-Management Services Administration, Division of Public Employee Labor Relations.
8. *Ibid.*
9. Wellington & Winter, *The Unions and the Cities*, (Brookings Institution, 1971), pp. 7-33.

employer. Therefore, all objectives sought by the union must be accomplished through dealings with this one entity. In the public sector, however, there are many management entities that can legitimately be called the "employer," including the police chief, director of public safety, city manager, personnel director, budget director, civil service commission, mayor, and council. Unless these employers take a coordinated approach in their relationship with the police union, the union will be able to accomplish objectives by going to one entity when another is not receptive to a particular union goal, or playing off one against the other. For example, if the police union is attempting to achieve two-man squad cars for all patrol assignments and fails to achieve this objective through collective bargaining with the city manager, it might then attempt to influence the mayor to force a change, especially where this politician owes a debt to the union because of its support during the last election.

One more subtle distinction between the two labor sectors is the relative equality of bargaining expertise between labor and management. The long history of collective bargaining in the private sector has resulted in both the unions and management developing the expertise necessary to come to the negotiating table on a relatively equal basis. Private sector unions generally have the financial resources available to hire leading labor negotiators. Employers in private industry often assign the responsibilities of collective bargaining and other labor relations matters to a separate division within the organization created solely for that purpose.

There is a noticeable disparity in public employment, however, between labor and management bargaining expertise, with police unions holding a decided advantage over public employers. This disparity becomes quickly apparent by examining police collective bargaining contracts. In many cities operating under tight budget restraints, management negotiators have given police employees pay raises significantly higher than other city employees, as well as other economic benefits, including educational incentive pay; time and one-half for overtime, off duty court time, and call back work; and shift differential pay.

In the area of negotiating over management rights, this

negotiating disparity is even more noticeable. One recent police collective bargaining contract contains a clause requiring that the union *agree* to any changes in working conditions during the life of the contract. Another contract form a New England city mandates pure seniority for specified job assignments and promotions. Several police collective bargaining contracts include a restrictive "Policeman's Bill of Rights," which deprives the police chief of several essential powers necessary to conduct an efficient internal investigation, e.g., require an officer under investigation to make a statement, take a polygraph, and answer questions relating to criminal matters. (10) This police union advantage in collective bargaining can be attributed to several factors, including the reliance on private industry union bargaining expertise and the earlier recognition by police employees of collective bargaining as the best means for regulating labor-management relations.

MANAGEMENT DEMANDS FOR AGENCY/EMPLOYEE IMPROVEMENT

One other significant reason for the disparity in labor-management negotiating expertise is the general conception among public administrators of the collective bargaining process. Most administrators view the bargaining process as one in which the union makes the demands upon management, and management only responds to those demands. Under this conception of bargaining, the union asks for x, y, and z; and the employer responds by stating that the city can give one-half of x, all of y, and nothing of z.

Viewing collective bargaining from the narrow perspective that the employer's role is to merely give, and the union's to take, is to have a gross misconception of the bargaining process. *Collective bargaining is a two-way process, and public employers not only can, but should begin to make management demands on police unions to the same extent that unions engage in this practice.*

Management demands are formulated in order to achieve

---

10. See PSLR, FEATURES: 1-60, for a discussion of this point.

employer bargaining objectives. Management objectives can take many forms, including the elimination of undesirable clauses in the old contract, e.g. a seniority provision for job assignments; increasing employee contributions to insurance or pension plans; or eliminating employee practices that are damaging to the city, e.g. employees' wearing police uniforms on off duty jobs. These objectives, in many instances, can be achieved through a bargaining strategy known as a "trade-off," in which the union accedes to the management demand in return for a concession by the employer of a union bargaining objective.

One form of management bargaining demand that has not been recognized in most jurisdictions, and where it has, put to limited use, is the demand to improve the police agency's standard of performance — i.e. productivity — and to improve individual employee performance standards. An example of management demand to improve agency performance would be the civilization of clerical, desk, and dispatching positions, thereby allowing officers previously assigned to these tasks to be placed on the street for patrol duty. An illustrative management demand to improve individual employee performance would be a requirement to be placed in the collective bargaining contract requiring every officer on the department to annually qualify with his firearm on the firing range.

ADVANTAGES TO BARGAINING OVER AGENCY/EMPLOYEE PERFORMANCE

Most programs tied to the improvement of police agency and employee performance represent a significant change from the status quo. The general response by police unions to changes from the status quo is resistance. An LEAA study completed by Dr. Hervey Juris and Dr. Peter Feiulle on police unions amply demonstrates instances where police unions have resisted such change concepts as civilization, education incentive, lateral entry, master patrolman, and minority recruitment. (11) Without placing a value on the desirability or undesirability of these programs, they do represent a departure from old management

---

11. Wellington & Winter, *The Unions and the Cities*, (Brookings Institution, 1971). pp. 7-3.

practices and, therefore, an attempt by police management to improve the agency through the change process. The union's resistance to programs of this nature is predictable in light of its role as the protector of present membership interests.

Union resistance to programs geared toward improving agency or employee performance can be eliminated, or at the very least, reduced, by management negotiators placing these programs on the bargaining table and negotiating them into the collective bargaining contract. Union resistance is eliminated or reduced because the contract mandates the unions *and* employees' agreement to the new program and, therefore, their cooperation. The failure of the union or employees to cooperate in supporting the program will result in a direct violation of the collective bargaining contract which is enforceable by the city filing an unfair labor practice before a labor commission, a grievance before an arbitrator, or an injunction in court as provided by local contract and statutory law.

Besides assuring union cooperation, or nonresistance, bargaining over programs related to improvement of agency/employee performance has the advantage of subjecting the programs to bilateral scrutiny. Collective bargaining is a process of discussion between labor and management, and any program of this nature would undoubtedly merit a great deal of attention and discussion between the parties. Bilateral discussion of new management ideas has the advantage of giving employees, through their union in this instance, a feeling of having a stake in the organization and of having had an opportunity to express viewpoints. This approach can both buttress employee morale and give the union a more positive view of management, thereby improving the labor-management, environment in the police department. It should be noted that subjecting programs related to agency/employee performance to bilateral discussion at the bargaining table does not signify that management is giving up its administrative power. If the union makes counterproposals on the program that are not acceptable, the management negotiator can either state that the union demand is unacceptable or withdraw the management program from the table.

The bargaining strategy for achieving management demand

related to agency/employee performance is simple — the demand is tied to a union demand that has high priority on the union's bargaining objectives. The management negotiator can make it clear that the union can only achieve its bargaining objective by acceding to the management program. If the union objective is economical, there is an obvious financial inducement for its agreeing to the management performance demand.

DISADVANTAGES TO BARGAINING OVER AGENCY/EMPLOYEE PRODUCTIVITY

Two disadvantages to bargaining over police agency and employee performance have been expressed by labor commentators. Many spokesmen for public employers argue that only economic issues should be negotiated, with issues related to management rights, or "prerogatives," being kept off the bargaining table. There is a fear among many public employment negotiators that bargaining over management rights issues can only lead to the police union wresting administrative control away from management; and therefore, agency or employee performance standards should be adopted unilaterally by the employer independent of collective bargaining.

This argument has several weaknesses. First, public administrators, who can no longer hide behind the piety that "management prerogatives" are nonnegotiable in collective bargaining statutes, specify that the scope of negotiable issues includes "terms and conditions of employment," a phrase that has been interpreted by many state labor commissions to encompass such management issues as promotions, job assignments, and discipline. (12) The term "management prerogative" is not a valid concept in today's labor relations arena. It can be better expressed as a power that management has been able to hold onto and the union has not taken away through collective bargaining.

Some police union leaders are equally disinclined to bargain

---

12. *Professional Policemen's Protective Association of Milwaukee, Plaintiff v. City of Milwaukee, Defendant*, 62, LC 67, 457 (1970).

over agency and employee performance standards. The argument made by labor leaders is that employee economic benefits should not be tied to agency and employee performance standards because this policy will only antagonize employees, whose sole concern in bargaining is the achievement of improved economic benefits. This argument raises the suspicion that the union is seeking to achieve a maximum of benefits from management with no expectation of a return on the investment. It would not appear to be unreasonable for management to take the position that it has the right to expect employees to perform their duties in a manner that will both improve the work production of the police agency and each employee, and to correlate this expectation with some increase in economic benefits sought by the union. Management is, in this instance, trying to emphasize that if the union expects economic increases for its membership, there must be an improvement in performance output by employees.

Public employers attempting to improve police agency performance are today applying a technique called *productivity*. Before examining how productivity can be applied to the collective bargaining process, it is important to first examine the concept itself. Productivity has long been applied in private sector management. The definition of productivity in its broadest sense is "the efficiency with which output is produced by the resources utilized." (13)

Productivity is simply the overall performance standard of the employer. The standard measure of productivity in private industry is the ratio of outputs, such as goods or services, to inputs such as labor, capital, or energy. Private employers have long tried to bargain wages (i.e. output) on the basis of employee accomplishment of work assignments (i.e. input).

There has been a long-standing negative attitude in the public sector toward the concept of productivity. This attitude is based on two premises. First, the public sector is not able to compete financially with private industry for the services of the best people available. A second objection to public sector productivity has been that many forms of public employment performance are not

---

13. Jerome Mark, "Meanings and Measures of Productivity," *Public Administration Review*, Vol. 32. p. 748.

measurable in quantifiable terms. For example, it is not a simple matter to assess the matter in which a police officer is able to achieve the cooperation and respect of the public in performing his duties. (14)

These objections to productivity in the public sector no longer appear persuasive. Many public employers have begun to realize that high quality public service can only be achieved by competing with the same labor market used by the private sector. This realization is reflected in the proportional increase of public employee salaries over private industry employees in the past decade. (15) Also, a number of jurisdictions are discovering that there *are* quantifiable measurements of employee performance in the public sector, and that there are other concepts independent of the measurement of performance for the improvement of agency productivity. The New York City productivity program, discussed below, is an outstanding example of a successful public sector effort to improve agency productivity.

The more contemporary view of productivity in public employment was best expressed on 1972 by Peter Peterson, former secretary of commerce, when he stated that:

Improving productivity in the public sector of the U.S. economy is fundamental to the success of the current federal effort to create through a variety of policy initiatives an environment that will spur a higher rate of productivity growth — over the long-term — in the economy as a whole.

It is fundamental, first, because the public sector is such a large and rapidly growing part of the whole. But it is crucial, also, because no government program to encourage higher rates of productivity growth in the private sector will succeed if government itself sets a bad example (or, because of inadequate measurement or popular mythology, is widely thought of as a bad example). (16)

---

14. See Ed Hamilton, "Productivity: The New York City Approach," *Public Administration Review*, Vol. 32, p. 785, for a further discussion of these.
15. See Bureau of Labor Statistics, Department of Labor.
16. Peter Peterson, "Productivity in Government and the American Economy," *Public Administration Review*, Vol. 32, p. 740.

PRODUCTIVITY IN NEW YORK CITY

During his tenure as mayor of New York City, John V. Lindsay made the decision to pay employees on a competitive basis with private industry. This course of action was accompanied by the correlative decision to demand from New York City employees the same high standards of performance that any firm in private industry would require. The deputy mayor of New York City, Edward Hamilton, expressed the new policy of the city of New York in 1972: "Public employees have the right to comparable salaries, but the taxpayer has an equal right to comparable productivity." (17)

In order to achieve the goal of improving *agency* productivity in New York City, management created a fourphase program for the improvement of both the quality and quantity of work per dollar by city employees. (18)

1. *Reducing unit costs.* Where particular jobs could be measured in quantifiable terms, the city attempted to increase the number of tasks performed on some measurable unit basis. (i.e., per man-day), with an accompanying reduction in cost. Three types of city employment obviously susceptible to quantifiable measurement include license inspectors (i.e. premises inspected per man-day), and sanitation workers (i.e. man-days per ton of refuse removed).

Police performance is not generally susceptible to simple measurement since many police tasks are judged on their qualitative rather than quantitative features. New York City, however, has been able to establish some criteria for police performance that can be measured quantitatively and which, through the development of new management programs, have resulted in increased police department productivity. (19)

    a) A reduction in the manpower that accounts for felony arrests.

    b) The increase of felony arrests per felony complaint

---

17. Note 2, *supra*.
18. *Ibid.*, p. 787.
19. "City of New York Productivity Program," published by the City of New York, 1972.

Specialization of detective assignments resulted in a 5 percent increase in felony arrests per felony complaint.
c) In narcotics cases, an increase in the percentage of drugs and money seized per arrest. An organized narcotics crime unit, concentrating on the top distribution of drugs, was able to increase the narcotic seizure percentage by 55 percent, and the money seizures by threefold.
d) Reduction in the span of control between sergeants and patrolmen. An increase of 450 sergeants resulted in a reduction of the span of control from 13.1 to 10.1.
e) The reduction of arrest processing time. The centralization of book-procedures resulted in a two-hour reduction in arrest processing time, for a savings of thirty-five man-years.
f) The reduction of patrol time and overtime. The assignment of an arrest processing officer to handle duties previously performed by the arresting officer resulted in a 75 percent reduction in lost patrol time, a 14 percent reduction in overtime, and a savings of forty-five man-years.

2. *Improving the deployment of personnel resources.* Since it is difficult to measure many aspects of some public employment services, especially police and fire, the second phase of the New York City productivity program concentrates on insuring that personnel resources will be available at the times and places when they are most needed. One of the notable police programs to achieve the maximization of personnel resources is the SPRINT system, in which a computer controls the dispatching of calls for service on the basis of present deployment, the work load situation, and the nature of the call. (20) This system has the multiple advantages of assigning calls on a statistical rather than random basis, reducing response time to calls for service, supplying the responding officer with information relevant to the call, and providing management with weekly information (as compared to prior monthly reports) of crime data and patrol car utilization. Another program to maximize the allocation of personnel resources in the New York City Police Department is the civilianization program, whereby civilians are hired to

---

20. Note 2, *supra*, p. 791, for a discussion of the SPRINT system.

perform clerical, administrative, and planning functions, thereby relieving sworn officers for street duty.

3. *Improvement of government processing procedures.* The third phase of the New York City productivity program consists of the imaginative use of computers. (21) Citywide application of this program has included the use of computers (and accompanying displacement of six clerical personnel) for the processing of welfare checks, payroll checks, tax billing, and parking violations. In addition to the SPRINT system, computers have been applied in the police department for scheduling and increased data bank on criminals and budgeting.

4. *The development of new technologies.* New York City has been active in developing new technological advances that improve the quality of service to citizens. (22) Two significant technological improvements include the discovery of methadone as a form of treatment for addicts and a plasticized rapid water for fire fighting. One difficulty with this phase of the productivity program is the excessive costs incurred in the research and development process, which simply cannot be borne by municipal governments. Private industry has also taken little initiative in technological improvements for city governments due to the limited market. New York City feels that the federal government should take a more active role in the funding of technology projects for local governments.

PRODUCTIVITY BARGAINING

The concept of productivity has a bright future in law enforcement, as evidenced by the experience in New York City. There is one major obstacle blocking a successful police productivity program, however, and that is resistance by employees and their primary spokesman, the union. A recognized technique for reducing or eliminating employee/union resistance to new programs that improve overall performance is called *productivity bargaining.* Productivity bargaining has been defined as "the negotiation and implementation of formal

---

21. *Ibid.*, p. 792, for a discussion of this concept.
22. *Ibid.*, p. 794.

collective bargaining agreements which stipulate changes in work rules and practices with the objective of achieving increased productivity and reciprocal worker gains." (23)

The basic objective of productivity bargaining is to improve an industry or agency's general performance level through negotiating innovative programs *into* the contract, and programs or policies which defeat productivity *out* of the contract. In return for management achieving these objectives, the employees are given a reciprocal economic benefit in the contract.

New York City has attempted to refine this concept even further. In 1970, the city announced that productivity standards for each city department would be established, and failure of employees to meet these norms would result in no salary increase at the next contract negotiations above a cost of living raise. (24) The philosophy of this approach is that employees would work harder to achieve the performance standards set for each agency.

The city does not actually bargain over productivity standards for a particular agency. Instead, the city bargains over the *right* to set these standards. This objective is achieved by bargaining over a contract clause offered at the initiative of the city, which reads as follows:

> The union recognizes the city's right under the New York City Collective Bargaining Law to establish and/or revise performance standards or norms notwithstanding the existence of prior performance levels, norms, or standards. Such standards, developed by usual work measurement procedures, may be used to determine acceptable performance levels, prepare work schedules, and to measure the performance of each employee or group of employees.

This clause is merely a glorified management rights clause, but it does achieve the goal of giving the city the unilateral right to establish productivity standards for each agency.

There is no question that productivity bargaining in the New York style can be applied successfully to those jobs where

---

23. Chester Newland, "Personnel Concerns in Government Productivity Improvement," *Public Administration Review*, Vol. 32, p. 808.
24. Note 2, *supra*, p. 786.

performance can be measured quantitatively. For example, the city can determine the tonnage of garbage collected by sanitation workers this year versus last year; and if there has been no appreciable change, refuse to award a salary increase above a cost of living raise.

There are two crucial distinctions in police productivity programs that militate against the New York City concept of productivity bargaining. First, the program is geared toward the improvement of measurable statistics that will elevate the overall performance of the agency — or, in the converse, programs that have no relationship to the individual performances of employees. The second observable distinction is that there can really be no productivity without the creative thinking and application of sound administrative techniques by *management*. The impact of employees and the police union on the success or failure of any police productivity program is minimal.

For example, the success or failure of anticrime patrol teams established in all precincts of the city (i.e., whether or not there will be reduction in the percentage of manpower who make the greatest number of felony arrests) is not keyed to the individual performances of employees for two reasons. First, the most crucial factor in the success of reducing the percentage of employees who make the greatest number of arrests is the creativity of *management* in developing a patrol concept to achieve this objective, and then effectively deploying that patrol force. Also, an emphasis by management on employees increasing the number of arrests would create obvious public relations problems so this approach could not be sanctioned. Contrast the importance of individual employee achievement for police productivity programs with a sanitation department productivity, where each employee must make a concerted effort to collect X tons of garbage per year for the agency to meet its standard.

It would appear immensely unfair to the police bargaining unit as a whole to deny any more than a cost of living increase on the basis of productivity programs that fail to measure up to established norms, since these programs have no relationship to individual employee performance and place the major, if not entire, burden on police management for their success. In actual practice, it would appear that the City of New York does not bargain over measurable statistics with the New York City PBA. Instead, the city uses productivity bargaining as a means of paying the union for its cooperation in the implementation of programs that are going to signify a radical departure from past practice and, therefore to draw considerable opposition from employees. Some labor commentators might suggest that this approach constitutes "buying off" the union, but even if looked at from this perspective, the New York City approach has the positive effect of achieving the smooth implementation of programs that will change departmental policies and programs, and hopefully, result in improved agency performance.

SOME CONCLUDING OBSERVATIONS ON IMPROVING AGENCY PERFORMANCE

The New York City productivity program is instructive because it emphasizes that overall police agency performance *can* be achieved through a sophisticated use of the bargaining process. The city has gained the cooperation of the PBA on many new controversial programs through correlating salary increases with the program. The ultimate effect is to gain the union's, and thereby the employees', cooperation in implementing these programs. New York City has achieved some important programs through this process, including new patrol tactics, reorganization, civilianization, and computerization.

It should be noted, however, that the New York City program emphasizes bargaining over the *right* to establish productivity standards, and not the standard itself. This approach simply provides management with the unilateral right to create new productivity programs, which is workable in the absence of union or employee resistance. Where the union objects to a new productivity program, however, management in many jurisdictions no longer has the *power* to implement the program unilaterally. Irrespective of the management right granted in the contract clause (i.e., the right to set productivity standards), the union can manipulate other facets of the government process to effectively reduce successful implementation of the program, such as appeal to a political body or officeholder, lawsuit, or referendum.

In this situation, a more sophisticated use of the collective bargaining process is necessary, and police administrators and other public officials involved in bargaining are urged to observe the following principles:

1. Where a new program or policy is being contemplated that represents a severe departure from past practice, and
2. Where there is likely to be resistance from the employee and the union, and
3. Where the union has internal power to the extent that the program cannot be unilaterally implemented by management, then
4. *Management should place the new productivity program itself on the bargaining table and tie this program to a high priority economic item of the union.*

These principles can be applied to any positive program which is geared to the improvement of the agency. Some of the possibilities include lateral entry, minority recruitment, reorganization, civilianization, and the master patrolman. This bargaining techique would have application for *negative* programs as well, such as elimination of a work rule that hinders management (e.g., a contract clause allowing only three shifts, with no flexibility therefore, for a fourth shift during peak crime hours). City government negotiators and police chiefs can undoubtedly think of many other applications of the bargaining technique.

There are three problems with bargaining over productivity programs which should be foreseen by management negotiators. First, once a productivity program is placed on the bargaining table, it can be subject to change through negotiating initiatives by the union. If the city feels that the union counterdemands are unacceptable and will result in an unsuccessful program, the city will have no choice but to withdraw it from the table. However, a responsible police union will most likely not attempt to sabotage a productivity program by making unreasonable counterdemands for two reasons — this form of bargaining opens the door for bilateral policy making, a hopeful sign for the union, and there is a desirable economic incentive that the union will receive in return for consenting to the new program.

A second problem will be that once the productivity program is in the contract, there might be a need for an adjustment in the program that will be restricted by the language in the contract. For example, if the contract calls for the hiring of ten civilians for clerical positions, and a subsequent determination is made by management to hire twelve civilians, this change could not be made until the next contract is negotiated, or the union approves such a change, thereby leaving management in a difficult position. Therefore, the city must negotiate a clause in the productivity program stating that management reserves the right to make adjustments in the program. If the union objects to this clause on the basis that it once again gives the management unilateral right to make productivity changes, management can offer a meet-and-confer clause whereby the city and the union must discuss any changes in the program prior to their implementation, with management still reserving the right of ultimate decision making.

One final problem is that placing a productivity program in a collective bargaining contract will subject it to the grievance procedure where the procedure permits grievances over interpretation, application, or enforcement of the contract. This situation could result in many harassing grievances over the substance of productivity programs. For example, if the program calls for an anticrime team to be created for the purpose of patrol in high crime areas, the union could file a grievance where the chief places the team in a low crime area for a purpose such as surveillance of a particular criminal suspect. Therefore, the productivity program should be excluded from the scope of grievable issues under the contract, except where the program affects the employment rights of one individual employee (i.e., the civilianization program is being used to put several older police officers out on the street as punishment for their union activities).

IMPROVING INDIVIDUAL EMPLOYEE PERFORMANCE

Productivity bargaining is a concept that applies to the improvement of the entire agency. The principles of productivity bargaining can be applied as well to the improvement of the performance of individual employees. City management can collectively bargain with the union over the right to set individual performance standards for employees as is done in New York City, or in the alternative, bargain over the performance standards themselves as suggested previously in this article. As with productivity bargaining, negotiating over employee performance standards will reduce or eliminate union/employee resistance to the implementation of new programs and will encourage bilateral decision making on performance standards, a positive benefit to both labor and management.

There are a variety of programs that can be established through bargaining that will improve employee performance. The Kalamazoo, Michigan, experience with this technique is illustrative. One bargaining objective of the City of Kalamazoo during negotiations in 1972 was an annual firearms qualification policy for all police officers. The city reasoned that it is essential for police officers to handle their firearms adequately for the safety of both the public and other police officers. This policy was discussed with negotiators for the Fraternal Order of Police (i.e., bargaining agent for patrolmen, detectives, and technicians) and agreement was reached that a firearms qualification policy was necessary. The resulting contract clause reflected this agreement.

Section 3: In order to ensure the safety of fellow officers and the protection of the citizenry, each sworn officer shall qualify at a minimum score of seventy-five (75%) percent of the total possible score on the course of fire that is being currently employed for training purposes. The Employer agrees to study the possibility of implementing a training course of fire that realistically trains the officer for instinct, combat situations, and requires the officer to make a mental decision as to whether he should shoot. The course(s) of fire may employ all of the above, or separate courses may be conducted to cover the areas of instinct, combat, and decision, separately. Before such course(s) of fire is implemented, it shall be the subject of at least one (1) Special Conference.

(a). Each sworn officer shall qualify at the minimum score on the course of fire currently used for training purposes at least once each year, on or before September 30, and shall do so with his issued departmental firearm. In order to assist officers so that they are able to meet the qualification, the Employer agrees to provide a reasonable amount of firearm instruction by one of the certified firearm instructors of the department (certified meaning certified by the National Rifle Association, and the Michigan Law Enforcement Training Council) during 'open range days' for officers without pay during off duty hours. An officer desirous of such firearm instruction, shall notify the Chief or his designated representative. If an officer does not qualify on or before September 30 of each year, he shall be given a reasonable amount of additional firearm instruction by one of the certified firearm instructors for such purpose by the Employer.

(b). Officers who are unable to qualify, except for a temporary or permanent physical disability, shall be subject to suspension until such time as they actually qualify. The purpose of such suspension is to allow the officer a concentrated period of time in which to practice, receive additional instruction and therefore meet the qualification.

Other employee performance standards established through the collective bargaining process include the following:

1. *Physical qualifications.* A requirement that each employee pass a physical examination, or meet a minimum physical agility test and weight requirement.
2. *Educational qualifications.* A requirement that officers seeking promotion must have achieved a specified number of college credit hours, or for supervisors, a requirement that these officers attend college education courses oriented toward police supervision.
3. *Off-duty time.* A requirement that employees not work certain types of secondary employment due to conflicts of interest (e.g., private detective agencies, use of police uniforms in security work), or a requirement that officers devote a specified amount of off-duty time each year to in-service training.

4. *Squad cars*. A requirement that officers keep their squad cars clean or pass an annual driver qualification test especially designed for police driving situations.

As with the concept of productivity bargaining, police chiefs and management negotiators can think of many other applications of this principle to the bargaining process.

One criticism raised against bargaining over employee performance standards is that the failure of an employee to measure up to standards results in punitive action (i.e., disciplinary action) which constitutes a negative approach to improving employee performance. For example, in the Kalamazoo police contract provision on firearm qualification, the failure of an officer to qualify will result in suspension until such time as he qualifies. Unquestionably, when an employee fails to meet a required standard such as a firearm qualification, corrective action is necessary. However, this remedial action by the employer is going to be applied irrespective of whether the performance standard is a part of the collective bargaining contract or simply a unilateral policy established by management. Both private industry and public sector employers have traditionally used discipline as the tool for correcting employee performance deficiencies. This argument therefore overlooks the broad application of discipline as the standard mechanism for improvement of employees, whether through bargaining or outside the bargaining process.

The application of discipline to an employee for failure to measure up to required standards does not, however, necessarily have to be punitive. Reprimands, suppressions, and discharge are not the only remedies available to the employer in this situation. More *positive* forms of corrective action can and should be taken to insure employee conformance to performance standards, such as roll call training, better supervision, and continuous in-service training.

BIBLIOGRAPHY

BOOKS

Black, Algermann: *The Police and Politics.* New York, McGraw-Hill, 1968.
Black, Donald J., and Reiss, Albert J. Jr.: *Patterns of behavior in police and citizen transactions. Studies of Crime and Law Enforcement in Major Metropolitan Areas: Field Surveys III, II, Section I.* Report to the President's Commission on Law Enforcement and Administration of Justice. Washington, D.C., U.S. Government Printing Office, 1966.
Blalock, Hubert M. Jr.: *Toward a Theory of Minority-Group Relations.* New York, Wiley, 1967.
Bopp, William J., and Schultz, Donald O.: *A Short History of American Law Enforcement.* Springfield, Thomas, 1972.
Bopp, William J., and Schultz, Donald O.: *Principles of American Law Enforcement and Criminal Justice.* Springfield, Thomas, 1972.
Bristow, Allen: *Effective Police Manpower Utilization.* Springfield, Thomas, 1969.
Burns and Peltason: *Government by The People.* Englewood Cliffs, Prentice-Hall, 1960.
Chevigny, Paul: *Police Power.* New York, Pantheon Books, 1969.
Clark, Donald E., and Chapman, Samuel G.: *A Foreword Step.* Springfield, Thomas, 1966.
Cloward, Richard A., and Ohlin, Lloyd B.: *Delinquency and Opportunity: A Theory of Delinquent Gangs.* Glencoe, Free Press, 1960.
Cook, Fred J.: *The Secret Rulers.* Des Moines, Duell, Sloan & Pearce, 1966.
Garner, Erle Stanley: *Cops On Campus And Crime In The Streets.* New York, William Morrow and Company, 1970.
Golembiewski, Robert T., and Gibson, Frank: *Managerial Behavior and Organization Demands.* Chicago, Rand McNally, 1967.
Hollingsworth, Dan: *Rocks In The Roadway.* Chicago, Stromberg Allen, 1954.
International City Manager's Association, Municipal Police Administration. Cushing-Malloy, Ann Arbor, 1969.
Kenney, John P.: *Police Management Planning.* Springfield, Thomas, 1952.
Kooken, Don L.: *Ethics in Police Service.* Springfield, Thomas, 1957.
Lane, Roger: *Policing The City.* Harvard, Cambridge, 1967.
Levy, Burton: Cops in the ghetto: a problem of the police system. In Massotta, Louis H. and Bowen, Don R., (eds.): *Riots and Rebellion: Civil Violence in the Urban Community.* Beverly Hills, Sage Publications, 1968.
Mass, Peter: *The Valachi Papers.* New York, Bantam Books, 1969.
Merriam, and Goetz: *Going Into Politics.* New York, Harper, 1957.

Messick, Hank: *The Silent Syndicate*. New York, MacMillan, 1967.
Moley, Raymond: *Politics and Criminal Prosecution*. New York, Minton, Balch, 1929.
Niederhoffer, Arthur: *Behind the Shield: The Police in Urban Society*. Garden City, Doubleday, 1969.
Novick, David, (ed.): *Program Budgeting: Program Analysis and the Federal Budget*. Washington, U.S. Governments Printing Office, 1965.
Pantaleone, Michele: *The Mafia and Politics*. New York, Coward-McCann, 1966.
Pfiffner, John M., and Sherwood, Frank P.: *Administrative Organization*. Englewood Cliffs, Prentice-Hall, 1960.
Pound, Roscoe: *Criminal Justice in America*. New York, Holt, 1930.
President's Commission on Law Enforcement and Administration of Justice: *The Challenge of Crime in a Free Society*. Washington, U.S. Government Printing Office, 1967.
President's Commission on Law Enforcement and Administration of Justice: Task Force Report: *The Police*. Washington, U.S. Government Printing Office, 1967.
Reid, (ed.): *The Grim Reapers*. Chicago, Henry Regency, 1969.
Reith, Charles: *The Blind Eye of History*. London, Faber & Faber, 1952.
Salerno, Ralph, and Tompkins, John: *The Crime Confederation*. New York, Doubleday, 1969.
Schultz, Donald O., and Slepecky, Michael: *Police Unarmed Defense Tactics*. Springfield, Thomas, 1973.
Schultz, Donald O., and Norton, Loran A.: *Police Operational Intelligence*. Springfield, Thomas. 1968.
Schultz, Donald O.: *Special Problems in Law Enforcement*. Springfield, Thomas, 1971.
Smith, Bruce: *Police Systems in U.S.*, New York, Harper, 1949.
Turner, William: *The Police Establishment*, New York, Putnam, 1968.
United State Chamber of Commerce: *Deskbook on Organized Crime*, Washington, 1969.
Van Allen, Edward J.: *Our Handcuffed Police*. Mineola, Reportorial Press, 1968.
Volz, Joseph, and Bridge, Peter, J.: *The Mafia Talks*. Greenwich, Fawcett, 1969.
Wildavsky, Aaron B.: *Politics of the Budgetary Process*. New York, Littlejohn, 1967.
Williams, Robin M., Jr.: *Strangers Next Door*. Englewood Cliffs, Prentice-Hall, 1964.
Wilson, O. W.: *Police Planning*, 2nd ed. Springfield, Thomas, 1958.
Wilson, O. W.: *Police Administration*, 2nd ed. New York, McGraw-Hill, 1963.

MAGAZINE ARTICLES

A death in the family. *Life*, Feb. 28, 1969.

Bibliography

Atwater, James: Detroit vs the mafia. *Saturday Evening Post*, May 20, 1964.
Beral, Harold, and Murcus Sisk: The administration of complaints by civilians against the police. *Harvard Law Review*. 77:499-615, 1964.
Big tab. *Newsweek*, Oct. 3, 1966.
Big spender. *Newsweek*, Oct. 14, 1963.
Brazen empire of crime: from a governor and a D.A., an offer of resignation. *Life*, Sept. 29, 1967.
Catlin, Robert E.: Should public employees have the right to strike? *Public Personnel Review*, Jan., 1968.
Copp, William C.: Let no one be fooled! *Law and Order*, Jan., 1969.
Cosa Nostra, the poison in our society. *Reader's Digest*, Dec., 1969.
Crime: kiss of death. *Newsweek*, Oct., 7, 1963.
Crime our thing. *Newsweek*, Aug. 19, 1963.
Draper, Theodore: The ghost of social-facism. *Commentry*, Feb., 1969.
Elam, Jerry: Close ranks — march. *Law & Order*, Feb., 1962.
Elam, Jerry: Wake up. *National F.O.P. Journal*, Vol. 44, No. 3, July, 1961.
End to big riots. *US News & World Report*, June 2, 1969.
How Mafia killers got their man. *Saturday Evening Post*, Oct. 31, 1964.
How the Mob controls Chicago. *Saturday Evening Post*, Nov. 9, 1963.
Investigations: Jersey bounce. *Newsweek*, Dec. 22, 1969.
Italy: a mother's pain. *Newsweek*, May 2, 1960.
Italy: guilty friars. *Newsweek*, July 15, 1963.
Italy: justice for Francia. *Newsweek*, Jan. 2, 1967.
Italy: Let them kill me. *Newsweek*, May 6, 1963.
Italy: the Sicilian canary. *Newsweek*, Oct. 14, 1963.
Kassalow, Everett M.: Trade unionism goes public. *The Public Interest*, Winter, 1969.
Kheel, Theodore, W.: Can we stand strikes by teachers, police, garbage men, etc? *Reader's Digest*, Aug. 1969.
Kreutzer, Walter E.: The elusive professionalization that police officers seek. *The Police Chief*, Aug., 1969.
Lundstedt, Sven: Social psychological contributions to the management of law enforcement agencies. *J Criminal Law, Criminology and Police Science*. 56:375-381. Sept., 1965.
Lutz, Carl F.: Overcoming obstacles to professionalism. *The Police Chief*, Sept. 1968.
Mafia rubs out a rebellion. *Life*, Aug. 30, 1963.
Mafia: the inside story. *Saturday Evening Post*, Aug. 10, 1963.
Mass, Peter: The story behind the crime hearings. *Saturday Evening Post*, Nov. 23, 1963.
McClellan, John L.: Weak link in our war on the Mafia. *Reader's Digest*, March, 1970.
McWilliam, Cary: Protest, power and the future of politics. *Nation*, Jan. 15, 1968.
More, Harry W.: The era of police collective bargaining. *Law and Order*, June

1969.
Murdy, Ralph G.: Civilian review. *FBI Law Enforcement Bulletin,* July 1966.
Neoling, Floyd M.: The police pay problem: a solution. *Law and Order,* Oct. 1969.
O'Brien, William P.: Unionization of police is main topic at ICPA annual conference, *The Law Officer,* Fall, 1969.
Oppenheimer, Martin: Strategies for the ghetto wars. *Nation,* Mar. 24, 1969.
Pomerleau, Donald D.: The eleventh hour. *The Police Chief,* Dec., 1969.
Schultz, Donald O.: Police review boards. *Valor,* Dec., 1969.
Schultz, Donald O.: Police unions. *Valor,* April 1970.
Singleton, Donald: How organized crime takes over business. *The American Legion Magazine,* April, 1970.
Skousen, W. C.: What about police labor unions? *Law and Order,* Oct. 1966.
Smith, Sandy: The crime cartel. *Life,* Sept., 1, 1967.
Stoddard, Ellwyn R.: The informal "code" of police deviancy: A group approach to blue coat crime. *J Criminal Law, Criminology and Police Science, 59*:201-213, 1968.
The conglomerate of crime. *Time,* Aug. 22, 1969.
The crime syndicate. *Newsweek,* April 14, 1969.
The four friars. *Newsweek,* March 26, 1962.
Williams, Gerald O.: Historical origins and development of political police. *Police,* March, 1969.
Winckoski, Bernard G.: The name of the game is collective bargaining. *The Police Chief,* Dec., 1969.
Wyrick, Ed.: Editor's comment. *Wisconsin Police Chief,* Jan., 1970.

NEWSPAPERS

Law a shield for organized crime. *Omaha World Herald,* Jan., 24, 1970.
Mafia thrives on fear, expands on legal loopholes. *Progress Bulletin,* March 27, 1969.
Mafia unlimited. *Omaha World Herald,* Jan. 25, 1970.

DEPARTMENTAL DIRECTIVES AND GENERAL ORDERS

Baltimore Police Department, *Code of Rules,* Baltimore.
Charlotte Police Department, *The Use of Force by Police Officer,* General Order #11, Charlotte.
Charlotte Police Department, *Training Bulletin* #7, Charlotte.
Charlotte Police Department, *The Chemical Mace,* Information Bulletin #31, Charlotte, October 11, 1967.
Department of the Army, *To Insure Domestic Tranquility,* Pamphlet #360-81, Washington, 1968.

Department of the Army, *Civil Disturbances and Disasters,* Field Manuel #19-15, Washington, 1968.
Kansas City Police Department, *Discharge of firearms,* Memorandum #67-37, 1967.
Kansas City Police Department, *Use of Mace,* Memorandum #67-10.
Kansas City Police Department, *K9 Squad,* Memorandum #68-32.
Kansas City Police Department, *K-9 Squad,* General Order #68-32, Kansas City, 1968.
Kansas City Police Department, *Control of Civil Disorders,* Procedural Instructions #69-4, Kansas City, 1969.
Kansas City Police Department, *Code of Rules.*
United State Army Military Police School, pamphlet, *A Platoon Leader's Guide for Civil Disturbance Operations,* Fort Gordon, 1968.
——— : Sixth Annual Report of the Police Advisory Board for the City of Philadelphia. December 31, 1964.

OTHER SOURCES

Juris, Harvey A., and Hutchison, Kay B.: *The Legal Status of Municipal Police Employee Organizations.* Working Paper No. 2, University of Wisconsin, July, 1969.
Kuykendall, Jack L: Police deviancy in the enforcement role: situational cooperation/compliance — response hierarchy of deviant and non-deviant power strategies. 1969, submitted for publication.
President's Commission on Law Enforcement, 1967, Task Force Report. Government Printing Office, 1967.
Staff Report to the President, *Rights in Concord,* U. S. Government, Jan., 18, 1969.
The FBI Annual Report, 1969.
U. S. Bureau of the Budget: Bulletin No. 66-3, October, 12, 1965.